Dead Ringers

Dead Ringers

How Outsourcing Is Changing the Way
Indians Understand Themselves

Shehzad Nadeem

PRINCETON UNIVERSITY PRESS ❀ PRINCETON AND OXFORD

Published by Princeton University Press,
41 William Street, Princeton, New Jersey 08540

In the United Kingdom: Princeton University Press,
6 Oxford Street, Woodstock, Oxfordshire OX20 1TW

press.princeton.edu

Second printing, and first paperback printing, 2013
Paperback ISBN 978-0-691-15965-2

The Library of Congress has cataloged the cloth edition of this book as follows

Nadeem, Shehzad, 1978–
  Dead ringers : how outsourcing is changing the way Indians understand
themselves / Shehzad Nadeem.
    p. cm.
  Includes bibliographical references and index.
  ISBN 978-0-691-14787-1 (hardcover : alk. paper)   1. Contracting
out—India.   2. Offshore outsourcing—India.   I. Title.
  HD2365.N23 2010
  338.8'7—dc22   2010031434

British Library Cataloging-in-Publication Data is available

This book has been composed in Bodoni with Futura display

Printed on acid-free paper.

Printed in the United States of America

10   9   8   7   6   5   4   3   2

For my family

Remember that you are an actor in a play, which is as the playwright wants it to be: short if he wants it short, long if he wants it long. If he wants you to play a beggar, play even this part skillfully, or a cripple, or a public official, or a private citizen. What is yours is to play the assigned part well. But to choose it belongs to someone else.

—*Epictetus, "Enchiridion"*

Contents

Acknowledgments

I owe a special debt of gratitude to John Skrentny. Jokes about my preference for working in "monastic isolation" aside, his guidance through all stages of this project was invaluable, and I cannot thank him enough for his kindness and generosity. Paul Frymer also provided a great deal of encouragement, especially when my motivation flagged. I am grateful to both of them for seeing potential in a project that, at its outset, could charitably be described as quirky. I appreciate greatly the efforts of Ethel Brooks, Pierre Feilles, Arlie Hochschild, Martha Lampland, Kiran Mirchandani, Michael Schudson, Gershon Shafir, and Harley Shaiken. This book would be a *much* poorer one were it not for their thoughtful and inspired comments. Syed Ali and Christopher Bonastia deserve special mention for their willingness to read the many, many drafts of the introduction, among other things.

The intellectual support of the Department of Sociology at the University of California, San Diego, where I attended graduate school, was extremely beneficial, and I'd like to thank Mariano Bargero, John Evans, Nadav Gabay, Paula Gutierrez, Michael Haedicke, Jeff Haydu, Jiangsui He, Caroline Lee, Isaac Martin, Akos Rona-Tas, Christena Turner, and Rika Yonemura, among others. Elsewhere, many people helped sharpen my thinking: Doreen Mattingly, Winifred Poster, Ananya Roy, Amandeep Sandhu, and Mohammad Warsi. In India, Lalit Batra, Anannya Bhattacharjee, Praful Bidwai, Ernesto Noronha, Ketaki Rege, Vinod Shetty, and Preeti Singh helped deepen my understanding of the labor issues at stake.

A generous fellowship from the UC Labor and Employment Research Fund financed the fieldwork. I am grateful to Sam Kernell for hiring me to teach at the UC-Washington Center, where I completed the first draft of this book. Alfreda Brock deserves mention for her friendship and assistance while I was there. My new colleagues at Lehman College—Kofi Benefo, Thomas Conroy, Dana Fenton, Elhum Haghighat, Barbara Jacobson, Susan Markens, Miriam Medina, Madeline Moran, Naomi Spence, Elin Waring, Esther Wilder, Devrim Yavuz—have been extremely welcoming. Grants from the Professional

Staff Congress–CUNY, UC Berkeley, the Institute for International, Comparative and Area Studies, and the Friends of the International Center (UCSD) supported my work at various stages. Prior to graduate school, I worked for a year at the Institute for Policy Studies, whose blend of intellectual and political commitment has served as a constant source of inspiration. I must also thank my undergraduate advisor, Bruce Busching, for his anarchic supervision of my first attempt at longish writing.

Opportunities to test some of my ideas in presentations made this a better book. Mary Blair-Loy's probing questions after a 2007 American Sociological Association panel on culture and work helped clarify some of the book's key arguments. Similarly, I am thankful to Jan Nederveen Pieterse for including me on a globalization panel at the 2009 ASA meeting, where Amit Prasad and others provided valuable commentary on my work. I also benefited from presenting an early draft of chapter 4 at a panel organized by Richard Applebaum and hosted by the UC Institute for Labor and Employment.

A different, slightly more academic version of chapter 3, "Macaulay's (Cyber) Children," was published in volume 3, issue 1 of *Cultural Sociology* in 2009. The same holds for chapter 4, "The Uses and Abuses of Time," which was published in volume 9, issue 1 of *Global Networks* in 2009. I would like to thank the editors and reviewers at those journals for their constructive comments, and publishers Sage and Blackwell, respectively, for permission to use portions of the articles.

At Princeton University Press, Eric Schwartz has been an exemplary editor. He has been nothing if not enthusiastic since day one, and I am very fortunate to have worked with him. Janie Chan provided friendly and ready assistance in preparing the manuscript, Nathan Carr expertly navigated the production process, and Richard Isomaki dutifully and painstakingly copyedited the text.

My heartfelt thanks to Asher Ghertner and Preetha Mani, Benjamin Rollman, Claire Tixeire, and their daughter Adele, and Matthew Strugar and Michelle Martinez for their enduring friendship and for extending their gracious hospitality to me in Berkeley, India, and New

York. Ritha and Gopal Patil allowed me to stay with them for some time in New Delhi, and I am extremely grateful for that.

None of this would be possible were it not for the encouragement of my lovely family. Ami and Abu are responsible for all that is good in my character and by extension all that is good in this book. I could not ask for more sisterly and brotherly affection than that provided by Erum and Sam. Their daughter, Nooria, has inherited their charm and good humor, and I'm excited for the day when she can read "Mamu book." I would be horribly remiss if I did not thank my extended family—a rather cold term for a web of warm affection and support that stretches from New Jersey and the DC area to Islamabad and Lahore (with a detour in Nairobi). And, finally, there simply would be no book were it not for the participants. They had nothing to gain by talking to a slight, notebook-clutching researcher but gave of their time freely, and for that I am infinitely grateful. I would thank them by name but human subjects regulations prevent me from doing so.

Dead Ringers

Would you rather have high hopes and have them routinely dashed, or have low expectations and rarely be disappointed? This was the question I pondered while listening to two Indian workers, Prashant and Anil, debate the merits of globalization. They are employees of Dynovate, an outsourcing company in northern Bombay that handles a number of basic financial processes for Western multinationals. As was their habit during breaks, the two had gathered in their building's sixth-floor stairwell for a smoke. Prashant is 24, dark-skinned, and stocky and has a Cheshire grin. He says he "likes to party" and is a deejay at nightclubs in his spare time. His favorite group is the Black Eyed Peas. Anil is two years his senior. His complexion is fair, his frame slender, and his attitude sullen. He does not party, does not drink, and favors Indian music. (Curiously, Prashant, the devotee of Western popular culture, smokes the domestic India Kings, while Anil, the self-professed skeptic of globalization, prefers Marlboros).

A dyed-in-the-wool PR man—he works in "media relations"—Prashant has an admirable capacity to see silver linings and half-full glasses where other might despair. While some have speculated that the Indian outsourcing industry faces a critical shortage of "employable talent," Prashant thinks that its future is bright and that it "isn't a bubble that's going to burst." His work, like much of that in the industry, is tedious, but he finds the "open" culture of the company exciting and he enjoys working with American clients. They are demanding but fair. What is more, he has learned how to be a professional. "Everyone likes professionals," he says genially. "They're the ones that get things done on time. They interact with various people in the right way, in the right manner. You give them something to do and they do it quickly." Prashant understands his work to be a performance, like his after-hours deejaying, and is anxious to please.

Anil, by contrast, is a grudging participant in the emerging drama.

He finds Western clients to be terse and unappreciative and grows tired of always having to put on a bright face. He also laments the long hours they have to put in at the office—at times, up to 12 to 14 hours. "They demand too much and they get too much," Anil says with slight resignation. The industry, moreover, "caters to lower skilled labor" and training is "minimalistic." He believes that management is not as transparent as it should be, especially in awarding bonuses and promotions. And while outsourcing has generated employment for some two million people in India, Anil doubts its long-term viability. "If our costs start increasing, what will happen?" he asks with knitted brow. "The jobs will move. The work will go."

This book tells the stories of people like Prashant and Anil, the purported winners of globalization. The animating paradox of their condition is that they are reaping the benefits of the corporate search for cut-rate labor but also bearing the burdens. Last I checked, Anil is still with the company and draws a steady if unspectacular salary. Prashant restlessly jumped from one firm to the next in search of better pay and more stimulating work, only to find that the ladders of upward mobility often end in midair. So, would you prefer a life of false hopes or one of dull monotony? Starving artist or couch potato? Peripatetic Prashant or austere Anil?

Globalization enthusiasts would respond that this is a false dilemma, that the "new economy" is characterized by an upward spiral of effort, innovation, and reward. And if the news reports are to be trusted, this enterprising constellation now applies to the developing world. By dint of the spread of information and communication technologies, many white-collar service jobs that were previously regarded as the sole privilege of the richer nations can be performed from almost anywhere. And there is no question that outsourcing has provided opportunities for many young Indians and has boosted the country's profile on the world stage. (Revenue from outsourcing is predicted to reach $71 billion this year.) The preponderance of evidence, however, including the extensive field research I conducted for this book, suggests that the promise of outsourcing-led development has been wildly oversold.

The usual moral dilemma about globalization—whether, as Paul

Krugman provocatively put it, bad jobs are better than no jobs at all—obtains here as well, but with a few twists.[1] As surveys in India indicate, the outsourcing industry draws its workforce from the privileged castes and classes, not landless peasants scouring scrap heaps for recyclables. These young and college-educated workers (mostly under 30 years of age) would easily have work even without outsourcing. And the pay is good by national standards, much of which is dispensed of forthwith at exurban malls, cafes, and nightclubs (though some charmingly sober-minded workers do support their families). In short, this is a population whose gains are assumed to be unambiguous. Yet as I shall argue, these workers are also shouldering the weight of the global restructuring of work.

First, they do indeed receive relatively high wages (in India), but they are also subject to what Marx called the "dull compulsion of economic relations," and the forms of discipline and surveillance issuing thereof. The room they presently have to bargain over the terms of their labor depends largely upon a contingency: the temporary condition of the labor market. If labor demand decreases or the supply increases, the situation of these workers may no longer look so enviable. And, still, the conditions of work can be strict: hours, by turns stress-filled and Chekhovian, monitored tightly.

Second, much attention has been paid to the broadening of workers' insecurity in the advanced industrial economies since the 1970s.[2] Downsizing, privatization, deregulation, and union decline have all undermined the position of labor. Beck, for example, writes about a new "political economy of insecurity."[3] This book builds on these observations by looking at how developing countries are integrated into this precarious environment. Globalization extends insecurity to workers in developing countries through a process of inclusion and marginalization. They are included through the "spatialization" of jobs and work.[4] Yet they are simultaneously excluded from core and creative activities, thereby ensuring their vulnerability, if not expendability.

Rhetoric about the "flat" and "borderless" world notwithstanding, then, globalization is not the great leveler it is often reputed to be. The Indian outsourcing sector, for example, is a niche and hugely dependent export-based industry. While offshore workplaces appear, at first glance, to be beacons of high-tech innovation, they are very often sites of rote tasks, such as customer service, data transcription, and basic software coding. The worker, moreover, uses the digital tools of the information economy to perform its grunt work. And while long and busy hours are no strangers to Americans, their lengthening and deepened intensity in the offshore context raise concerns about labor conditions. Drawing on extensive fieldwork in India and the United States, I argue that this offshore workforce is something of a white-collar proletariat. (See the appendix for a discussion of research methods.)

This interstitial position is well reflected in a newspaper photograph I saw recently. Indian call center employees are pictured working under a banner that reads, "Life Means More." The banner is part of the décor—a motivational device?—and I wish I could have asked the employees what they thought of it. Has outsourced work enabled them to make more of their lives? Or has it raised hopes without providing the means to realize them? I pose these questions to the reader. In so doing, I hope this book serves as a corrective for the many sensationalistic and polemical accounts of globalization now circulating. My goal was to move back and forth from corporate headquarters and trade fairs to offshore workplaces and the spheres of everyday life to paint a more accurate picture of its costs and benefits. And as the focus is on the supposed beneficiaries of globalization, I pay close attention to the cyclical humiliations *and* joys of life under transnational capitalism. "Outsourcing" has become a public spectacle, and I try to capture its many, often absurd, facets.

Truth in Outsourcing

> Things are not what they appear to be; nor are they otherwise.
>
> —*Surangama Sutra*

Globalization is a polysemic term, a floating signifier.[5] Of its various attributes, none are perhaps thought to be as defining as transparency. Yet as corporate operations are increasingly globalized, truth becomes less immediately verifiable and trust becomes more a matter of faith. To mitigate these problems, companies have created international standards for a wide variety of practices. This way, it matters little whether a practice is performed in-house, across the country, or overseas. Universal standards smoothen geocultural friction. They build confidence. And as confidence grows, not only is work outsourced, but so are intangibles like accounting and human resource practices, management styles, and even names and accents. But sometimes the confidence falters. As the following examples illustrate, globalization is defined as much by smoke and mirrors as by transparency.

The news came as a shock but was not altogether surprising. In January 2009, Ramalinga Raju, the founder and chairman of Satyam Computer Services—the first Indian technology company to feature on the Nasdaq—was arrested after admitting that he had cooked the company's books. If Satyam was not a world-class company, the thinking went, it would pretend to be by posting fictitious earnings and assets to lure investors. And the act was convincing. The company had gained the patronage of over a third of the Fortune 500, such as General Electric, General Motors, Cisco Systems, Coca-Cola, Sony, Nestlé, Nissan Motors, Caterpillar, and State Farm Insurance. Having revealed that he exaggerated the firm's cash reserves by about $1.4 billion (around 94 percent of the cash on the company's books), chairman Raju—recipient of Ernst and Young's 2007 entrepreneur of the year of award—wrote in his resignation letter that the process "was like riding a tiger, not knowing how to get off without being eaten." Raju as well as Satyam's former chief financial officer are being investigated on suspicion of conspiracy, forgery, criminal breach of trust, and falsifying documents. *Satyam*, I should add, is Sanskrit for "truth."

According to C. B. Bhave, India's chief markets regulator, the disclosure was of "horrifying magnitude."[6] As one of the biggest corporate frauds in Indian history, questions were immediately raised about regulatory oversight, accounting standards, and corporate governance in the country. While the full repercussions of "India's Enron" have yet to be realized—and the Indian government has moved to stanch them by deposing the entire Satyam board—the revelations have already rattled investors' confidence in India and cast fresh doubt on the viability of the offshore outsourcing model.

But the outrage elicited by the confidence trick had only partly to do with the company's economic might. Satyam mattered because it, like other homegrown tech giants Infosys and Wipro, embodied an idea: the idea that from acorns mighty oaks grow. From its small beginnings in 1997 in Hyderabad, where a handful of energetic workers wrote software code and processed data, Raju's company capitalized on concerns in the United States and United Kingdom about potential software bugs at the turn of the millennium by providing upgrades. Satyam now employs 53,000 workers and has operations in 67 countries, including eight offices in the United States. It provides a range of activities to some of the world's largest multinationals, from information technology to customer service and, ironically, has even managed some clients' accounting and finances. A model corporate citizen, Satyam sponsors a number of nonprofit organizations that focus on improving the life chances of the rural poor.

The fear is that Raju's fall from grace is not his alone, that he might take the "new India" with him on his tumble from corporate headquarters to Hyderabadi prison cell. India's lucrative information technology and back-office industry, according to the *Wall Street Journal*, has become the "poster child for India's economic liberalization and rapid growth," the beaming face that modern India proudly shows to the world. Thus the scandal cannot be written off as a holdover from India's bad old days of corporate and bureaucratic corruption. Satyam is a new type of company. It is also a global company that has been audited for the past 10 years by the Indian affiliate of Pricewater houseCoopers.

And Raju himself is a product of Western training. The son of a farmer, he earned his master's of business administration degree at Ohio University in the late 1970s. As Taube explains, upon his return to India he was determined to emulate Western best practices:

> Having studied and learned business in an environment different from the Indian one, he brought back home not modern technology but rather western business culture. Many other engineers or managers working in American companies experience a different organization of work, usually much more flexible and open, especially high-tech companies in Silicon Valley. A major difference is the less hierarchical structure with more freedom and responsibility.

Eventually he established a very untypical modern organizational structure at his company modeled after what he had seen in the U.S.[7]

(Perhaps his scheme should be conceived neither as purely Indian nor purely Western but instead as hybrid, where the twain meet.) Instead of serving as an example of the universalization of transparent accounting standards, as in notions of a "rationalistic world culture," Satyam made a hash of them, and PricewaterhouseCoopers failed to sound the alarm.[8] While there is certainly some truth to the claim that global integration has expanded the reach of rationality, transparency, and accountability, such arguments now require a quite lengthy list of qualifications, especially in light of the Enron and WorldCom debacles, Madoff's Ponzi scheme, and the recent financial crisis.[9] The same holds for critics who tell a counternarrative of rationalization run amok, recalling Weber's famous invocation of the "iron cage."[10] The iron cage, even a digitized one, is not the appropriate metaphor for today's realities. Rather, a central argument of this book is that the "rational" and "nonrational" are intermingled.[11] They coexist and sustain each other.[12] Close scrutiny of global processes in situ reveals a complex mixture of contrary elements, giving everyday life a surreal, *Through the Looking Glass* quality.

A most vivid example comes from the Indian call center industry, which frequently requires employees to don Western identities in providing inbound (customer service) and outbound (telemarketing) service. Workers also undergo training in Western accents and popular culture and are discouraged from disclosing their geographical location on the phone. (If pressed, many are simply told to lie.) This results in masked accents, masked names, and masked locations. Whole offices of workers act like Americans and Europeans and live as if they are in time zones a world apart. The rationale for these obfuscating practices is that they allow agents to serve customers better. But another reason, less discussed, is to mute the political backlash in the West over the morality of outsourcing.[13] To employers and executives, these are white lies. To Indian workers they are tainted gray. To Western workers they are soot black. They are lies that justify, complicate, and deceive. But the paradox is that outsourcing is also a material truth, a series of concrete, mimetic practices. A forged truth. In a word, a masquerade.

The Fugue of Globalization

How are we to conceptualize the foregoing? And what does it tell us about globalization more generally? Two different perspectives dominate discussions of the trend. The first tends to see it as a force that is homogenizing the globe, in fact, turning it into McGlobe, all rights reserved. Partisans of this approach include subscribers of updated versions of modernization theory, such as Thomas Friedman, who see globalization as challenging power asymmetries, as well as denouncers of the neoliberal imperium, who see it as consolidating them.[14] The main problem with this picture is that the brushstrokes are too broad and linear; it misses a whole range of diverse ideas, patterns, and forms that have emerged despite and in consequence of increased global interconnectivity.

The second view, which also crosses ideological lines to include proponents of globalization as well as academics who study things closely, sees not sameness but "hybridity." While attention to syncretism is certainly welcome, this camp is guilty of missing the "prime mover": were it not for the expansion of transnational capitalism, we would not be having this discussion.[15] (You may find a McAloo Tikka Burger with Cheese or a Chicken Maharajah Mac only in India, but it is still McDonald's.) That is to say, the global interplay of culture, capital, and commodities is not purposeless; it is motivated by the impulses and desires of economic and political elites.[16]

The first perspective loses the trees for the forest, the second, the forest for the trees. What is needed is an approach that combines sensitivity to empirical detail with an awareness of the broad direction of change. That is, we must remain alive to the "local and determinate ways" in which globalization unfolds.[17] To this end, I argue that globalization produces similarity and difference simultaneously. On the one hand, offshore spaces of work are constructed in the Western corporate image. On the other, existing values and organizational forms cannot be extended to new social groups without being transformed in the process. Workplace identities and relations are therefore composed of a variety of influences, not just corporate impositions on an amorphous Indian mass.

In the case at hand, globalization can be likened to a fugue, a technique of imitative counterpoint in musical composition. The first line announces the major subject or theme, which is followed by an "answer" in imitation, but in a different key and often distinct enough to form a counterpoint. Likewise, the mimicry of modes of work, consumption, and ways of being does not result in a one-to-one correspondence; it is a practice of emulation, which necessarily takes on distinctive characteristics.

This notion of difference-in-similarity is also suggested by this book's title. The term *dead ringer* refers to one who strongly resembles another. In its original meaning, a ringer is a fast horse that is furtively entered into a competition in place of a slow or injured one. Here workers in the global south are substituted for their more expensive counterparts in developed countries. To all outward appearances, the names and neutered accents, the workplace cultures and structures, the identities and lifestyles resemble those of their country of origin. Upon closer inspection, however, you see how they diverge from the mold.

As the book's organizing motif, the idea of imitative counterpoint allows us to capture a wide spectrum of responses to globalizing pressures that occur within a context of unequal political and economic relations. It is capacious enough to apply to instances of resistance (i.e., using the colonizer's language and categories to undermine colonialism), ambivalence or pastiche (i.e., Bollywood movies), as well as acquiescence (i.e., out-and-out mimicry). The idea also provides purchase on the dialectic of freedom and constraint, or agency and social structure, as it is called in the academy. Mimicry is not a crude caricature of other ways of being, nor is it the unproblematic transplantation of foreign norms; it signifies their appropriation and transformation as they are anchored in different terrain.

So, by most accounts, India has done very well in integrating itself into the global service market. I wrote *integrating*, but I might also have written *ingratiating*. The rules of the game are set by already dominant transnational corporations, and if India wants to play it has to adhere to them.[18] This is not, then, a story of a country's belated "modernization." Rather, it is a tale of the imperfect reproduction of (shifting) Western patterns abroad, which, I think, can tell us much about the dynamics of global capitalism and development. India reinvents itself, somewhat paradoxically, by modeling itself on the advanced consumer economies. The trick is to recast the necessity of adhering to the Western mold as an emphatic choice.

Looking Ahead

As much as globalization is a political-economic reality, it is also a promise. A promise that hard work and the exploitation of comparative advantage are redemptive and that the old division of the world into center and periphery, into First and Third, is no longer relevant. By virtue of globalization, India would be built not by backbreaking labor but, even more heroically, by "mind work." The bureaucratic time servers that were the foundation of the state-directed economy (and the labyrinthine "license Raj") would be replaced by a new generation of urban, tech-savvy professionals. The fetters of caste and tradition would be washed away by the rising tide of modernity. In more fanciful prognostications, India would glide past industrialization to a "knowledge-based society," to the status of an "information superpower," with the ease of a film dissolve.

Promises sour, horizons dim. Allegations that workers are "cybercoolies," that work sites are sweatshops, that outsourcing is a technologically updated version of colonial subjection, and that India is merely the "electronic housekeeper to the world," hold a particular sting. Critics are told that although the "long hours and erratic shifts invariably confuse people's biological clocks," that although workers "tend to put on weight" as they "eat and smoke more and down more coffees during night shifts," there "can be no possible argument against call centres." Outsourcing provides "employment, salaries and facilities to youth who might otherwise be unemployed." "It is a virtual godsend." Trade unions for all their fussing about labor conditions are accused of "killing the golden goose."[19] But the hard reality is that the eggs were never golden and the goose is quite ordinary.

My purpose in the pages that follow is to explore the cycle of hope and disappointment that has come to define the globalization story in India and elsewhere. In so doing, I consider noneconomic factors, such as managerial styles, workplace culture, and family and social relations, to be of more than secondary importance. They enable the economic; they are its condition of possibility.[20] To this end, I focus on the culture of the economy—the exuberant banality of economic life—as well as on the economy of culture: the strictures and structures by which social life and human creativity are hedged.

The book is structured as follows. First, I lay out the mottled backdrop against which this drama unfolds. When service outsourcing was first registered on the public radar, it set off something of a moral panic in the United States and Western Europe. Some believed it to be salubrious in the long term and consistent with broad trends of economic restructuring. To others, it betokened a new era of job loss and economic vulnerability. In both cases, as I discuss in chapter 1, the international trade in services became a synecdoche for the promise and peril of increasing global interdependence. Chapter 2 anchors the book theoretically. It explores how place-bound practices, policies, and identities are being reconfigured by cross-border processes. It also establishes the basic characteristics of global outsourcing and the historical and institutional context in which it takes place.

I invite readers of a less theoretical bent to begin with chapter 3, which explores how globalization affects the identities and aspirations of workers, managers, and employers. Briefly, workers find the adoption of foreign accents, identities, and timings both exciting and disorienting. They increasingly identify with lifestyles and customs that are global in reach. (For others, perceived maltreatment leads to disenchantment.) Executives and managers, too, use their close engagement with the West to define themselves as something other than the "traditional" Indian. It is a cultural distancing act predicated on unacknowledged class privilege.

Chapter 4 focuses on what I call *time arbitrage*. The extension of work hours through global outsourcing means that a 24-hour work cycle is a near possibility. This means long hours for offshore workers, as they often stay past dusk to work with Western clients. The other option is the direct adoption of Western timings in offshore offices. This translates into the permanent night shift for workers as spatial and temporal disorientation are neatly combined. In both cases, companies exploit both Western and Indian work norms to increase the length and density of work time. Unsurprisingly, these long, busy, and odd hours estrange workers from family and friends and the "ordinary" rhythms of the society. What is more, the inversion upsets circadian rhythms and adversely impacts health.

Chapter 5 traces the offshoring of work from the United States to India as it occurred at one company. It looks at the types of work being moved, the labor conditions under which they are performed, and adumbrates my argument about white-collar proletarians. While the complexity of services offered from India is increasing, there are presently limits to how high subsidiaries and subcontractors will move up the so-called value ladder. That is, they depend on standardized work for the bulk of their revenues. This translates into extreme levels of work rationalization, or the Taylorization of information work, and consequently, high turnover.

The next two chapters address the globalization of corporate culture. I find that outsourced practices and norms mirror those in the West in a double sense. Strictly, they are attempted copies. But they are also a mirror held up to the desires and disappointments of managers and executives. Frustrated by what they perceive to be the submissiveness and excessive "Indianness" of their employees, management attempts to instill nominally Western professional values in the workforce (chapter 6). This project of moral reform ultimately misfires as workers are counseled to take ownership of work that is fragmented. The worker is thus torn between the poles of obedience to rules (an attitude befitting routinized work) and self-direction (one that requires greater control over projects). But the problem is not just the ends but also the means. Workers tell of managerial overreach, favoritism, and other unethical practices in this effort to shape employees' character.

Chapter 7 considers the cultural dynamics of the offshore work-place from the perspective of an American executive in Bombay. It traces his journey from intense optimism about globalization, when he cofounded an outsourcing company, to the melancholic uncertainty that causes him to leave India. The "juggernaut of job creation" he helped create no longer looked so impressive when weighed against the inherent limitations of the industry and the poverty of workers' culture. Chapter 8 considers the normative visions that animate globalization: namely, the cosmopolitan ideologies of global capitalism and labor's internationalist challenges to them. I use the idea of an *economy of utopia* to illustrate how these universalizing ideals are transformed through their application in particular contexts. The conclusion revisits the central themes of the book and explores their relevance for development strategies. The appendix is a detailed discussion of the research methodology.

CHAPTER ONE. **Leaps of Faith**

The cover illustration of the February 3, 2003, issue of *Business Week* was of a white man in a business suit dangling from a pallet of cargo that is being hoisted into a clouded, pale-yellow sky. The juxtaposition of sartorial elegance and emblems of manual labor (the ship and crane are out of view, but their presence can easily be inferred) suggested that white-collar jobs were now vulnerable to the same gale-force economic winds that had spirited away the country's manufacturing base. Moreover, the dubious coloring of the sky seemed to pose a suggestive question: Is this the twilight of American economic preeminence and the dawn of a brave new global age? In case the symbolism was lost on the casual business reader, the headline read in tall white letters: "Is Your Job Next?" followed by a synopsis of the cover story: "The next round of GLOBALIZATION is sending upscale jobs offshore. They include basic research, chip design, engineering—even financial analysis. Can America lose these jobs and still prosper? Who wins? Who loses?"

It was the first in a long series of reports loudly documenting the offshore outsourcing of white-collar service work to the developing world.[1] The debate, or rather feud, about what was now simply called "outsourcing" was to intensify a year later during the U.S. presidential campaign. The chairman of the White House Council of Economic Advisers, N. Gregory Mankiw, gave voice to the views of orthodox economists, saying, "I think that outsourcing is a growing phenomenon, but it's something that we should realize is probably a plus for the economy in the long-run. . . . It's just a new way of doing international trade."[2] The qualifiers "probably" and "long-run" did little to allay fears, and even President Bush was forced to distance himself from the young chairman's frankness. It soon became customary for advocates of "free trade" to cry crocodile tears over the localized pain that is the inevitable by-product of salutary economic forces.[3] But, *at the end of the day*, they argue, to make an omelet you must break a few eggs.

Such sententious hand-wringing, however, would fail to win over globalization's "protectionist" critics. The resonant note of betrayal was sounded by Democratic presidential hopeful John Kerry, who railed against "Benedict Arnold CEOs" who throw scruples to the wind in pursuit of greater profits.[4] CNN anchor Lou Dobbs broadcast a list of companies he accused of "exporting America."[5] Protestations of outrage aside, little was done to fetter or accelerate the trend, though worker anxiety mounted as jobs continued to be relocated offshore. The unease was palpable. A Pew survey found that a large majority of "Americans believe that the outsourcing of U.S. jobs abroad has had a decidedly negative impact on American workers."[6]

What gave the theme of betrayal traction was the sense that a promise had somehow been broken. Were not the "creative" and "knowledge-based" jobs being sent to India and elsewhere the selfsame ones that had been promised a restive populace in the wake of the first wave of offshoring? The tech bubble had burst; the contours of the "postindustrial" economy were shaky and uncertain.[7] What would Americans be asked to reinvent themselves as this time around? And how were workers to be able to compete with their counterparts in the developing world who would work diligently for a fraction of the cost? Whereas an experienced software programmer in Silicon Valley earned $77,690 a year plus benefits in 2004, according to the Bureau of Labor Statistics, the same job paid $10,900 in India.[8] Other comparisons reveal similar differentials. Figures 1.1 and 1.2 illustrate the salaries in select countries. The first figure displays salaries in information technology (IT), which includes things like software development and IT maintenance. The second shows salaries for business process outsourcing (BPO) (i.e., accounting, claims processing, customer care, debt collection, and human resources).

Offshoring is about reducing labor costs, as many firms are finding it cheaper to buy goods and services from suppliers abroad rather than provide them internally.[9] The savings are largely a product of the wage differential between workers in advanced capitalist and emerging

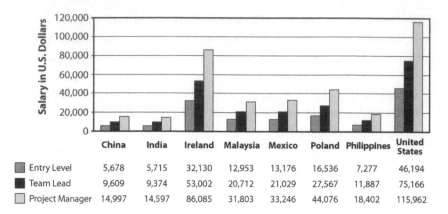

	China	India	Ireland	Malaysia	Mexico	Poland	Philippines	United States
Entry Level	5,678	5,715	32,130	12,953	13,176	16,536	7,277	46,194
Team Lead	9,609	9,374	53,002	20,712	21,029	27,567	11,887	75,166
Project Manager	14,997	14,597	86,085	31,803	33,246	44,076	18,402	115,962

Figure 1.1 Average Salaries for IT.
Source: NeoIT, "Offshore and Nearshore ITO and BPO Salary Report," *Offshore Insights Market Report Series 4(4):1–23 (2006).*

economies.[10] The new phase of offshoring began in the 1980s when major multinationals like British Airways, American Express, and General Electric began shifting slices of service work to developing countries like India. Until that happened, it was mainly manufacturing work that got offshored. But the combined effect of technological ad-

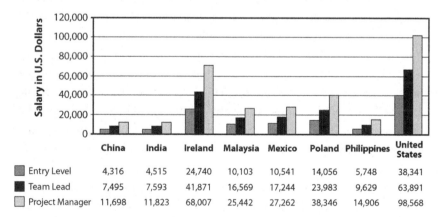

	China	India	Ireland	Malaysia	Mexico	Poland	Philippines	United States
Entry Level	4,316	4,515	24,740	10,103	10,541	14,056	5,748	38,341
Team Lead	7,495	7,593	41,871	16,569	17,244	23,983	9,629	63,891
Project Manager	11,698	11,823	68,007	25,442	27,262	38,346	14,906	98,568

Figure 1.2 Average Salaries for BPO.
Source: NeoIT, "Offshore and Nearshore ITO and BPO Salary Report," *Offshore Insights Market Report Series 4(4):1–3 (2006).*

vances like the Internet, the declining costs of transportation and communication, and promarket reforms in Asia and Eastern Europe and the consequent "oversupply" of workers, is that the provision of services is increasingly being ceded to overseas subsidiaries and subcontractors.[11]

Public statements by executives have done little to soothe matters. At a meeting with members of Congress, Carly Fiorina, then the CEO of Hewlett-Packard, divined the intentions of the Divine, declaring that "there is no job that is America's God-given right anymore."[12] The CEO of a software company called Autodesk put it similarly: "When you can get great talent at 20 percent of the costs, it isn't about waving the American flag. It's about doing what's right to have a good company." (In the wake of the economic collapse, the company has suddenly gone red, white, and blue in its eagerness to access taxpayer funds.)[13] The CEO of Symantec shared a similar sentiment: "U.S. corporations' first responsibility is to their shareholders. You cannot say, 'I'm going to put national interests ahead of shareholder interests.'"[14] One should call these tumbrel remarks—displays of singular class arrogance in one's last hours—but for the fact that the jobs of workers, not employers, are the ones being wheeled to the metaphorical guillotine. Indeed, the pay ratio between U.S. CEOs and U.S. and Indian call center workers is 400:1 and 3,348:1, respectively.[15]

The issue turns on the relationship between national and corporate interests. For critics, the two are misaligned.[16] But for free traders, they converge. Citing Adam Smith's famous dictum about dinner and self-interest, the authors of an outsourcing manual write that by maximizing profits and returns to shareholders, corporations are indirectly, even unwittingly, serving the public interest.[17] The logic is roughly as follows: countries are better off when they focus on sectors in which they have a comparative advantage, that is, lowest opportunity costs of production. By ridding themselves of inefficient processes (which can be done quicker and cheaper elsewhere), companies are free to do what they do best, thereby raising productivity and freeing up resources for investment in new products and services. This boosts economic growth. Consumers also benefit from lower prices. And the rising tide creates more jobs than it destroys, while also allowing firms to remain competitive in the global economy.[18]

But discerning advantage has proved much tougher on the ground. The major news media seem to paint a contradictory picture. On the one hand, it reported that the majority of jobs being sent offshore were low-end, such as customer service, basic software coding, and data entry. As economist Jagdish Bhagwati wrote, there is "little evidence of a major push by American companies to set up research operations in the developing world."[19] But, at the same time, we heard that sophisticated things like engineering, software development, and financial and medical services were being performed abroad as well. As columnist Thomas Friedman, who has done more than any writer to promote service globalization, would write:

> The dirty little secret is that India is taking work from Europe or America not simply because of low wages. It is also because Indians are ready to work harder and can do anything from answering your phone to designing your next airplane or car. They are not racing us to the bottom. They are racing us to the top.[20]

If tax returns could be prepared, X-rays read, cartoons colored, students tutored, and patents filed 9,000 miles away, what could not be, and what was left of the country's competitive advantage? Worry not, wrote Friedman. Factory jobs are indeed limited, but *"there is no limit to the number of idea-generated jobs in the world."* Some workers therefore will have to "move *horizontally* into new knowledge jobs," while "lower-skilled" workers "will have to move *vertically*, not horizontally. They will have to upgrade their education and upgrade their knowledge skills [?] so that they can occupy one of the new jobs sure to be created."[21] That is to say, the causalities of offshoring have to retool and become "entrepreneurial employees" to remain competitive in a globally integrated labor market. Quite rightly, Friedman concedes that such optimism requires a "leap of faith."

The issue is further clouded by the fact that the federal government does not require companies to report data on offshored jobs. Thus the estimates of job losses are highly speculative. A sample: Forrester Research estimates that about 3.3 million U.S. service jobs will be shifted abroad by 2015, led by IT-related work. In 2004, Goldman Sachs estimated that offshoring accounted for roughly half a million layoffs in the prior three years. Another study estimates that 14 million U.S. jobs are vulnerable to being outsourced.[22] Further confounding matters, even the estimates are open to interpretation. Fact and value, the descriptive and normative, become conflated. While some hold the projected job losses to be significant, others say that they are inconsequential when compared to the normal "churn" in the economy by which millions of people change jobs every year.[23] Just "another business sea change," says a venture capitalist.

In any event, executives are firm in their belief that displaced workers will find new places of work. As Robert Bailey, president and CEO of PMC-Sierra, a multinational that produces semiconductors, put it at an industry conference:

> If you were to ask someone who had a factory jobs some years ago about unemployment, we've lost millions of factory jobs in this country and they're not here anymore. Forty percent of imports now come from overseas subsidiaries of U.S. corporations. So no steelworker has worked for 20 years? No, a lot of them moved down to Texas and other places, and that's the beauty of our economy. It is extremely resilient. And you go to Pittsburgh now and it's a biotech Mecca. I mean, things change. Steelworkers didn't go to school and become biotech engineers, but things changed and evolved, and everybody found work.[24]

Michael Corbett, a consultant whose small stature belies his immense enthusiasm for outsourcing, writes similarly:

> Some may not be willing or able to rise to the challenge of competition in a global market and will find themselves doing the same work for less money. But many more will find ways to compete and win. They will earn their current and higher salaries by getting better, learning new skills, and doing so ahead of the pack. Others will move away from the more technical parts of jobs entirely toward elements of their jobs where they add greater value, for example, customer-facing activities.[25]

I met Corbett at a conference. He was all smiles and handshakes. But such goodwill cannot hide the fact that wages in the nontechnical service sector (where workers drift in his last scenario) are low compared to "knowledge based" jobs and even manufacturing jobs, which pay 23 percent more than service sector jobs on average.[26] Moreover, the Bureau of Labor Statistics reports that between 2003 and 2006 over a third of displaced workers remained unemployed and many that found jobs took significant pay cuts. Thus, while the editor of *Wired* magazine could muse, "It is not hard to see how outsourcing to India could lead to the next great era in American enterprise," the skepticism of the public is fully understandable.[27] Furthermore, optimistic projections of job creation are simply that: projections based on historical trends. There is no guarantee that the promised high-skill, high-paying jobs will materialize or that the United States will enjoy an absolute advantage in these new areas, which would prevent a further round of offshoring.

Mutual Benefit or Zero-Sum

Critics have asked questions that nobody seems prepared to answer; about concession bargaining, about the denial of workers' rights in export-processing zones, and about the impact on wages and working conditions in the United States.[28] Nobel laureate Paul Samuelson upbraided fellow economists for perpetuating "the popular polemical untruth" that the U.S. economy will necessarily benefit in the long run from all forms of trade. The assumption that "the gains of the American winners are big enough to more than compensate for the losers," Samuelson argues, is "only an innuendo."[29] Just as offshoring is not a zero-sum game in which a job lost in the United States is a job gained in India, neither is it necessarily one of mutual benefit to workers the world over. As economists Gomory and Baumol write, there are "inherent conflicts in international trade" in that outcomes "that are best for one country . . . [can often] be disadvantageous for its trading partner."[30] While trade between a prosperous and a poor nation could be mutually beneficial, it could also depress wages and conditions in the higher wage country. Or as the "factor-price equalization" theorem would have it, trade between countries with similar technology and skill sets but different wage rates may increase the price of labor in the poorer country while reducing it in the richer country until workers in both countries end up earning similar sums.[31] But as Polaski writes,

> Until the [global] labor surplus is worked off, we can expect to see higher profits and stagnant or declining wages in the high-wage countries. These trends already have affected the manufacturing sector, which has been transformed during the past decade. Now they are beginning to affect service industries.[32]

Such considerations led a frustrated Samuelson to comment, "If you don't believe that changes the average wages in America, then you believe in the tooth fairy."[33]

And while some studies predict that offshoring will benefit the U.S. economy in the form of increased jobs and wages, media reports suggest otherwise. Bank of America, for example, cut nearly 5,000 U.S. jobs while outsourcing up to 1,100 jobs to India in 2003. In July 2004, the firm announced that it planned to cut another 12,500 U.S. jobs in the next two years. Adding insult to injury, while the bank continues to offload thousands of jobs to Indian subcontractors, the severance pay of many soon-to-be-fired workers is made contingent on the training of replacements.[34] Even the venerated "Big Blue" succumbed to the pressure to downsize and offshore. While IBM was laying off 13,000 U.S. and European workers in 2005, it was reported that it planned to increase its Indian workforce by more than 14,000. Its 53,000 Indian employees are its group largest outside of the United States, and it expects to invest $6 billion in the country over the next few years. (In the wake of the current recession, it was leaked that IBM planned to axe 5,000 U.S. jobs and move the orphaned work to India.) Arguably of greater moment is its decision to contract with Indian outsourcing company HCL Technologies to design its signature Power Architecture chips.[35]

While the overall implications can be debated, two points can be established. The first is that the majority of white-collar work being offshored is of the back-office and low-skill and clerical variety: that is, application processing, data entry, invoice and payroll preparation, customer service, basic software coding.[36] While outsourcing boosters speak with much gusto about what is to come, more than half of all export-oriented FDI projects were related to call centers in 2002–3.[37] Moreover, work has been standardized and digitized, making it easier for particular tasks to be moved. According to a former managing director at Lehman Brothers, "Even companies that have been outsourcing for 10 years haven't outsourced entire projects."[38] Asked what should and should not be offshored, Randy Altschuler, co-CEO of OfficeTiger, an outsourcing company, said that core activities usually stay onshore while "noncore" and repetitious functions can be moved: "I think you look at, frankly, how repetitive is the process? Because if the process is repetitive, you can apply technology, process improvement, and labor savings to generate efficiencies. If the process is too complicated, maybe outsourcing isn't the best solution."[39]

The second point is that while offshoring is occurring mostly in low-skill segments, there is little stopping the gradual expansion into more complex activities as firms become more comfortable with the practice. That is, services offshoring may follow the trajectory of manufacturing, from low-skilled to high-skilled labor. "From a trickle to a flood" says a consultant of the increasing scope and scale of offshoring. Raman Roy—dubbed the "father of Indian BPO" for starting the outsourcing company Spectramind and for his work at GE and American Express—told an eagerly assembled crowd at an outsourcing conference that "the sky is the limit. We are only limited by the imagination."[40] Between 1995 and 2002, 20 million factory jobs were lost in the 20 major economies because of globalization.[41] If these numbers are anything to go by, then Alan Blinder, a former vice chairman of the U.S. Federal Reserve Board and former economic adviser to President Bill Clinton, seems justified in describing offshoring as the "third industrial revolution." He writes, "We have so far barely seen the tip of the offshoring iceberg, the eventual dimensions of which may be staggering."[42]

Indeed, offshoring has crept into sectors that we previously thought were untradable internationally. The news agency Reuters offshored basic business coverage to an office in Bangalore. Legal services firms in Bombay and Gurgaon draft patents and contracts for multinationals and have recently started offering Troubled Asset Relief Program (TARP) services. Indian radiologists read X-rays, MRIs, and CT scans for less than half the cost of their U.S. counterparts, and workers process tax forms and mortgages, handle insurance claims, burnish PowerPoint presentations, and assist on special effects for movies. The market for outsourced clinical drug trials is also growing rapidly in India, where an "ethnically diverse, largely treatment-naïve populace can be recruited about three times faster than in the United States."[43] Westerners now travel to exotic locations for joint and heart-valve replacements, for dental work, and for Botox injections—a practice known as "medical tourism." Even maternal surrogacy is being outsourced internationally.[44]

And while the services sector is much larger than manufacturing, only 10 percent is presently traded internationally, compared to 50 percent in the latter. Moreover, the tradability of services affects companies in all sectors and is proceeding at a quicker pace than manufacturing. As the United Nations Conference on Trade and Development reports, "Services that are offshored may be more footloose than relocated manufacturing activities because of lower capital-intensity and sunk costs."[45] Additionally, venture capital firms are increasingly "imploring" companies to offshore as much as possible.[46] There is, thus, reason to believe that the trend will only continue.

The View from India

The murmur of somber departures is drowned by the hubbub of gay arrivals as the jobs that vanish in the West reappear in India and other "emerging" economies. In transit, work deemed fit for the young, those in-between jobs, and even rural housewives acquires a sudden sheen, its promise almost comically exaggerated. There is talk of socialist corners turned, of entrepreneurial India mimicking its way into global markets. An editorial in the *Times of India* observed that "catering to Americans" offered "immense foreign exchange opportunities" and that "IT-enabled or remote services could be the key mantra" in "getting rid" of the prickly problem of educated unemployment.[47] The evidence of this optimism is not everywhere visible, but, once found, is mesmerizing in its garishness.

On my first research trip to New Delhi I took a taxi down National Highway 8 to Gurgaon, an alleged former backwater and present-day outsourcing hub and "mall capital." When crossing the flyover that connects the two cities, my gaze drifted from the craggy fields below to the billboards above, one of which featured an outsized call center worker's comely visage, fair and framed by raven-black hair, flashing a winning smile. (A similar but exoticized photograph of a traditionally bejeweled Indian worker with a headset appeared on the cover of *Time* magazine the same year, illustrating how the imagery of the "new" India migrates across borders like the flow of work it depicts and advertises.) Welcomed by a quaint sign that read, "Thank you for visit," we passed through a toll and armed checkpoint and entered a relatively barren stretch of road. Then, almost without warning, the new metropolis started from the dusty plain like a strutting peacock. Its plumage was fine but its calls were loud and course. The taxi driver's teenage son stared with mouth agog at the iridescent whirl of office towers, apartment blocks, hotels, and fine restaurants. He said slowly and with wonder, "Call center-walleh idhar rahte hai" ("The call center ones live here"). It was not Dubai, but Gurgaon had that "city of tomorrow" feel: cement trucks, proletarians, scaffolding, and cranes offset by smartly dressed professionals shopping for Western brands at malls named Ambience, Amusement, Galaxy, Marriage, Scottish, and Specialty; the hot gleam of dynamic steal and glass facades in the afternoon sun balanced by the haze and roar of traffic and construction. These were marvelous and moving sights.

But the embrace was not entirely rapturous. The high-rises were impressive, the signage luminous, and the private clubs cozy, but there were also power outages and water shortages and slum neighborhoods. (The real estate bubble has since burst, halting mall construction and depopulating office parks and luxury housing complexes, one of which famously featured a golf course and "cigar lounge.") Misgivings about the industry that had underwritten Gurgaon's rapid rise were muted but multiple. Talk of poor labor conditions, dead-ends, graveyard shifts, accent neutralization, and identity shifting gave some a postcolonial pause. The same news media that had so loudly sung the industry's praises began expressing concern. "Stressed Techies Losing Sex Drive," read one headline. "Stressed Youth Turn to Acupressure," warned another.[48] We came to know that call center work "turns brains into soup" and people with "high ambitions either leave call centres for something better or get fired."[49] Still, outsourcing was creating jobs. And this fact was its trump card, so to speak. (Already, opponents must start with a concession: if there were no jobs, there would be nothing to criticize.) Framed in this manner, the petty problems of individuals dissolve in the immeasurable immensity of the economy.[50]

Additionally, the power of novelty should not be discounted. The outsourcing of information and communication technology (ICT) work upsets conventional assumptions about the international division of labor, wherein the production of certain goods and services is concentrated in some places and not others. Marx, in his time, wrote that the world was divided "into a chiefly agricultural field of production for supplying the other part which remains chiefly an industrial field."[51] This changed, of course, and the "new international division of labor" saw a historic shift of manufacturing from First to Third World regions. The geographical dispersion of ICT work complicates this picture. As one of the fastest growing forms of employment in the global economy and the most vulnerable to being offshored, it has been touted in respectable quarters as a solution to global unemployment and a shortcut to modernization, emerging as something of a new development paradigm.[52] Figure 1.3 illustrates the favored offshore destinations for various services.

On whole, the *Economist* estimates that India accounts for about 80 percent of the low-cost offshore service market, though this figure seems inflated.[53] Seventy percent of the exports are to the United States.[54] The number of young university graduates (those with seven or less years of work experience) in India is thought to be around 14 million, which is 1.5 times that in China and nearly double that in the United States. Furthermore, India adds 2.5 million new graduates each year.[55] So, despite rising wages and an impending "talent

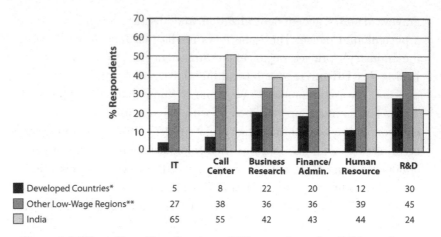

	IT	Call Center	Business Research	Finance/ Admin.	Human Resource	R&D
Developed Countries*	5	8	22	20	12	30
Other Low-Wage Regions**	27	38	36	36	39	45
India	65	55	42	43	44	24

Figure 1.3 Where Does Your Company Offshore or Intend to Offshore the Following Activities? % Respondents (N = 239)
*Developed countries: Canada, United Kingdom, Western Europe
**Other Low-Wage Regions: Africa, China, Eastern Europe and Russia, Latin America, and Asia and Pacific
Source: Diana Farrell, Noshir Kaka, and Sasha Sturz, "Ensuring India's Offshoring Future," *The McKinsey Quarterly* (2005), 76; retrieved from www.mckinseyquarterly .com/links/18836.

squeeze," India will likely continue in its role as the "world's back office" for at least the near future. And as India is "the preferred destination for offshoring of virtually the whole range of services," it is the most logical place to explore what happens when service work is moved abroad.[56]

CHAPTER TWO

Variations on a Theme

The Royal Stag Corporate Music Carnival was held in New Delhi's Mittal Gardens in late 2005. Sponsored by Seagram's, the alcohol distiller, the event featured a competition between bands composed of BPO and IT workers who played an array of American and British hard rock and heavy metal songs, such as Metallica's "The Unforgiven," Radiohead's "Creep," U2's "With or Without You," Limp Bizkit's "Take a Look Around," and Green Day's "Boulevard of Broken Dreams." While the performers represented companies like General Electric, E-funds, Wipro, EXL, and Daksh (IBM), their black T-shirts read Iron Maiden, Deep Purple, Bon Jovi, and Judas Priest. (The band registration fee of 30,000 rupees [$663] was paid by participating firms.)[1]

The neutralized accents on amplified display—which one onlooker described as the "weirdest in the whole wide world"—were courtesy of employer training programs, while the torn jeans, exaggerated gestures, and of course tunes came via globalized media. The night was capped by a performance by Saif Ali Khan, a Bollywood star and Royal Stag Whiskey "brand ambassador," of AC/DC's "Highway to Hell": "Hey Satan, paid my dues / Playing in a rocking band / Hey Momma, look at me / I'm on my way to the promised land . . ."

Afterward, Khan left for Goa to shoot a Lay's "magic masala" potato chip commercial.

❁ ❁ ❁

Globalization, we frequently hear, has led to the declining significance of place.[2] Kenichi Ohmae, for example, writes that "country of origin does not matter. Location of headquarters does not matter. The products for which you are responsible and the company you serve have become denationalized."[3] While at best an exaggerated truth, such assertions make Marx and Engels's proclamation that "all that is solid melts into air" seem an apt description of the current historical moment.[4] Through the diffusion of communication technologies, local work relations are dissolved and reconfigured across vast distances. Along the way, they alter our experiences of place and truncate the turnover time of capital. (And, as the anecdote above attests, they also influence the music we play, the clothes we wear, and the food we eat.)

But while goods, services, and investment now move at a rapid clip, labor, relatively speaking, is wedded to place.[5] What happens, then, when white-collar work is shifted overseas? Workplace culture, structures, and identities cannot simply be exported and reproduced abroad like so much capital or technology; they must be anchored in new terrain. Understanding the concrete ways in which cultural and economic forms are reinvented on the ground is thus of the utmost importance. As Yeung writes, one should be mindful of

> the ways through which capital is geographically embedded in distinct national, social, or institutional structures. . . . Geographical embeddedness of capital refers to complex and ongoing articulations of its home-country characteristics and host-country operating environments.[6]

This book is largely a story of the attempted reproduction of these home-country characteristics in India. And so the inevitable question: If offshoring relies on the mimicry of workplace norms, management strategies, and even identities, is it not a force for Westernization?

The question of globalization's impact is usually framed in a binary form, that is, cleared fields or rocky climbs, global village or Tower of Babel. My contention is that globalization does not substitute the dynamism of modernity for the complacent solidity of tradition nor the Occident for Orient. Its genius and mystery lay in the balancing of diametric modes. But while its overriding principle is hybridity, the intermingling does not occur at random or without purpose.[7] It occurs according to a plan. But not all things go as planned. To understand this difference-in-similarity, it is helpful to first explore how place is being transformed by global capitalism.

Whither Place?

If the thesis that place is of diminishing importance is at least provisionally accepted, it is necessary to consider what, if anything, it is being replaced by. Castells, for example, contrasts the "space of place" with the "space of flows."[8] The latter, he writes, "is becoming the dominant spatial manifestation of power and function in our societies." We will return to the tendential organization of space later, but what is important in his formulation is that place is a kind of space. As the geographer Tuan writes, "The ideas of 'space' and 'place' require each other for definition."[9] Place has commonsense associations of security and stability, the homely and familiar. It connotes tradition and the past. Space, by contrast, is a realm of freedom and uncertainty and possibility. It is an arena of movement; when you pause in space, you stop in a place. Place thus is space invested with meaning. One does not speak, for example, of a strongly felt sense of space. Space acquires shape and meaning through human activity. Tuan explains:

> The human being, by his mere presence, imposes a schema on space. Most of the time he is not aware of it. He notes its absence when he is lost. . . . Cultures differ greatly in their elaboration of cultural schemata. In some cultures, they are rudimentary; in others they can become a many-splendored frame that integrates nearly all the departments of life.[10]

Corporations, societies, and states, too, impose schemas on space; in Lefebvre's terms, they "produce space."[11] In the academic literature, the place-space dichotomy is applied in almost unmodified form to the relationship between labor and capital. Beynon and Hudson, for example, write that space is a "domain across which capital is constantly marching in pursuit of greater profits," while place denotes the "meaningful situations established by labor."[12] Peck argues that neoliberal strategies "attempt to reduce place to space."[13]

Capital, then, transforms the concrete realities of a particular place into the manifold possibilities of space, which is conceived of as "something usable, malleable, and therefore capable of domination through human action."[14] The implementation of this vision of timeless time (24-hour society) and placeless space (network of flows) becomes the site of struggle and negotiation between capital, the state, and civil society. And because space is not an empty container but an arena of lived experience that, like a palimpsest, retains the impress of the past, development becomes a process of "creative destruction" by which those elements of a place that are not conducive to state consolidation or capital accumulation are effaced, "pulverized" in Lefebvre's words.[15]

The struggle between labor and capital can thus be seen as a struggle over the definition of space. In recent years, capital has had the better of it. The term *neoliberalism* is used to signify the corporate revanchism whereby social welfare protections are undone by programs that privatize, liberalize, and downsize (an inversion of Polanyi's "double movement" of capitalism).[16] The contemporary period is also marked by the expanded use of subcontracting, temporary and self-employment, and the geographical dispersion of work. As with manufacturing, the standardization (and now digitization) of tasks enables corporations to globalize their operations: "By increasing the range of possible substitutions within a given production process, capitalists can increasingly free themselves from particular geographic constraints."[17]

Offshoring, in this regard, entails the extreme rationalization of jobs, projects, and tasks. Only when broken down into component parts could work be exported, and executives agree that decomposed projects are rarely made whole in the offshore office. As an executive at Proctor & Gamble remarked at an industry conference, offshoring is about "standardizing it and extracting value." Said another executive: "There is a lot of compartmentalization of tasks."[18] Thus, just as the globalization of manufacturing "brought a wave of competitive Fordist industrialization to entirely new environments," the same could be said of service offshoring and the ethos of flexibility.[19] Following Lipietz's characterization of the labor process in offshore factories as "peripheral Fordism," we can describe the present phase of globalization as involving "peripheral flexibility."[20] This produces a pockmarked economic landscape in which different modes of production ("informational," industrial, agricultural, etc.) overlap.[21]

Capital thus seems hardwired to traipse around the world in search of surplus value, pausing in space, thus in a place, like a bee stopping to pollinate.[22] To use Deleuze and Guattari's terminology, capital is territorialized (emplaced in a certain location), deterritorialized (capital and job flight), and reterritorialized (anchored in another area).[23] Through each territorialization, capital in conjunction with the state produces space. This occurs in a paradoxical way. On the one hand, it involves an indifference toward, if not a disdain for, the specificity and stubbornness of place and past. On the other, places have specific, a priori attributes that attract capital in the first place—skill sets, resources, infrastructure, cheap labor, malleable governments. These assets are seized upon and developed in accordance with specific short- and long-term interests. In other words, capital does not confront an empty plane, but an uneven landscape. The thrust may be towards uniformity and repetition, but space is not created ex nihilo.[24] Rather, it is produced "in a contested institutional landscape in which newly emergent 'projected spaces' interact conflictually with inherited regulatory arrangements."[25]

Stalk these shimmering spaces long enough and you soon realize that their creation is often predicated upon displacement and hardship. In West Bengal, for instance, the governing Communist Party of India (Marxist) has decided to industrialize the region, uprooting peasants to free up land for foreign companies, such as Dow Chemical, in the process. On March 14, 2007, police were sent to quell protesting peasants in Nandigram, a collection of villages south of Calcutta. Fourteen were shot dead and dozens were injured.[26] A similar scenario unfolded in August 2008 in NOIDA (New Okhla Industrial Development Authority), a charmingly named satellite town of Delhi, when farmers demanded higher compensation for land that had been acquired for development. Several lives were extinguished by a clutch of excitable policemen, and dozens were injured. In China, the number of people displaced by large projects and urbanization runs into the millions. Thus does Harvey describe such processes as "accumulation by dispossession."[27]

The state therefore plays a pivotal role in facilitating the circulation of capital, recommending itself as a reliable partner in the production and extraction of surplus value. Yet it must still attend to va-

TABLE 1.1
Estimates of the Development of Export Processing Zones

	1975	1986	1997	2002	2006
Number of countries with EPZs	25	47	93	116	130
Number of EPZs or similar zones	79	176	845	3,000	3,500
Employment (millions)	n.a.	n.a.	22.5	43	66
Employment in China (millions)	n.a.	n.a.	18	30	40

Source: International Labor Organization, "Database on Export Processing Zones" (2007).

riety of obligations and serve a broad range of interests. It is a vehicle for promoting the public good as well as the interests of particular classes. It must also perpetuate itself. What makes the contemporary situation unique is that political elites in developing countries are increasingly seeing their needs as coincident with the short-term interests of foreign capital.[28] (The paradigm shift from import-substitution to export-orientation is evidence of this.) And to reap the benefits of increased employment, exports, and foreign exchange, states must first foster "good business climates." This is often though not exclusively accomplished through the creation of export-processing zones (EPZs) and special economic zones (SEZs). India currently has 578 approved zones, which are designated as "foreign territories" for the purposes of trade and tariff.[29] (Table 1.1 illustrates the growth of EPZs over time.)

They provide not only cheap labor but a range of fiscal and policy incentives to exporting industries, such as "tax incentives, government services, and such features as 'total or partial exemption from laws and decrees of the country concerned.'"[30] Additionally, the mobility of capital "reduces overall costs of production while it strengthens the bargaining position of corporations vis-à-vis local governments competing for foreign investments."[31] This form of competitive bidding is an intranational matter as much as it is an international affair.

But while they continue to sprout in the global south, these seemingly homogenous zones are surprisingly diverse. As the International Labor Organization reports:

> Zones have evolved from initial assembly and simple processing activities to include high tech and science zones, finance zones, logistics centres and even tourist resorts. Their physical form now includes not only enclave-type zones but also single-industry zones (such as the jewellery zone in Thailand or the leather zone in Turkey); single-commodity zones (like coffee in Zimbabwe); and single-factory (such as the export-oriented units in India) or single-company zones (such as in the Dominican Republic).[32]

Furthermore, an intention should not be confused with its realization; the blueprint differs from happenings on the ground. This is because designs and schemas interact with the raw material of social life. Space is also appropriated for human needs, which is what gives a place its distinctive local stamp. "Desire," writes Lefebvre, "which preceded needs and goes beyond them, is the yeast that causes this rather lifeless dough (the homogenizing capitalist city) to rise. The resulting movement prevents stagnation and cannot help but produce differences."[33] Consequently, postcolonial urbanism has its own distinctive forms and cannot be reduced to Western precursors and coevals.[34]

The Production of Space in India

How did India become the "world's back office"? Briefly, starting in the 1980s, India instituted a series of probusiness reforms that helped boost the productivity of established industrial and commercial firms in the country, such as the removal of price controls, the relaxation of industrial regulations, the encouragement of capital-goods imports, and the reduction of corporate taxes.[35] The reasons for this shift are unclear, though pressures from domestic big business and the market-oriented ideology of key decision-makers in government played a part.[36] While the focus was initially on domestic deregulation, the political class began encouraging entrepreneurial activities and integration into the world economy.[37] According to Pederson, a "quiet revolution" occurred within Indian industry, whereby a new breed of industrialist that had emerged as a result of early policy changes began pushing for a new development strategy.[38] The macroeconomic picture also changed. While current revenues had previously exceeded expenditures, the surplus turned into deficits as a result of lax fiscal policies. To finance investment and consumption India had to borrow heavily from the World Bank, International Monetary Fund, and bilateral donors.[39] The situation was compounded by domestic political instability and rising oil prices during the Gulf War.

The reforms of 1991 were more comprehensive and far-reaching. In consequence of indebtedness and a foreign exchange crisis, India partly opened its economy to global trade and investment under the counsel of the World Bank and the IMF.[40] This "New Economic Policy," initiated by the finance minister, Manmohan Singh, consummated a dramatic shift in development strategy that had begun a decade earlier, as the emphasis was now decidedly on exports and a greater reliance on market forces. Changes in trade policy allowed access to imports and technology at low rates of duty. Foreign direct investment was also sought, "driven by the belief that this would increase the total volume of investment in the economy, improve production technology and increase access to world markets."[41] Majority and even 100 percent foreign ownership is now allowed in many key industries.

Given its large pool of educated and English-speaking labor, India fast emerged as the favored destination for business process outsourcing and information technology. In the 1990s General Electric established a joint venture in the country and subcontracted software development and maintenance and back-office work to Indian suppliers, such as Wipro and Tata.[42] Other multinationals, such as Microsoft, Cisco, Xerox, and Honeywell, soon followed suit. A former managing director at Lehman Brothers puts the rationale plainly at an industry conference: "The country offered us cheap labor and skilled people." Additionally, many expatriate Indians who had set up "bodyshops" in Silicon Valley, which imported high-tech workers on H1-B and L-1 visas, established service operations in India.[43] As an executive put it, "Immigrants become knowledge workers except they enter through portals rather than ports." The end result, writes Krugman, is that "India's surge into world markets hasn't followed the pattern set by other developing nations, which started their export drive in low-tech industries like clothing. Instead, India has moved directly into industries that advanced countries like the United States thought were their exclusive turf."[44]

A nonexhaustive list of companies offshoring services to India: Accenture, Adobe, Amazon.com, American Express, AT&T, Bank of America, Barclays, Boeing, British Airways, Chevron, Churchill Insurance, Cisco, Citibank, Dell, Delta, Deutsche Bank, EDS, Gateway Computers, General Electric, GE Capital, GlaxoSmithKline, Hewlett Packard, HSBC, IBM, Intel, JC Penney, J.P. Morgan Chase, Kodak, Merck, Microsoft, Novell, Oracle, Phillips, Proctor & Gamble, Reuters, Royal Sun & Alliance, Siemens, Standard Chartered, Sun Microsystems, Texas Instruments, United Airlines, and Washington Mutual.[45]

India's export revenues in IT and IT-enabled services (ITES) are reported to have grown from less than $0.5 billion in 1994 to $40.4 billion in 2008. The industry's share of the country's GDP reached 5.2 percent in 2007. The number of workers employed in the sector is estimated to have grown from 830,000 in 2004 to over two million in 2008.[46]

While I know of no large-scale survey of the workforce, the following can be said of its demographic makeup. It is young, well educated, and urban, as English and computer literacy are necessary conditions for employment. The majority of workers are Hindu and upper caste. They also tend to have been educated at English-medium and often private schools.[47] Generally speaking, software and IT workers tend to be better educated and earn more than BPO/ITES workers, though the latter still do well by national standards. The ratio of men to women is reported to be 69:31 in IT and reversed in favor of women in BPO/ITES, according to the industry group, Nasscom.[48] Indeed, call center managers routinely describe workplaces as gender-desegregated.[49] Most surveys, however, suggest a more balanced gender ratio in the latter.[50] All told, the outsourcing workforce constitutes less than 1 percent of the overall population. Its privileged status can be seen in the fact that some 74 percent of households in India earned less than $2,000 in 2002, while these workers earn more than double that sum.[51]

TABLE 1.2
IT and ITES/BPO Sector Performance in India in U.S. dollars (in billions)

	FY2004	FY2005	FY2006	FY2007	FY2008
IT Services	10.4	13.5	17.8	23.5	31.0
Exports	7.3	10.0	13.3	18.0	23.1
Domestic	3.1	3.5	4.5	5.5	7.9
ITES-BPO	3.4	5.2	7.2	9.5	12.5
Exports	3.1	4.6	6.3	8.4	10.9
Domestic	0.3	0.6	0.9	1.1	1.6
Other	2.9	3.8	5.3	6.5	8.6
Exports	2.5	3.1	4.0	4.9	6.4
Domestic	0.4	0.7	1.3	1.6	2.2
Total	16.7	22.5	30.3	39.5	52.0
of which exports are:	12.9	17.7	23.6	31.3	40.4

Source: National Association of Software and Service Companies, "Indian IT Industry Fact Sheet" (2008).
*Includes engineering services and R&D and software products.

There is little natural about India's relative advantage in services. What is neglected in conventional narratives of India's rise is the state's promotion of scientific and technological development over time. This can be seen in the international reputation of its seven Indian Institutes of Technology; its 1998 National IT Action Plan, which created software technology parks throughout the country; and its improved telecommunications infrastructure. Yet it is common to hear that the Indian outsourcing industry has succeeded in spite of, rather than because of, state policies. As the former CEO of one of India's largest outsourcing companies told me, "The reason for the success of IT companies was that they were never regulated. Once things took off, there were all sorts of ministers asking what else they could do. They wanted a stake in things. We would say, 'Please, nothing.'"

Nonetheless, the state has taken an active role in attracting foreign investment. A newly minted Ministry of Information Technology has

TABLE 1.3
Employment Figures in the IT and ITES/BPO Sector

	2000–1	2001–2	2002–3	2003–4	2004–5	2005–6	2006–7	2007–8
IT Exports & services	162,000	170,000	205,000	296,000	390,000	513,000	690,000	860,000
BPO exports	70,000	106,000	180,000	216,000	316,000	415,000	553,000	700,000
Domestic market	198,114	246,250	285,000	318,000	352,000	365,000	378,000	450,000
Total	430,114	522,250	670,000	830,000	1,058,000	1,293,000,	1,621,000	2,010,000

Source: National Association of Software and Services Companies, "Indian IT Industry Fact Sheet" (2008).

been tasked with converting the country's notorious red tape into "a red carpet" for multinationals. Export production in special economic zones and software technology parks "is organized on an internationally competitive basis with requisite infrastructure, tax holidays, subsidized land, dependable power supplies, and duty free imports, among other things."[52] Deeply linked to major nodes in the global economy, these spaces have an ambiguous relationship to their immediate environs: companies pay little to no taxes and are largely removed from the domestic market. The BPO policy of the state of Karnataka, whose capital is Bangalore (India's "Silicon Valley"), describes some of the features of SEZs:

> BPO units set up in SEZs are specifically delineated duty-free enclaves treated as a foreign territory for the purpose of industrial, service and trade operations, with exemption from customs duties and a more liberal regime in respect of other levies. To promote foreign investment and other transactions, domestic regulations, restrictions and infrastructure inadequacies are sought to be eliminated in the SEZs for creating a hassle-free environment. . . . The State is committed to simplify[ing] all the relevant enactments for the BPO sector. The barriers, including employment of women at night, flexi working hours, [and] mandatory weekly offs, have all been removed . . . to create an optimal environment for the growth of the BPO sector in the state.[53]

Even the government of West Bengal, which has been led by the communist Left Front for over three decades, has tried to erase its image as a land of refractory labor by offering similar concessions and reforms. The state's IT policy, which reads like a marketing brochure, states that its incentive package is "significantly more competitive than that offered by other states" and is "the best of the breed in the country."[54] It quotes Pramod Bhasin, president of GE Capital, offering the following accolades: "This is a very detailed proposal and addresses every concern raised by us. In fact, we have not been able to keep pace with that of your government." Likewise, the aforementioned former CEO says that labor laws are "pretty flexible" for the industry: "When we went to Calcutta, we met with the chief minister. West Bengal is the only state to declare IT essential services alongside the fire brigade and police, which outlaws strikes in a place where there are a lot of strikes." (He, however, is incorrect; various states have since designated the industry a "public utility.") The Government of Haryana explains the implications of the "simplification" of labor laws:

> The IT-ITES industries have also been added to the First Schedule of the Industrial Disputes Act, 1947 for the purpose of declaring the sectors as "Public Utility Services," which will prevent the occurrence of strikes as well as lockouts without due notice. This provision is expected to go a long way in preventing industrial unrest in Haryana's IT-ITES sectors. . . . The Haryana Government has adopted a liberal policy in granting the players in this segment exemption from the provisions of the Punjab Shops and Commercial Establishment Act, 1958, regarding opening and closing hours. . . . The Government has also taken a policy decision to allow the employment of women workers during night shifts, to encourage employment of women while ensuring the sufficient protection of their rights.[55]

In consequence of this increased flexibility, the outsourcing industry is characterized by an extensive use of temporary and contract labor, individualized employment relations, and high turnover.[56] Like restless spouses experimenting with open relationships, companies are freed from the usual constraints on hiring and firing workers. As Robert Bailey, president and CEO of PMC-Sierra, remarked of the company's Indian operation at an industry conference, "There's a scalability factor, where you can dramatically increase headcount very, very quickly. There's also flexibility: you can bring it down very quickly as well, without the inertia, the internal inertia you usually have." It is not all hire-and-fire policies and economic insecurity, however. Flexibility works both ways: labor demand presently exceeds supply, resulting in pay raises and various perks, job-hopping, and decent working conditions.

Reification and Mimicry

> Nature creates similarities. One need only think of mimicry. The highest
> capacity for producing similarities, however, is man's. His gift of seeing
> resemblances is nothing other than a rudiment of the powerful compulsion
> in former times to become and behave like something else. Perhaps there is
> none of his higher functions in which his mimetic faculty does not play a
> role.
>
> —*Walter Benjamin*[57]

Global capitalism proceeds through the production of spaces, such as
quasi-national special economic zones, that are relatively homogenous
in form and yet distinct in content. (This project is a collaborative one
between capital and the state.) In this section, we look at how this process unfolds in practice. It works, first, by obfuscation, by masking its
operations (e.g., *dead ringers*), and, second, through the imitation and
repetition of certain cultural, economic, and political forms (e.g., *imitative counterpoint*). The notion of reification is helpful here. First, reification can be understood as "the effacement of the traces of production."[58] This is intensified by global integration. As Willis writes, "If
as Marx defined them, commodities are the containers of hidden social
relationships, certainly these social relationships are all the more con-
cealed by the movement of production to the Third World."[59] (The
danger is that if these traces become evident, the consuming public
will feel angry or anxious.) That India is referred to as the "world's
back office" implies that many of these activities were already out of
view to begin with. Few ordinary workers interact directly with corporate clients. ("We don't allow anybody from India to talk to clients in
the U.S. or anywhere," says an Indian executive.) In those activities
where interaction is unavoidable, such as customer service, smoke-
screens are deployed to obscure the location of workers. (This can
even apply to intrafirm technical support, such as at General Electric.)
The combined effect is that the geographic signature—"Made in
India"—is occluded.

The second sense of reification—the "transformation of social relations into things"—is equally important.[60] Once objectified, cultural

models can be exported and copied. Thus accompanying material flows across space is a whole train of representations. As I shall argue, in the execution of work previously performed in the West, offshoring is mimetic in a number of senses. Yet mimesis would seem an odd concept to use in discussing economic affairs. The faculty to copy, the impulse to become like another, is thought to be premodern and "beyond reason."[61] For Habermas the concept "appears to be a placeholder for primordial reason," which "recalls to mind the model of an exchange of the subject with nature that is free of violence."[62] As applied to social relations, it denotes a sympathetic and accommodating attitude:

> Imitation designates a relation between persons in which the one accommodates to the other. There is an allusion here to a relation in which the surrender of the one to the other does not mean a loss of self but a gain and an enrichment. Because the mimetic capacity escapes the conceptual framework of cognitive-instrumentality . . . it counts as the sheer opposite of reason, as impulse.[63]

But as Benjamin writes, this "powerful compulsion in former times to become and behave like something else" is deeply involved in our "higher functions."[64] How is this so? Whereas for Adorno and Horkheimer, mimesis once denoted a relationship to nature in which the "outside world [serves] a model which the inner world must try to conform to" for purposes of survival, it was later subjected to conscious control through magic (by which "shamans warded off danger by means of images imitating that danger") and has finally (and tragically) been appropriated by instrumental rationality.[65] What we are getting at is not the demise of mimesis but its mutation:

> Civilization has replaced the organic adaptation to others and mimetic behavior proper . . . by rational practice, by work. . . . Uncontrolled mimesis is outlawed. . . . The ego has been formed in resistance to mimicry. In the constitution of the ego reflective mimesis becomes controlled reflection. . . . In the bourgeois mode of production, the indelible mimetic heritage of all practical experience is consigned to oblivion. . . . Science is repetition, refined into observable regularity, and preserved in stereotypes. . . . Technology

[works] by automation of the mental processes, by converting them into blind cycles. With its triumph human statements become both controllable and inevitable. . . . The pitiless prohibition becomes mere fate; the denial is now so complete that it is no longer conscious.[66]

Offshoring can be seen as a highly "sublimated manifestation of mimicry"; it is mimicry subject to rational control and the rules of capital accumulation. Work processes are standardized, replicable, and predictable, one task following the other in serial progression. Call center personalities involve a form of emotional mechanization as well as the carefully choreographed mimicry of Westerners. Even in some aspects of IT work, where employers try to construct new work identities, the reformed personality is to be based on a stereotype of the Western professional and is yet another form of rationalized copying. For those on the permanent night shift, this also means living as if they were in the same time zone and imaginative space as American and British consumers.

This does not mean, however, that offshore workplaces are facsimiles or faithful copies of those in the home country. Given that offshoring relies on plans abstracted from concrete reality, the offshore workplace is both a copy and a "copy that is not a copy."[67] This latter point registers the way that things resemble each other yet take on a life of their own; how things are "almost the same, but not quite."[68] As Sontag writes, "The life of an institution cannot be appreciated by examining a blueprint of its structure; run under the auspices of different feelings, similar structures can have a different quality."[69] In Deleuze and Guattari's terms, you could say that offshore sites "form a rhizome" with onshore offices, a relationship marked by "an aparallel evolution."[70] The notion of imitative counterpoint captures this difference-in-similarity.

Mimed forms are transposed into a different key. Offshore workplaces resemble those in the United States and Western Europe, but they perform work that is at the lower end of the skill and value spectrum, often work that those in the home office would prefer not to do. These high-tech spaces seem to glow with the prospects of development, but they are outposts of Western economic hegemony, not exactly servile but not independent either. Memes like the *flexible professional* and the *entrepreneurial employee* mean something altogether different in the Indian context, as we will see. It is thus not the case that mimicry is "consigned to oblivion." Rather, capitalism has arrogated the mimetic faculty and transformed it into something more organized and less intuitive.

Modern Mimicry

> Not all people exist in the same Now. They do so externally, by virtue of the fact that they may all be seen today. But that does not mean that they are living at the same time with others. Rather, they carry earlier things with them. . . . In general, different years resound in the one that has just been recorded and prevails.
>
> —*Ernst Bloch*[71]

If Bloch could write so insistently about "the non-synchronicity of synchronicity" and the "simultaneity of the non-simultaneous" in the 1930s, one cannot conclude that today's juxtaposition of "outmoded" and "modern" ways of being is nonpareil. The Baroque fugue, for example, was described by Adorno as "the most technical achievement of musical rationalization."[72] Yet, as Said pointed out, what made the fugue radical was its "union of antiquated contrapuntal devices with a modern rational subject."[73] Offshoring is a provocateur in this sense. It unsettles the sense of spatial and temporal continuity by combining experiences and values of different times and climes.

The foreign and familiar, the alien and the accustomed, are promiscuously intermingled. Anachronistic elements flourish in the midst and even at the expense of the modern or contemporary. On the one hand, we see "motives and reserves from precapitalist times and structures" and the "surmounted remnants of older economic being and consciousness" manifest themselves in the docility of workers and the high-handedness of management.[74] On the other, the individualism unleashed by the comparatively open workplace atmosphere takes on an unexpected character in a context of high labor demand. Rather than translating into increased responsibility and professionalism as management intends, it takes the form of possessive individualism and skittish job-hopping. The deferent worker fresh out of school and buffeted by managerial demands for professionalism therefore enacts a unique form individualism that partakes of contrasting qualities: workers can be surprisingly servile *and* astonishingly assertive. Likewise, managerial power is simultaneously personal and arbitrary as well as rational and transparent. Its motivational techniques are both highhanded and forward-thinking.

Globalization is full of contradictions that generate uneasy balances. The resurgence of religious-political conservatism and its embrace of economic liberalization, as evidenced in the Hindu nationalist Bhara-tiya Janata Party's 2004 election slogan, "India Shining," is one such incongruity. The decision by the communist Left Front government of West Bengal to alter labor regulations, displace peasants, and offer generous incentives to attract foreign capital is another. Additionally, India's quick integration into global markets—what some call its "second independence"—belies its semiperipheral position in the world economy.

Globalization also tampers with time. The temporal orientations of border-bending capitalism and Indian social life become enmeshed in each other. Postindustrialism has certainly provided some respite from the drudgery of rigid routine. But this era of flexibility has also ushered in longer and busier hours. Culturally, women's employment rankles conservative sensibilities, especially with the night shift's intimations of prurience: call centers, call girls. But while it troubles the boundaries of the patriarchal family, it does not undermine it. The ghost of history is apparent in the reactionary provincialism—the nostalgia of tradition—that ranges itself against the relativism of spendthrift workers.[75] These antithetic romanticisms of past and future shape the cultural politics of outsourcing in India.

So, in many ways, the tired tropes of modernity and tradition obscure more than they clarify. The Indian middle class, for example, is at once heralded as a harbinger of modernity and bemoaned as a bastion of conservatism. In this connection, Dirlik suggests that we have moved from a "temporalization of difference (modern versus primitive, backward, pre-modern or traditional, etc.) into a re-spatialization of difference," whereby spaces are created that stake conflicting claims to modernity.[76] It follows that there are multiple modernities, not a universal global modernity. That a plethora of social forms coexist in the present, however, does not solve the problem of the lingering past as Bloch posed it. As Thrift writes, "Nearly all spaces bear the freight of their past."[77]

Instead of viewing modernization as a linear process or as an ahistorical collection of modernities, the process must be understood dialectically: The modern defines itself against the traditional and, by reviving its memory, brings it into being. The same holds for space and place, for rationality and nonrationality, for maturity and immaturity, for regressive and flexible forms of labor organization, for servility and professionalism, and so on. In other words, it would be wrong to speak of the past as a lingering residue that will soon be washed away like so much flotsam by the high tide of modernity. Rather, modernity provides the conditions of possibility for the resurgence of the "primitive," for the "return of the repressed," and for the appearance of "living and newly revived nonsynchronisms."[78] De Certeau, for example, writes that "popular practices" that have resurfaced "within industrial and scientific modernity . . . cannot be confined to the past, the countryside, or primitive peoples. They exist in the heart of the strongholds of the contemporary economy."[79]

Modernization therefore entails the "perpetual disruption of temporal and spatial rhythms."[80] If tradition did not exist, modernity would have to invent it.[81] It must range itself against something, which it invariably portrays as stolid, slow, and obsolete. As we shall soon see, the Indianness of employees is constructed as "traditional" by employers and managers, as something that is jarringly out of place in today's whirling world. And once this representation of the dilatory and deferent Indian—which borrows heavily from Orientalist discourses—is solidified, the ground is cleared for the creation of the mythic Western professional on native soil. But the process is always incomplete: if one fossilized tradition is effaced (*homo hierachicus*), another is fashioned (*homo bureaucraticus*) and duly politicized.[82] In this way, the construction of the modern is predicated on the invention of the traditional.[83]

The world then seems a confusing mess, but Dirlik poses an important question that allows us to make some sense of it: "Does the recognition of heterogeneity necessitate the repudiation of the existence of structural forces globally?"[84] Characterizations of globalization as a "hybridization which gives rise to a global mélange" are accurate but, to my mind, seem overly descriptive and lacking in structural context.[85] Economic globalization is not aleatory but is shaped by the needs and aspirations of multinational corporations. Thus while capital's various destinations all put their own distinctive stamp on the production process, mimicry generally does not work both ways, or at least not on the same scale. While acknowledging difference, then, it is important not to fall into a sort of culturalist hybridity fetishism that celebrates difference, fragmentation, and dislocation and glosses over historically and structurally determined inequalities.[86] Offshoring, and by extension economic globalization, is largely a corporate strategy and not a reconfiguration of political and economic relations, however rapidly the international division of labor seems to change.

The Seductions of the West

If, as Taussig writes, the history of mimesis is profoundly tied to "Euro-American colonialism," then today's variant is deeply connected to corporate globalization.[87] (A key difference is that it works in a much more diffuse way.) Colonialism pitted "civilization" against "savagery"; economic globalization pits "developed" against "developing." Both produce a strong compulsion to imitate, particularly on the part of privileged strata in the so-called developing world. Today, with the waning appeal of postcolonial nationalism, consumer-oriented mimicry has emerged as an integral component of class and personal identity.

Parvati has lost favor to Lakshmi.[88] Postreform India has done away with moral squeamishness about open displays of wealth. As Mehta writes, "In the old days, if you had it, you hid it. We were a poor country and self-denial was solidarity."[89] The newfound individualism is expressed in consumerism, drinking, lavish celebrations, Western-style "love marriages," a preference for English, and even the patron-age of multinational fast food chains like McDonalds, Pizza Hut, and KFC whose clientele is generally well-to-do. "All devotion," write Adorno and Horkheimer, "has a touch of mimicry about it."[90]

By a kind of Hegelian ruse of history, what seems at first blush a modernist impulse to create an authentic identity, can be interpreted as its opposite; namely, the sensual, prerational, and childlike ten-dency to copy. If mimesis, as Alford writes of its original sense as a relationship between people and nature, "appears to be an impulse without an appropriate object," the mimetic aspirations and commod-ity lust of workers and employers, too, appear spontaneous and dream-like.[91] The second sense of reification—the transformation of social relations into things—also applies to the seductions of the West. Peo-ple develop sympathetic relationships to its figurations whether as commodities, as lifestyles, or as other forms of popular culture. Through its reification and global diffusion, "the West" becomes a cathetic object that is invested with emotional energy. As in children's games, which are "everywhere interlaced with mimetic modes of be-havior," identity-shifting at call centers is seen as a space of "play" by some workers.[92] Ironically, the practice is pushed on them as job re-quirements at multinationals, the primary forces of "modernization."

Thus while Adorno's point about the rationalization of mimicry is well taken, it is perhaps overstated. In Benjamin's view, this "regres-sive" and subconscious capacity to copy is reinvented by modern means. As Buck-Morss writes of Benjamin's views on film and photography:

He noted . . . that the camera arrests the flow of perception and cap-tures the most subtle physical gestures. "Through it we experience an optical unconscious as in psychoanalysis we first experience the instinctual unconscious." Film provides a new schooling for our mi-metic powers: "Within the enlargement space is stretched out; within slow motion, movement expands," revealing "entirely new structural formations of matter."[93]

In their immediacy, images unlock and open up; they elicit emotion and invite the spectator to identify with them. The intimate texture of the other is experienced in sensuous detail. The far is brought near. In this connection, how much does the *habitus* of the call center worker, and the young upper-middle-class Indian for that matter, owe to the globalization of Western imagery, television, film, and music? That these forms are copied more closely and comprehensively than before can be seen in such things as the Royal Stag Corporate Music Carnival, which I alluded to in this chapter's introduction. The point here is that even "prerational" and playful forms of mimicry can be put to profitable use.

Lefebvre contrasts the "abstract space" of domination and homogenization with the "absolute" space of human appropriation.[94] Put otherwise, if space is the domain of abstract rationality, rules, bureaucracy, and institutions, then place is the "politically enabling" realm of intimacy, feeling, and belonging.[95] But this realm of everyday life is not necessarily one of hope or resistance. Consumerism and possessive individualism, for example, trouble such an easy distinction. They are "freedoms" that do not contest power but confirm it. In Lefebvre's terms, consumer capitalism—"the bureaucratic society of controlled consumption"—aims to "cybernetize society by the indirect agency of everyday life . . . [T]here are powers, colossal and despicable, that swoop down on everyday life and pursue their prey in its evasions and departures, dreams and fantasies to crush it in their relentless grip."[96] In consumer society, power works through "seduction rather than repression."[97] Absent an equal and opposite response, "abstract space" and "absolute space" merge into one depressing consumer spectacle.

This can even be seen in how labor problems are dealt with. The politically disabling conditions of work—particularly the stress of the graveyard shift, long hours, and an intense work pace—are assuaged not through collective organization but by the individualized consumption of stimulants to stay alert. The sweet, milky tea that workers imbibe at all hours has a historical antecedent in industrializing England. Tea with sugar (the fruit of slavery and colonial rapine) "was the first substance to be part of the work break." Along with other sucrose-laden foods, it supplied "quick energy" and "stimulus to greater effort without providing nutrition."[98] The thin columns of cigarette smoke rising from India's technology parks, moreover, are symbols of the underside of the digital revolution, just as the black clouds of soot bellowing from factory smokestacks stood for the pernicious effects of the Industrial Revolution. Of course the physical and emotional hardships exacted by the latter were far greater than anything India's ICT workforce will ever face.[99] The irony is that rather than seeing them as necessary evils in a topsy-turvy work culture, the stimulants and junk food of the global "24-hour society" are extolled as emblems of choice in the postmodern apotheosis of the consumer-citizen.

Globalization, then, makes other cultures more emulatable. It provides the conditions not for the declining significance of place but for the emergence of a "global sense of place."[100]

CHAPTER THREE. **Macaulay's (Cyber) Children**

> We must at present do our best to form a class who may be interpreters
> between us and the millions whom we govern; a class of persons Indian in
> blood and colour, but English in taste, in opinions, in morals, and in
> intellect.
>
> —*Lord Babington Macaulay, "Minute on Education," 1835*

South Delhi is a dense settlement of middle-class homes and shopping markets, pitted with occasional slums, gardens, and Mughal landmarks. Its ethos is largely consumerist. The banner headline of a community newspaper during the Hindu festival of Diwali asks, "Want to Get Wealthy?" The question is material but the speculations are airily religious. "What pleases Goddess Lakshmi [the goddess of wealth]? When does she bless us with all the riches and comforts of the world? Different people have different answers: some say, it is the gem that you wear, the goddess that you worship, the colour that you paint your walls in or how big is your wealth vase [sic]."

The dance floor of an area night club is occupied by tight clusters of young men and women in designer clothes, all of whom, one presumes, have rather large wealth vases. Rita, a 22-year-old call center worker, has drunk five cocktails priced at 250 rupees a piece, approximately $25 in total—a large sum in a country where 35 percent of the people live on less than $1 a day. Although city regulations require bars to stop serving alcohol at midnight, the club simply locks the front door and allows the intoxicating flow to continue. After a night of dancing, Rita's head is beginning to spin. Her growing dizziness and fatigue are amplified by the kaleidoscopic whirl of strobe lights and a dance floor that undulates "boombonically" to a Bhangra remix of rapper 50 Cent's "In Da Club."

Rita is out with her team of six call center workers—the excursion is sponsored by their company to foster camaraderie within the group. Her long swaying hair cannot hide her pale face, which is a knot of exhaustion and sickness. Noticing her obvious discomfort, Deepak, her junior manager, gathers the rest of the team that is gyrating to the hybrid beats. They board a black Toyota Qualis with tinted windows, one of hundreds hired by the company to transport workers to and from work. When they arrive at Rita's house, Deepak steps out of the vehicle, walks confidently up the dimly lit driveway, and rings the doorbell. He is followed by Rita, who is being assisted clumsily by another inebriated worker. Rita's mother answers the door.

"Hello, Auntie, here is your daughter," says Deepak, drawing out the last rolling syllable sinisterly, barely able to contain his mirth. We may picture her, a housewife dressed in a nightgown with a diaphanous shawl draped over her frail shoulders (for it is late and a bit cool) standing in the doorway, one hand clutching the doorknob, the other on the jamb to support her weight, gazing over Deepak's shoulder and around his smile. What thoughts pass through her mind as she catches sight of her only daughter, her hair bunched into a loose ball by a supportive coworker, leaning awkwardly over an outer hedgerow thick with the first spring growth? Is she shocked and dismayed by the sight? Is she afraid of calling out and waking the neighbors? One thing is certain: her daughter's behavior has proved the alarmists right. The outsourcing industry is a den of sin and immorality, tempting the young and chaste with refulgent, air-conditioned offices in chrome and glass towers, with therapists and destressing rooms, and, of course, parties.

While outsourcing has provided welcome foreign investment and employment, the resulting cultural change is not easily reconcilable with certain aspects of Indian social life. Though not yet fully articulated as such, as in Williams's notion of "structures of feeling," what the clash supposes is two different moral worlds.[1] The first is one in which marriage is arranged by family, gratification is delayed, and the individual is engulfed and defined by a dense web of family and social obligations. The second posits an autonomous, pleasure-seeking self that no doubt derives succor from family, but is defined more by the voluntary choices it makes. At a remove from the traditional sources and enforcers of societal values—extended families, lifelong neighbors, religious authorities—workers construct their own, but not from scratch.[2]

The identities and aspirations of the ICT workforce are defined increasingly with reference to the West. Outsourcing has emboldened a class of cultural emulators and made their protest visible. Radical in their rejection of old values, conspicuous in their consumption, workers construct an image of the West that is used to benchmark India's progress towards modernity. The infusion of new money and jobs, however, feeds popular anxieties that stretch virtue into vice: too much personal freedom, too much consumerism. In this chapter, I argue that globalization does not herald an era of unprecedented personal or consumer freedom, a belated "modernity," nor does it signify a crisis of the "traditional" Indian family. Rather, it gives rise to an Indian morality play where the pleasure principle clashes with the demands of custom and obligation, where *kama* (pleasure) and *dharma* (duty) meet in uneasy suspension.

The New Middle Classes and the Bird of Gold

In 1841, the French writer and diplomat François-René de Chateaubriand asked what a "universal society" would look like. "Would the fusion of societies result in a universal idiom," he wondered, "or would there be a dialect of transactions serving daily usage, while each nation spoke its own language, or would a different language be understood by everyone?"[3] Such questions are again apposite in an era in which "our world and our lives are being shaped by the conflicting trends of globalization and identity."[4]

One school of thought on globalization understands it to be a force for the elision of cultural difference.[5] As modernization theory would have it, developing countries, with varying degrees of enthusiasm, are steadily moving toward the norms and cultures of the West by dint of transfers of technology and capital.[6] "The crucial sociological question," writes Bell, "is whether we still may have 'national' cultures that set off countries from one another."[7] Appadurai counters that if indeed "a global culture is emerging, it is filled with ironies and resistances."[8] In response to the seeming simplicity of the homogenization thesis, globalization is now viewed in terms of contestation, overlap, and disjuncture. Cultural fragmentation and modernist homogenization are said to be "equally constitutive" features of global reality.[9]

It is difficult to take issue with these compromise positions, for they are almost too reasonable. But while it has become fashionable to speak of postcolonial identity in terms of hybridity, the term obscures the direction of cultural change.[10] British colonialism in India, for example, produced not an exact copy of British English but a new variant, Indian English. Yet one must acknowledge that it also resulted in the relative Anglicization of the subject population. Likewise with corporate globalization. However partial and contested the process, recent years have witnessed the diffusion of a consumerist ethos in developing societies. Terms such as *invidious distinction* and *conspicuous consumption* have acquired a renewed significance.[11] The elaboration of a culture of consumerism is not merely a superstructural consequence of the formation of the middle class.[12] As Liechty writes, it is one of "the most important cultural processes through which an emerging middle class actually creates itself as a sociocultural entity."[13] Consumption has become a "privileged site for the fabrication of self and society, of culture and identity."[14]

As auto-rickshaws are displaced by taxicabs, tandoori kitchens by fast food chains, and teahouses by Internet cafes, the consumption of high-end goods and the emulation of Western lifestyles become markers of socioeconomic position. (Some see these developments, considered in the long sweep of Indian history, as evidence that the "bird of gold," a reference to the country's once renowned marketplace, is again taking flight.)[15] The "new middle class" exhibits many of the cultural contradictions—the undermining of the classic work ethic by a culture of consumerism and "hedonism"—that a vexed Daniel Bell considered in his book on postindustrial America.[16] Status distinctions based on ascribed characteristics like caste are giving way to those based on education, occupation, and income.[17] Economic liberalization is further razing the walls—the traditions of sobriety and thrift, the government sinecures and stable career paths—that have hitherto kept India's middle class in modest comfort. In their place rise ladders of corporate ascension as well as the multiplied possibilities of free fall.

How are we to understand this growing convergence of identities and lifestyles and even structural conditions? First, globalization must be disaggregated. Insofar as the relevance of classificatory devices—First and Third World, East and West—has been undermined by new forms of communication and production, the idea of a unitary "global village" is yet a fiction.[18] The village is traversed by historical fractures and political and economic divisions that have proved more difficult to elide than geography. Moreover, people are positioned differently with respect to these divisions, and they experience and interpret them accordingly. Attention must be therefore paid to the concrete practices of particular groups.

The argument about the fugue-like character of globalization is relevant here. While offshore spaces of work are structured according to Western conventions, local realities impart a unique coloration. As Mirchandani writes:

> While Indian workers are taught to mimic American work norms, there is a slippage between the information they are presented about Americans and the ways in which they interpret this information. In this sense, mimicry involves not only the colonizer's construction of the Other, but also the Other's construction of the colonizer.[19]

Moreover, as Jameson argues, the appropriation of another culture means first "inventing the culture of the other group" as an object of prestige and envy—effectively adding another layer of mediation.[20] As I have argued, corporate globalization produces sameness and dissimilarity simultaneously.

Women, Wine, and Water

The National Capital Region, encompassing New Delhi and the satellite industrial cities of Gurgaon and NOIDA, is host to over 30 transnational call centers. I scheduled a meeting in Gurgaon with Deepak, Rita's junior manager, at Café Coffee Day, the largest retail café chain in the country. It is a favorite of middle-class youth, and most of the gossiping and whispered backstabbing takes place in a mix of Hindi and the former colonial tongue, which is ever a mark of distinction. Even if you place your order in flawless Hindi, the smiling cashier will respond in thickly accented English.

Deepak arrives 15 minutes late. Clad in faded jeans, leather jacket, and black patent shoes that reflect the ceiling lights in bright flashes, he walks to the table with a swagger. The rings and creases about his tired eyes mar an otherwise clear and youthful complexion. Because of the necessity of working the night shift, BPO employees, more often than not, are exhausted, however much they are able to recalibrate their internal clocks to the intent rhythms of the global economy. Deepak has recently been promoted to junior manager, and the small salary increase has been accompanied by a haughty boost in status. Deepak the manager consorts not with other workers but with the likes of the company vice president. He evinces a casual disdain for those beneath him, the poor souls like Rita that remind him of his former, easily duped self.

Monetary incentives alone, he explains, are no longer effective in retaining people in an industry with extremely high turnover—on the order of 25–40 percent annually. "No matter how much you give them in salary and bonuses, it's never enough. One guy uses his money to buy a dress for his girlfriend. She's happy. But then she wants something more, like a necklace or flowers. It never ends. Now we're trying nonmonetary incentives like, you know, packets of cigarettes, taking them out drinking," Deepak carps in the manner of an exasperated parent. Then, leaning closer, he says in a tone of conspiratorial bonhomie, "My VP has a philosophy [to reduce turnover]. Women . . . wine . . . and water."

However nonsensical and off-putting the alliterative "philosophy," it illustrates the lengths companies will go to retain (at least male) workers. Because of a labor market in which demand outpaces supply, they make gestures toward indulging workers' perceived bacchanalian instincts. The CEO of a call center firm says that parties are a necessary "motivational tool in BPO culture. Everyone has to do it." Even a new union that is trying to organize BPO workers initially threw large parties to attract workers. Little organizing was actually accomplished, as workers were more interested in the alcohol than the union charter. And much to the chagrin of employers, the industry's reputation for promiscuity has even earned it visits from the government health ministry's AIDS awareness program. But aside from such ethically questionable "perks," there are more routine ways that companies shape the identities and behavior of the employees *within* the workplace.

"Neutralizing" Accents and Identities

"Are you calling from India?"

"No, I'm calling from Modesto, California."

"Well, you sound Indian."

"I've only been here for two months and haven't got the accent right."

Thus transpired a conversation between an American customer and a 22-year-old call center worker. "Sean," like many other "telecallers," is insecure about his accent and was telling only a partial lie. True, he was not calling from Modesto but south Delhi. But he has only been at the call center—his virtual Modesto—for two months and has not had sufficient time to "neutralize" his Indian accent. Sean, unshaven and dressed in a red sweatshirt, white high tops, tartan socks, and rumpled jeans, speaks with a tortured Americanized twang. The son of an industrialist, he considers his employment to be short term; in a few years he and his brother, who is seated at the adjacent workstation, plan to join the family business. As he introduces himself to me, I ask if Sean is his real name or his work name. He affirms both:

"Sean is my work name but I go by it now."

"Meaning your family and friends call you Sean as well?" I, the pop-eyed interviewer, inquire.

"Yes," he replies calmly. "Everyone calls me that now."

I look over to his brother, who has since removed his headset and is listening in. He nods slowly in confirmation. In what can be construed as either a remarkable instance of cultural self-alienation or youthful insouciance, Akhil is Sean in and out of the workplace.

Initially, workers were trained in specifically American and British accents, but the preference is increasingly toward a "neutral," global accent, as it allows workers to be shifted around to serve various markets without additional training.[21] At best, the resulting speech is not so much neutral as measured and devoid of the local inflections that would conspicuously mark it as "Indian." At worst, it is a mélange of British, American, and Indian English. (One worker sounded like a muddled Sean Connery trying to the find the whereabouts of Red October.) But in either case, it serves the purpose of obfuscation.

The demand for globalized speech has led to the creation of specialized institutes for accent "neutralization." "Those with extremely good skills don't want BPO," says Kiran Desai, a veteran accent trainer. "What you get is a lot of people that don't speak very well and aren't from the best schools in Bombay. Lots of dropouts from college," she adds in a crisp British-Indian accent. Schools do not concentrate on phonetics enough "and so they pick up sounds from their mother tongue. We teach them to get rid of mother tongue influence." To sensitize trainees to the subtleties of American culture, they sit for viewings of popular movies, such as *American Pie*, *Independence Day*, and *JFK*. The serial *Friends*, Desai says, is "a soap that works. It provides insight into American culture through the jokes they crack." The trainers even show videos of pet shows to convey Americans' intense fondness for pets—so that they understand that to an American, "a cat is like his baby." For Desai, these are purely technical issues, mere business requirements; she is adamant that these practices do not lead to a "loss of culture." Yet, she says uncomprehendingly, that there is sometimes "resistance" to training: "They say, 'I'm an Indian and I speak fairly well. Why do I need to change?' I don't know why [they object]. Maybe it's a fashion." (One call center manager describes his workers disparagingly as neither Indian nor American, but "half-baked.")

There is thus more at stake than phony identities and neutered accents. As opposed to physical labor, service work involves "emotional labor," wherein workers are called on to amiably display a particular emotional repertoire.[22] In call centers, these management technologies penetrate to the very core of your identity. During training sessions, employees are told that the customer can see their smile and sense their mood through their voice. Workers must be able to "pass" as American or British. Maintaining your composure in the face of sometimes racist abuse by irate customers is simply part of the job.[23] "What is of importance," writes Aneesh, "is the very endeavor to erase from view the disjuncture of different worlds, different time zones, different subjectivities, languages and accents."[24]

In describing the problematic aspects of labor practices in call centers, the question that often goes unconsidered is why workers are mostly indifferent, sometimes exultant, about their apparent cultural alienation.[25] Where some see tight control over emotions and personality and "dramaturgical stress," many workers see the freedom to create an identity. Even when companies try to relinquish the practice of using pseudonyms, workers are often reluctant to let their fictive personas go. One small company in Bangalore, for example, reached a compromise with its employees. They may take a Western first name but they must keep their given surname. "Thus we now have Britney Gupta," says an executive, rubbing the bridge of his nose with bemusement.

The term *cyber-coolie*, however polemical in intent, is thus perspicacious.[26] It conjoins the technologies and freedoms of globalization with traditional modes of subjection. (India is not a global leader in high-tech innovation, but in rote, back-office services.) Yet workers do not view themselves as ground down or subservient. Rather, as trade unionists learned during organizing drives, they are resentful of such characterizations. The reason is that mimicry is foremost a privilege, the product of a negative liberty. In order to separate oneself from the common rabble, to meaningfully identify with an outside culture, you must be able to afford its trappings. And just as the status of the colonial mimic men was dependent upon the structures of British colonialism, today, the social position of workers is contingent upon the continued patronage of Western corporations.

"The Road of Our Dreams is Under Construction"

While the West represents the pinnacle of individualism and consumer choice, India is at a crossroads. Should it choose the right path, it too will have its day in the sun. Such were Nila's sentiments, a female IT worker in Chennai, a teeming city of five million on the Bay of Bengal. Unlike Bangalore, where IT advertisements line the neatly paved streets, Chennai is still a work in progress, a "second-tier" ICT city. While outsourcing-generated wealth has dramatically altered its topography and complexion, it remains a modernizing city with a conservative outlook, or so the guidebooks tell us.

"Before I wasn't using pants, I used to wear saris," says Nila, who is wearing a floral-patterned blouse and black dress pants. "Right now, I'm using everything. My parents weren't accepting to all these things, but now they're OK with it." Freedom in fashion signifies the right to choose. And this leeway, this quiet discretion over personal affairs, she says, attracts women to the IT sector, in contrast to engineering, where women are not treated with respect. "It's different with IT, which is secure and safe. Take Bangalore, it's like the U.S. This city is changing, too. Three or four years back it wasn't like this. There are malls everywhere. Chennai is booming like anything," she says with a sparkle in her eyes.

Chennai's "road to prosperity" is a state-funded, six-lane, access-controlled, elevated, "world-class expressway" being constructed 200 feet behind the international airport. Once completed, you will be able to approach the multiplying technology parks directly from the airport, thus bypassing the dirt and smog-choked city center. Land prices in the area have risen dramatically. Homes and shopping arcades along the route have been demolished, and squatters have set up residence in abandoned buildings. At one congested intersection by the corridor, which seems in a perpetual state of disrepair, a small metal sign reads: "The Road of Our Dreams is Under Construction. Thank you for bearing with us." Delays notwithstanding, the corridor is an example of the Chennai to come. "It's supposed to be like in the U.S. On either side you'll have IT companies. Once they complete the freeway, it will be just like in America. Earlier there were very few supermarkets. Now there are supermarkets and restaurants. Cars used to be a big deal. Now IT guys, everyone is buying. Chennai is going to be luxurious!" Nila gushes.

While they are quick to point out the country's long-term economic potential, even Indian executives aspire towards something other than India. Narayan Murthy, the founder of Infosys, a leading IT firm, was reported as saying, "We live in a make believe world. . . . Right now, when you come to our campus, you are leaving India behind."[27] One is leaving India behind and going where? The Infosys campus, situated in the aptly named Electronics City in Bangalore, features a UN-style conference hall (which can supposedly host the largest video conference call in the world), a pool hall, gym, and many other perks. India, however, is not far away. The company's large canteen, a senior executive warns, does not serve "continental food"; rather, two buffet lines offer "north" and "south" Indian cuisine for well under a dollar.

More poignantly, only 100 yards from the polished marble floor of the Infosys lobby and the gleaming pyramidal theater opposite the putting green is Shikaripalya, a slum village composed of corrugated iron, cement blocks, mud bricks, gunny sacks, bamboo poles, and other flotsam. But the globalized sleekness of the modern office excludes the reality outside.[28] A cheerful, Oxford-trained economist at the World Bank's office in Chennai, which handles payroll and accounting functions for the headquarters in Washington, keeps his office window unshuttered to remind him that he is in India. "Otherwise, it's very easy to forget," he says with a smirk, looking out on a hazy vista of crumbling storefronts, doddering mendicants, and passing traffic. Or take Mindspace, an ICT complex spanning 5 million square feet in the suburbs of Bombay. It hosts a high concentration of firms as well as residences, restaurants, and shops. Social and class distinctions are physically instantiated in walls and private security that exclude the hoi polloi. The sense of separateness is also reinforced symbolically: the 17-story apartment towers go by pacific and awkward names like Quiescent, Whispering, Serenity, and Celestial Heights. Residents dine at Ruby Tuesday and Pizza Hut.

Escapist middle-class desires have raised the ire of many prominent Indian social critics. Varma, for instance, writes, "For all the achievements of the Indian State in the last fifty years, there is, for its middle and elite classes, a crippling ideological bareness which threatens to convert India into a vastly unethical and insensitive aggregation of wants." Middle-class Indians, in their preening self-regard, desire to secede from the "other" India that exists outside "their narrow little worlds."[29]

The idea of the middle class carries immense symbolic and historical weight in India, however elusive it may be as a definable sociological entity. The class has played a pivotal role in recent history, whether in its incarnation as the nationalist vanguard that won independence through self-sacrifice or later as sober civil servants powering Nehruvian modernization. As opposed to these images of civically minded discipline and frugality, the "new Indian middle class" has few of the moral scruples of its predecessors. Accompanying the program of economic liberalization in the 1990s was a redefinition of national progress. Concerns about class and caste stratification gave way to a focus on wealth and consumption as indicators of development. Consumerism fills the vacuum left by the lost sense of civic duty.[30]

The outsourcing-related strand of the Indian middle class is something of a comprador bourgeoisie.[31] Like the compradors in the colonial period, their livelihood and economic well-being are directly dependent upon Western business. Regarding executives and managers, there is an obvious resonance in their roles as intermediaries between foreign capital—overwhelmingly American and British—and Indian labor.[32] The new compradors act single-mindedly in their class interest and, some would say, to the neglect of national considerations. As Mazzerella writes, the middle classes' desire to consume is "at one" with its "political impatience," which often takes the form of longings for authoritarian rule—an instance of what Lasch has called "the revolt of the elites."[33]

Atul Gupta has spent the majority of his professional life in the United States. He recently returned to India to manage the subsidiary of an American bank and is now its chief operating officer. The gray light of dusk gives an ashen pallor to his already solemn features as he sits in a leather office chair. Our conversation is arid, but when asked his opinion about the sustainability of the industry, his guard drops and he leans forward with interest. The country's overtaxed infrastructure, particularly the poor roads and power outages, he says, could spell disaster. Looking carefully to his right and left, Gupta confides in a hushed tone, "You know what we need in this country? We need a dictatorship for 12 years. Then . . . back to democracy."[34] No more power outages, strikes, and work delays. What is needed is an IT leviathan. While India's entrepreneurs and their political allies have been successful in pushing an agenda of economic reform—entailing the liberalization of trade and investment, deregulation, and a weakening of the "license Raj"—nothing is more vexing than the bureaucratic inefficiencies of democratic governance.

"The Sweatshop Has Become the Boudoir"

After five years of managing an Indian workforce, Tyler, a young American BPO executive, has come no closer to cracking what has become a nagging question: "Why does everyone want to be American?" That American culture exercises an irresistible fascination on the minds of ICT workers is undeniable. Western popular culture gives form and implicit coherence to their desires, which are both vague and soaring. They are chasing dreams, dreams that lead some of them into casual affairs, binge drinking, and hard rock music competitions sponsored by whiskey distillers. By relaxing familial and pecuniary constraints, outsourced jobs give workers the ability to act on their wishes.

In the beginning, Indian society was not very kind to BPO workers. Despite their comparatively high salaries, the transgressive combination of graveyard shifts, competitive consumption, and partying cast workers in a dubious light. Reports flourished in the press suggesting that workers were not only adopting Western accents but promiscuous lifestyles as well. An article in the *Times of India* titled "Sex in the City" described the raffish call center demimonde, causing many a middle-class tongue to click in consternation:

> There is a newer, freer workplace, a lot less inhibited and radically
> different from the one that the self-styled censors would have you

believe. This is a part of India where freedom knows no bounds, love is a favourite pastime and sex is recreation. The sweatshop has become the boudoir: this new workspace is redefining the man-woman relationship.[35]

Mohandas is the owner of a domestic telecom company. He has a neat moustache and wears square gold-rimmed spectacles and a dress shirt unbuttoned just so, exposing a masculine tuft of chest hair. I ask him about call center workers' supposed penchant for drinking and partying. Perched perilously near the edge of his seat—eyes wide, brow arched—he says excitedly, lifting an index finger, "You know, there was an article in the paper, the *Economic Times*, that mentioned an HR manager who was giving out condoms to her workers! It's terrible." The HR manager did no such thing. But the actual text is irrelevant. The salient point is how easily rumors of the lasciviousness of workers, of condom-choked sinks in call centers, spread. Outsourcing is now the subject of a best-selling novel (*One Night at the Call Centre*) and even a television series (*India Calling*).[36] It is not an issue of promiscuity per se; the often sensationalistic stories of romance and rebellion are symptomatic of a gradual shift in gender relations wherein women have increased mobility. BPO lifestyles are allegorized as struggles between purity (knowing your place in the family and social structure) and contamination (dating and drinking) or freedom and constraint, depending on one's ideological leanings.

For women, the night shift is a source of considerable stigma. Risha, a secretary at a call center, says that initially people in the community used to look down on her. "You were no longer seen as marriageable," she says softly.[37] "Nobody directly questioned you, but you could tell what they were thinking . . . by the look in their eyes," remarks Usma, an assistant manager at a BPO, who is dressed "conservatively" in a red *shalwar kameez*, her hair pulled back tightly in a ponytail. "When I first joined five years ago, there was no boom. I had no clue what a BPO was. All I knew was that they paid more than the standard. The shift job wasn't famous in India. This is something new," she says. It is not seen as "respectable, especially for women. If a girl wants to get married, the first thing they ask is, does she work at night? They don't like it." Wilson, a 23-year-old call center agent with a gleaming pate, emphasizes that the stigma applies to male workers as well: "Nowadays you can't get married because you work in a call center. The name *BPO* shouldn't be written anywhere in your offer letter. Arranged marriages are complicated. Prestige, money, and property all matter. Love marriages by comparison are simple."

According to workers and managers, the freedom and mobility provided by the jobs fostered amorous relationships between workers. When parents found out about the clandestine romances, they often pressed marriage upon their children. Inevitably, the charm faded and many unions were dissolved. But not all call center romances end in divorce or separation. "Tracy" met her husband at a call center and feels that they are "the best place for females to work." "It's cushy. For a guy it's not a great career, but it is good for people like housewives," she says confidently. But because of "the weird timings, the girls are getting Western." For example: "Girls smoking in the open wasn't common before, but this is normal at a call center. Here you'll see every girl smoking. They tend to stay away from the family. Society's changing."

For parents, the media hype has shed little light on what actually takes place at work. As an HR manager explains:

> It wasn't only that older parents did not understand the rationale for outsourcing, though that too was the case. BPO is relatively new and still hasn't gotten social recognition. Parents have given up trying to figure [it] out. Some company pays their son or daughter a hell of a lot. It's mysterious. They don't understand the mechanics. If someone in India is answering an American's call, they say, "But why would they make an STD [long-distance] call to India?"

The fear is that outsourcing, to quote a senior police officer, is causing a "breakdown in the fabric of Indian family life."[38] What is threatening about globalization is its emphasis on individualism, the sense that personal skills and achievement, not family, caste, or class, are what make a person. As Sennett writes, "The social bond arises most elementally from a sense of mutual dependence."[39] Economic independence can therefore mean freedom from family. Statements like

"I'm my own boss" exemplify the more egoistic aspects of the new ethos. Female workers often find the loosening of family bonds especially bracing, particularly as it leads to a recasting of gender roles and control over one's sexuality. Gainful employment is not synonymous with "empowerment," but in a social setting where women are often considered repositories of family honor, being able to work at night with men is no small matter. (While 118 out of 133 workers surveyed gave "housewife" as their mother's profession, 40–50 percent of BPO employees are women.) That they may use this freedom in ways that middle-class moralists disapprove of is somewhat inevitable. The domination of the patriarchal family is replaced by the burden of public disapproval.

The rumors are not all apocryphal, however. Workers do indeed express relaxed attitudes towards sex, alcohol, and club drugs. One study finds that four out of five workers interviewed have "had a workplace affair and that the majority of those were married. In another recent poll one in four call centre staff said they regularly had casual affairs."[40] BPO workers talk openly about premarital "flings," which more than once were described perplexingly as "emotionless." It is hard to imagine a relationship, even one that is purely platonic, that provokes no emotion, suggesting that even in their minds such narrowly personal affairs rank lower in value than those sanctioned by family and confirmed in matrimony.

One must view the disclosure of such intimate details with caution, however, as the young workers seem almost too willing to boast of their rebellion. Take Vikash, a 23-year-old call center worker with heavily pomaded hair. When asked what he does in the small hours of the morning after returning from work, you might expect him to say that he has breakfast, takes a nap, or watches television, something that would suggest an attempt to connect with the normal course of things. But his conversation is strictly limited to the rebellious transgression of social mores. "Me and my friends, we go back to one of our apartments and we take shots of vodka," he says, savoring the last word as if it were a final sip of the real stuff. "What on earth are you talking about? At 9:00 a.m.?" I ask. "Of course," he replies with a sly grin. He also likes working at the call center as he is able to flirt with female employees without rebuke. But even if you take Vikash at his word, it remains an open question whether this transvaluation of values is an instance of youthful exuberance, a generational dynamic, or a serious reappraisal of Indian culture.

"If a Cat Tries to Bark It Doesn't Become a Dog"

To understand the extent of the stigma attached to workers, you could do worse than talk to Krishna, a portly and vigorous executive at an IT company in Chennai. Krishna is of venerable upper-middle-class stock and his profile recalls a dignified eagle (in a moment of leisure) and an English sparrow (in an espresso-permeated hour of work). He has spent most of his working life in the United States—something many BPO workers would like to do often but lack the means to achieve. Migrating home after such a long absence, he is alive to his native culture's faults and is vocal about the vices of the BPO parvenus, particularly their tendency to imitate fantasy Americans. From his glass-walled office, he casts a worried eye to a clouded future:

> India's middle class is definitely bulging. But then I'm not sure people are being prudent. Overnight richness doesn't really do good to people. They don't know how to handle it. I think the culture is not going in the right direction. Just because they work for a U.S. company, I don't see why they should lose their culture. Just because they work for a U.S. company, McDonalds doesn't become the life. It's not the life in the U.S., right? You also go to McDonalds and you also watch MTV once in a while but that doesn't drive you. Here this newfound money drives. There is a call center here in the building. The guy, you look at him, he looks like a junkie to me. He has a goatee. . . . He walks into the lift and I don't know, he looks dirty. Downright dirty. He works in a call center, so obviously they taught him how to speak with an American accent. Looking at him you say this fellow is shabby, probably came out of a shabby area. He's talking with an American accent as if he's lived all of his life in the U.S. When I walked out, a colleague said, "Krishna, how long did you live in the U.S.?" I said quite a few years. "But you don't

speak with an accent." I said why? Why do I need to? Do you understand me without an accent? If you do, then that's good enough. Just because they do this they don't become something. If a cat tries to bark it doesn't become a dog. This is exactly the way they're behaving. It's bad! I mean, it's pathetic! Personally, I feel very, very disgusted with this because you're getting the very worst of both Indian and American culture.

Told of Vikash's matutinal habits—hearty draughts of vodka at 9:00 a.m.—he is driven to distraction. "Can you think of a responsible American doing it? Probably somebody does that when they're in the university. Those are junkies, you think. Here these people earn good money and that's their behavior. It's disgusting. Really disgusting," he mutters, shaking his head and shocks of silvering hair. "Anyway, they make in one month what their parents earned in a year."

Ten thousand rupees a month will not buy one a car or house, but it can keep one in drink and designer clothes. As the *Washington Post* observes, "Because many BPO workers spend their days dealing with Americans and their credit cards, they have a comfort level with debt that other Indians might not."[41] ATMs are placed in company canteens, restaurants and all-night bars operate outside workplaces, and workers are given corporate credit cards. A report on the BPO industry accuses credit card companies of "working in tandem with call centre employers to give huge credit limits to young people working in call centres, in order to make them too indebted to leave their jobs."[42] A labor lawyer who is working on the case of a call center employee says that the "industry should take some responsibility for the lifestyle it promotes."

But not all outsourcing is the same. Societal perceptions distinguish between the IT and BPO industries. Whereas the social rank of BPO and call center workers is uncertain, particularly because of the night shift and the perception that the work is low-end, IT and software workers are publicly admired. Employment in BPO can endanger your marital prospects but has the opposite effect in IT, because of higher pay and the possibility of emigrating to the West. BPO workers occupy an inferior position in a privileged social universe. The "positional suffering" that results is no less real because it occurs among a relatively well-off group in class terms.[43]

Conspicuous consumption invites invidious distinction; workers are acutely class conscious. They differentiate between small and large companies. The former are referred to as *garibon ke call centers* ("poor people's call centers") as they pay less and supposedly have a deficit in "pretty faces." What makes for the pretty faces is more spending cash, the ability to exteriorize your superior class position through brand-name clothing, expensive haircuts, and cosmetics. Workers at smaller centers, for their part, construct salacious images of other workers—alcoholic, profligate, loose—as a means of self-validation. More generally, BPO workers tend to take their aggression out on people in respectable but less lucrative occupations like the civil service rather than cast aspersions at the software workers above.

With the growing familiarity of outsourcing, the night shift has become more acceptable. According to one manager, "Sometimes we have more of the girls working here than the boys. You feel proud of that. Slowly and steadily, India is also becoming Westernized." Risha, the soft-spoken secretary, notes with a smile that the sons and daughters of those who used to glare at her are now "all working in call centers." As Jayesh, a BPO worker, says:

> A fresh commerce grad will make three to four thousand rupees [$75–$100 monthly] as a junior accountant. He's lucky if he makes seven thousand [$175]. Here, the starting salary is eight to ten thousand rupees [$200–$250]. People have more spending power. Initially, the industry was for those who couldn't get jobs elsewhere. Now, engineers, doctors, chartered accountants, law graduates are joining. Initially, they felt ashamed. They thought it was a mindless job: "You can't get a job anywhere else. That's why you're in that industry."

Despite the growing acceptability, Jayesh's friends in finance and accounting ask him why he is still at a BPO. According to Wilson, such perceptions reflect "government thinking":

> You work fifty years and then you quit. They don't understand that as you grow, you don't have to do the night shift. But how to explain this to people? When you tell them this, they ask how long? But those that say it earn 10 times lesser salaries. They work like dogs, we don't work like dogs. We work in an air-conditioned facility.

For Wilson, discretionary income is a means of status compensation; it makes up for his precarious standing on the middle-class social scale. But the victory is bittersweet. Even relatively high pay and modern facilities do not change the nature of the work. As the Indian-American CEO of an IT-services company put it, U.S. employees perform the analytic and creative work, while those in India do the "dog work."

Power Words and Bonded Labor

Seated on the veranda of a bungalow overlooking the thinly populated Aksa beach in northern Bombay, Archana and Anil discuss their experiences as call center workers at one of the city's larger call centers. In the warm twilight, they describe how an exciting opportunity to earn a respectable income in a decent work environment turned sour. Anil quit the job because of poor management; Archana, an anomaly in the industry at 40 years of age, has filed a lawsuit against their employer for wrongful termination. Nonetheless, they show a passionate fondness for their work as booking agents for the British rail system.

"Oh, I absolutely loved it," says Anil, leaping up spontaneously from a garden chair with every sign of genuine pleasure. "How may I help you, Mr. Brimsley?" he exclaims in a British accent, theatrically describing an arc in the air with his right arm. Then tracing a crescent with his left arm and twisting his features into childish pout, he says with mock concern, "What seems to be the matter, Mrs. Grant?" While the daily rigors of emotion management can be very taxing, they also have their rewards. A successful booking, the proper handling of an inquiry, can be intensely satisfying.

There were proud moments. Archana's company received an appreciatory call from a British customer in which she, "Kate Brown," was described as a "treasure." She also won accolades for achieving the highest sales in a week: 53.85 percent of her calls.[44] "It was great fun for a time. But there were problems," Archana says. "If you haven't taken the person's name, you haven't taken 'ownership' of the call," she says with heavy irony. "We were told to use 'power words.' You're going from Leeds to London—fantastic! Oh, you're going with your family—

great! Going to a funeral—fantastic! For six to seven hours you're ex-pected to talk like this," Anil interjects, slapping at the bothersome mosquitoes as if they were so many niggling middle-managers.

Pedantic company decrees, overweening management, and dispirit-ing prescribed dialogues cut at their sense of professionalism and self-respect. "We were conditioned to say certain sentences. Other-wise, you're marked down on quality. On top of this, an agent never gets seven or eight hours of undisturbed sleep. But when they come into work tired they have to be on in terms of accent, quality, and tim-ing. You just can't be 'on' every day," Archana remarks. The nightly negotiation of accents and language is particularly difficult. "Indians don't speak English very well. We know Hindi, Marathi, and other lan-guages, but agents make grammatical errors and translate into English very literally. It's impossible to keep this up for seven hours a day," says Anil, who seems to smile inwardly as he firmly crushes a mos-quito that had alighted on his forearm.

Just as the contradictions of colonialism turned agreeable subjects into nationalists, Archana's and Anil's enthusiasm for globalization has been irreparably damaged. "We're treated as a bonded labor," Archana says with a catch in her voice. One of her "lapses" was re-turning from the toilet one minute and 50 seconds late. Other modes of control include surveillance cameras and locked doors and gates. Not only are calls recorded but companies also use software that analyzes wave frequencies to assess one's emotional disposition, which can range anywhere from irritation and duplicity to delight and even sex-ual arousal.[45] "Today we are given into the slavery of the foreign pow-ers," she says, "And this in India, a country that achieved freedom without violence."

Conclusion

Lord Macaulay's image of a class of pliable intermediaries adopting the culture and language of the colonial power has left an enduring im-print on the collective psyche. So much so that it is common to discuss colonial and postcolonial subjectivity in terms of neurosis. Fanon explored the inferiority complex of the colonized in *Black Skin, White Masks*; Naipaul, colonialism and cultural displacement in *The Mimic Men*; and the theme later resurfaced in the academic vocabulary of postcolonial studies.[46] The anguished oscillation between modernity and tradition, and the reach for cultural mimicry as a way of solidifying one's social status and identity, has been given a new twist by economic globalization, and in particular, by international outsourcing.

Thus come the questions: Is globalization akin to colonialism in some of its cultural effects? Can middle-class Indians be meaningfully described as today's "mimic men" (and women)? (As Plato warned, the actor's mask is "apt to become his face.")[47] To ask these questions is to answer them. In their accents, speech ("bucks"), and dress, in their comportment and aspirations, they bear the imprint of Macaulay's vision. While these aspirations do not have a clearly defined object, they cluster around an idea of the West as the locus of modernity. The West's mystique derives, no doubt as it did in the colonial period, from the fact that it is seen as the author of dramatic change. But this also prompts a certain anxiety among the middle class that such change is somehow corrupting.

Yet the paradoxical aspect of colonial Anglicism was that the social class it ushered into being eventually used the language of British liberalism—self-determination, constitutionalism—to undermine colonial rule. To what extent will the tools of corporate globalization be used to sabotage its machinery? The tentative answer is that any such stirrings are incredibly faint at the moment. While Appadurai's point about the contested nature of globalization is well taken, one finds little resistance to Western hegemony in the Indian ICT industry.[48] There is scattered disenchantment, but it is far from coalescing into a movement that could challenge the rules of globalization. Even the rare worker that delights at the prospect of "stealing" jobs from developed countries often conceives of the matter in terms of "beating the West at its own game." And as the executive Gupta's comments attest, the Indian middle class and its political allies are willing to do whatever necessary to play the game better.

Nevertheless, it is easy to see why the public feud over outsourcing has so enraptured urban middle-class India. It has all the dramatic elements of a Bollywood movie: the struggle between instant and de-layed gratification, arranged marriages and romantic love, consumerist and ascetic religious values, and the ominous prospect of generational rupture. It is in this sense that workers, managers, and employers exert a cultural influence that extends beyond their small numbers (as a per-centage of the population). In the cases here described, austere family values are buffeted by the open celebration of relative affluence. That workers sometimes earn more than their parents shifts household dy-namics, and this reversal can unsettle parental authority.

As India continues to liberalize, the cultural changes occurring among urban workers and their families prefigure those that will likely take place among the broader middle class. (As Fernand Braudel once observed, the city is a transformer that intensifies the pace of change.)[49] But while it is tempting to forecast a tectonic shift in social relations, what seems to be occurring is a subtle redefinition of urban family re-lations. This redefinition allows workers to assert their autonomy while retaining familial bonds. Sons and daughters may be scolded but they are not ostracized. And many rogue romantic relationships are ulti-mately approved by parents so long as the couple gets married. Even neighbors that once looked askance at night shift workers eventually come around, so to speak. Workers, after all, make decent money. And this is what causes the stigma to fade: the spectral power of money and the commodity image as families adjust to the lures (and snares) of a growing consumer society.[50] And so, in the short term, the clash be-tween the values of "modernity"—as exemplified by fantasies of a Western-style utopia—and reinvented "tradition" may grow more acute. But if the ability of many families to accommodate change is any indicator, it is perhaps more likely that the drama will find some-thing of the neat resolution of a Bollywood film.

CHAPTER FOUR

The Uses and Abuses of Time

> For hundreds of decades we have been sleeping in the dark and waking in
> the light. When we attempt to do the opposite of this set body program, we
> are fighting against generations of programming. . . . However, it is not
> impossible to reset the internal biological clock—all it requires is a little
> effort from our side to consciously regulate the biological clock so that it
> depends on us and not on daylight or darkness for its functioning. . . . And
> all along a "mantra" that you should keep in mind is: "My 2 a.m. is the rest
> of the world's 9 a.m."
>
> —*From "Surviving Night Shifts," a flier distributed*
> *to workers at a Bangalore call center*

On any given night, from the empty parking lot behind Kalkaji post
office and across a pitted road, you can see a narrow band of yel-
lowish light emanating from beneath a propped metal door. Behind the
door and down the concrete steps are about 40 call center workers and
their boss, Ajay, a young entrepreneur who has started over 20 outbound call centers throughout northwest India. In contrast to the steel
and glass modernism of the India's burgeoning technology companies,
Ajay's unprepossessing center is run out of a basement in south Delhi.
Whereas the interiors of many multinational call centers are painted
bright shades of blue, orange, and canary to create an atmosphere of
fun and play, the walls here wear a somber gray. And instead of air
conditioning, wall-mounted fans keep the place cool. There are no
windows on the work floor, which matters little as the daylight has long
expired when workers arrive.

As is the case in the industry at large, most of Ajay's employees are
recent college graduates, though he just hired someone who had only
completed his 12th standard. As a smiling, mustachioed manager re-

marked, "The less educated, the cheaper. Freshers accept lesser pay."
The workers have a sharp handle on English, which is a necessary
condition of employment as the calls are to American and British consumers. Their speech, however, is laced with a North Indian lilt as
Ajay cannot afford to offer extensive "accent neutralization" training,
which is intended to obliterate "mother tongue influences." The employees dress down in sweatshirts, sneakers, and jeans—all but the
manager, who is dressed in a lace-edged purple *shalwar kameez*, high
heels, and matching lipstick and lords over the staff as a matron does
her charges.

Some slouch at their stations. Others sit stiff and straight. Anita, a
fey 22-year-old Christian from Manipur in northeast India, does both.
The daughter of a pastor, she works the full-time night shift, which is
around nine hours, six days a week, including national holidays. She
lives in a joint family of eight, and the combined monthly income of
her family is below 20,000 rupees ($445). Anita herself makes 7,000
rupees ($158) a month, which translates to about 30 rupees or $0.67
an hour. (At the time of writing, most call center workers made about
double this sum.)

Working the graveyard shift, Anita says, is a health hazard. Asked
of any job-related health issues, she mentions backache, eyestrain,
earache, reduced appetite, insomnia, and stomach cramps. There is no
time for domestic activities; her only leisure is on Sunday, when she
prefers the stony silence of sleep to soporific church sermons. Her
voice is small but confident. She feels that call center jobs are "good
for women; otherwise, I'd be home." When asked if she considers her
employment to be a career option, she replies matter-of-factly, "I want
to live a long life. If I live like this, I won't live long."

Anita's case is not untypical of the more than two million people
working in India's outsourcing industry. Even in cases where the night
shift exacts an appreciable toll on their health, workers are willing to
give it a go, viewing their employment as a stopgap arrangement more
than a career. It is thus important not to overdramatize their plight. At
times, they are very happy. Especially so when they indulge in consumption binges at shopping malls or arrange romantic trysts at suburban night clubs or cafés. Such are the consolations of a relatively hefty

paycheck. Their experiences speak eloquently of the cyclical pleasure and pain of life under the new dispensation.

The central concept driving offshoring is *labor arbitrage*, which one company defines as the "ability to pay one labor pool less than another pool for accomplishing the same work, typically by substituting labor in one geography for labor in a different locale."[1] In addition to cost-savings, multinationals doing business in India also benefit from a strategic use of time. Consequently, I argue that transnational companies make use of *time arbitrage*. Time arbitrage can be defined as the exploitation of time discrepancies between geographical labor markets to make a profit. This operates on two scales. At the geographical scale, many companies exploit time zone differences to approach a 24-hour business cycle. At the labor process scale, time arbitrage can mean the extension of work hours or the acceleration of the labor process. As one executive says of his Indian employees, "You can get more out of them." To be sure, the raison d'être of offshoring remains the reduction of labor costs. Time arbitrage is simply the endeavor to put time to profitable use.

There is, however, a tension between the network time of corporate globalization and the prosaic rhythms of ordinary life. While flexibility is heralded in developed countries as a means of recalibrating the work-life balance, it means something entirely different to the Indian software programmer who stays late into the evening for a conference call with New York or for the call center worker on the permanent night shift. The temporal displacement resulting from employment in the ICT industry has potentially serious implications for the mental and physical health of Indian workers. Because of long hours and the permanent night shift, workers report various health problems and complain of growing alienation from family and friends.

So, in the Indian case, time arbitrage has resulted in long work hours, an intense work pace, and temporal disorientation. Given that 73 percent of Fortune 2000 companies say offshoring is an integral part of their overall growth strategy, it is increasingly possible to speak of a trend in global time arbitrage.[2] This chapter addresses the following questions: How are companies using time to their advantage, to reap the full benefits of a globally dispersed labor pool? What impacts are these temporal changes having on the health and social lives of workers?

The chapter is divided into three sections. The first focuses on how time arbitrage plays out in the workplace, through the stretching of work time and the speeding up of the labor process. The second section deals with temporal displacement: namely, the adverse impacts of time arbitrage on workers' health, safety, and social life. I close the chapter with a discussion of time as it relates to the balance of forces between capital and labor.

Time Arbitrage

The View from Above

Harvey writes that "the history of capitalism has been characterized by a speedup in the pace of life, while so overcoming spatial barriers that the world seems to collapse inwards upon us."[3] Globalization and the spread of ICTs have engendered a new temporality, what has been variously called "real time," "timeless time," and "network time." Simultaneity and instantaneity replace succession and duration, compressing time and space. Local and seasonal rhythms stand opposed to the forward march of network time, whose parameters are defined by the imperatives of transnational corporations.[4] The space of "flows" supplants that of "place."[5]

Heeks and his coauthors argue that global IT relationships must either "synch or swim," underlining the importance of aligning organizational cultures.[6] Being in synch temporally is equally important. As urban centers in the global south are integrated into global production and service networks, they must adapt to network timings.[7] Global software parks, such as TIDEL Park, the largest of its kind in the southern state of Tamil Nadu, are in accord with the ceaseless rhythms of the global economy. Its promotional material proudly proclaims that "TIDEL Park understands that the IT world has its own clock." Timeless time cannot afford to stop.

Although time seems a free-flowing ribbon, place still matters.

After a gulp of milky coffee, an IT worker whose company supports an investment bank describes India's locational advantages:

> Geographically, India is located in a pretty good position to support the needs of the East and West. In the morning, around 7:00 a.m., you can talk to clients in Singapore, Australia, and Hong Kong. Between 12:00 and 4:00 p.m., you can cover the Middle East, Luxembourg, and the U.K. And between 5:00 and 8:00 p.m., you can talk to the U.S. guys. India is geographically positioned to cover most of the global markets.

There are chiefly two ways in which offshoring companies deal with the 9.5- to 12.5-hour time zone difference between the United States and India. They can offshore work that requires synchronous or asynchronous coordination: A call center worker in Delhi receives and places calls somewhere from 10:00 p.m. to 9:00 a.m. Indian Standard Time, while a junior lawyer in Bombay working for an American client works during the Indian day. Companies see opportunity in both of these possibilities: the night shift allows employees to talk directly to customers; having an Indian lawyer prepare a draft patent during the day means that it will be in the client's inbox first thing in the morning.

With the offshoring of synchronous work, such as customer service queries, Wall Street's clock is exported across the globe. In migrating asynchronous work, such as IT maintenance, national timings are preferable as they allow firms to root out unproductive times and to approach a 24-hour work cycle. Where there has to be synchronous coordination in the latter, such as with conference calls between the "onsite" and "offshore" offices, Western timings trump national timings; workers and managers are required to stay late. There are thus multiple ways to exploit time differences, and many companies employ both night and day workers.

The global reorganization of service work marks the confluence of the business ideals of "flexible capitalism" and the "24-hour society." Outsourcing signals the hollowing out of the vertically integrated corporation. Offshoring allows corporations to farm out peripheral and repetitive tasks to contracted Third World labor, while the home office is left to busily contemplate its core functions. Through the fashioning of a globally dispersed network of suppliers, businesses can operate longer, if not continuously. The global marketplace, however, despite Thomas Friedman's rhetoric about the "flatness" of the world, is still dominated by the large transnational corporation.[8] Power is not evenly distributed throughout the far-flung business network; control operates according the principle of "centralization without concentration."[9]

Moreover, corporate flexibility has come of age in an era of labor casualization and downsizing. Whereas scientific and technological advancements were supposed to increase both productivity *and* leisure time, working hours have remained static or became longer and often more intense.[10] The advanced technologies of the new economy coexist with "temporally regressive" methods of labor control—the former tightening the screws of the latter—leading some critics to speak of "electronic sweatshops" and "assembly lines in the head."[11] "Lean" production methods are applied to service work with the goal of maximizing productivity and eliminating dead time.

There are a number of ways to compress time. The work process can be intensified. The sequence of tasks can be reordered. Flexible schedules and just-in-time production reduce "nonproductive" work times.[12] The merit of a comparative lens is that we are able to see how different types of employees are affected by these various methods. Whereas the workday of an IT worker is built around a series of tasks, that of a BPO worker is built around a designated number of hours or numerical targets. This translates into a difference in the method of time-discipline. In IT, time is stretched (overtime), while in the BPO it is condensed (quickened pace). This does not mean that call center workers do not have to work overtime or that IT workers work at a relaxed pace. Rather, task-orientation and time-orientation correspond loosely to the distinction between professionals (often salaried, who have to work longer hours without being paid overtime) and workers (whose time is closely monitored). In IT, while workers do have to log in hours, time-schedules are relatively elastic and breaks irregular. In BPO, breaks are fixed and even the time elapsed during bathroom visits is noted. Incentive schemes are also structured to take these differences into account. In fact, workers actually billed a project for idle hours at one IT firm—time they spent waiting for work from the U.S. office—something almost unheard of at BPOs.

Work Speedup: Compressing Time

While offshoring is motivated by the prospect of significant cost-savings, many companies have reported substantial productivity gains, ranging from 15 to 25 percent.[13] Consultants McKinsey report that one "British bank's call-center agents in India not only process 20 percent more transactions than their counterparts in the United Kingdom but also do so 3 percent more accurately."[14] Gains can be accounted for by the fact that wages are lower and thus companies are able to spend more on supervision and training. Workers may also be more motivated as the jobs have higher prestige in India than in the United States and United Kingdom. An executive says that Indian employees are more productive because "they're better qualified, they're better educated, they're younger." Additionally, managers often give cultural explanations, arguing that Indian industriousness is a product of the culture's emphasis on education. One manager speaks admiringly of the "Indian psyche."

In call centers, at least, gains in productivity may have less to do with age, motivation, or cultural inheritance than with an accelerated work pace and technologically induced efficiency. Larger call centers use automated dialing technology, through which numbers are dialed automatically and workers are fed only live calls. According to one manager, the rate of calls is variable: on average an American worker might have 45 seconds to one minute between calls, whereas an Indian worker would have only 5 to 10 seconds. By eliminating "idle time," nominal working hours remain the same but *real* working hours are lengthened.[15] One worker, Adnan, says that in a day they handle about 200–250 calls, of which 80–90 last a minute and 50–60 last between three and five minutes. "It's a source of stress. You don't have a long gap after every call," Adnan says. His coworker, Preethi, adds, "It's seconds. There isn't a break after every call, though I would rather do an 8-hour than 10-hour shift with longer breaks." Busy hours do not preclude an extension of the workday when necessary. A former worker complained that her shifts occasionally extended from the required 8 to 10 hours and that she handled hundreds of calls daily.

Workers also complain about not receiving their promised salaries. Managers respond that this is because a large portion of one's "salary" comes in the form of incentives, which are based on performance and adherence to predefined parameters.[16] Two major components relevant to our argument are talk time (the quicker you can dispatch a customer the better) and the intervals between calls (a matter of seconds). The result is an internalization of time-discipline, which is manifested in a psychological pressure to perform. "If I can't achieve target, it leads to an in-built stress. We know what we have to do every day. It's our own mind telling us, 'You have to do it.' The only thing we do is talk, talk, talk. We have about two seconds for the next call. Sometimes, though, you do have a long break. Those are the times we party," says Preethi, looking at Adnan, who is looking at a coworker who is looking out the window.

Yet even breaks are a matter of dispute. Despite the bright furnishings and the game rooms, the conditions of work can be exacting. Breaks (including dinner, which might take place at two in the morning) are strictly monitored, and one worker complains that they "are not given on time, if at all." One worker says that they are denied weekly days off and that "sometimes we aren't even getting breaks if call flow is high." Leave policies are another matter of contention:

> You can't fall sick. You have to plan your sick leave in advance. It's almost like having to say, "I'm planning to be sick in three weeks." They don't have a real sick leave policy. Someone had a bad fall once and they wouldn't sanction the leave at first. She came to work in intense pain and only then was told that she could go. They want you to come in first. Also, if one is sick, then they don't get incentives because the sick days are construed as leaves, unless planned.

Another worker says that he cannot attend out-of-town gatherings because of work timings. Leaves are hardly an option: "If we take more than one leave, then we will have to pay from our salary. And without money we cannot fulfill our social and family requirement."

At the same company, workers must ask permission from a superior to use the bathroom—the visits of which are timed. In one case, a worker named Neeta was dealing with a particularly cumbersome in-bound call. Thirty minutes in, she requested permission from her team leader (TL) to use the restroom, the normal protocol being that another worker or superior would handle the call from there. But the TL did not allow her to get off the line, and 20 minutes later when the call was completed, he congratulated her with a paternalistic smile and said, "I knew you could be a good rep if you put yourself to it." In this, Neeta's company is hardly unique. According to one study, "62 percent of managers say that their employees have little or no discretion to handle unexpected requests that arise in the course of customer calls and 70 percent say there is little discretion to handle customer complaints."[17] For the company, the end result was an uninterrupted and successfully handled call. After writing a letter to management itemizing this and other abuses, Neeta's services were suspended, officially for "dropping calls." Another of her "lapses," like Archana in the previous chapter, was returning late from the bathroom. She claims that she vomited after her meal and had to be assisted back to her seat. As another worker at the firm carped, "The food is not good. They contract service out to different caterers who prepare meals on a cost-cutting basis. This causes health problems and some have had food poisoning."

The authors of a recent study of the call center industry by the Indian Labour Ministry–funded V.V. Giri Labor Institute, argue that the constant surveillance in firms creates an atmosphere similar to that in "19th-century prisons or Roman slave ships."[18] My observations suggest that while surveillance is indeed tight and can be a major source of stress, most employees would not make such comparisons. Many describe their work environments positively. However, poor management and excessive monitoring can create a hostile atmosphere. Says one worker: "Everything is monitored. They record every damn thing." Additionally, workers are often expected to work six days a week and forego national holidays, and they often complain of unpaid mandatory overtime.

Long Hours: Stretching Time

Executives, often Indians trained in the West, lament their compatriots' lackadaisical attitude toward time. They claim that Indians take more breaks and have difficulty dealing with deadlines. And, indeed, an intense focus on family and social life does not mesh well with the rigidity of organization time and clock discipline.[19] Very commonly, IST—Indian Standard Time—is jokingly referred to as Indian "stretchable" time. The rigid status distinctions prevalent in Indian society and the often servile attitude of workers toward their superiors, however, ensure that when workers are called on to put in long hours, they do.

While productivity and quality are said to be at least as good as they are in the United States, Indian workers in IT firms regularly work longer hours than their American counterparts. This expectation on the part of employers, especially at the elite IT services firms, is rationalized by the notion that the company is a global business that works on a 24-hour cycle. The compensations for workers are high salaries, comfortable facilities, the status boost of working for a multinational firm, and occasional opportunities to work "on-site" in the United States, where they are paid in dollars rather than rupees. But as employees of a company with a "24-hour work culture," they are expected to be available at all hours. And while some managers say there is a longer learning curve for Indian workers, they are able to condense a good deal of training into a short period of time. One worker at an IT firm said that her team of trainees had to stay in the office for over 24 hours twice during their three-month training.

Even on his days off, Amir, an employee of an IT firm, receives a steady flow of messages on his Blackberry. The device, a source of both pride and annoyance, rarely leaves his person. His company maintains IT infrastructure for a variety of transnational companies, including Wal-Mart. He once spent two continuous days in the office. "I took meals at my desk. Afterwards, I could barely walk. I just collapsed there at my desk and went to sleep," Amir remarks wearily, as if reliving the exhaustion. He is also required to travel extensively and says that Western workers feel threatened by his work ethic. He quit twice because he felt that his services were underappreciated only to be lured back by pay raises.

Erran Carmel, who is no enemy of capitalism, writes that offshoring involves various hidden costs and time delays. These hurdles, however, can be cleared. "If Infosys has an elixir for the time zone gap," writes Carmel, "it is its organizational culture that expects a heightened commitment from employees." He continues:

> This commitment is to work longer hours and work off-hours. In short, it is a culture that expects heroics. . . . India-based engineering staff members are also expected to perform heroics by being time-zone flexible. They work longer hours and sometimes they time-shift. Managers are used to staying late to overlap with U.S. time. For example, one delivery manager said that he works 9-to-9 many days. The Infosys campuses in India are 24-hour campuses.[20]

Despite a culture that exacts "life style sacrifices" and expects "heroics" of its employees, Infosys is highly selective in its hiring, accepting less than 1 percent of its million applicants each year. "Infoscions," as they are called, earn very good salaries and benefits by Indian standards. "In return for being hired, employees know they are expected to contribute more than just their talent," Carmel concludes.[21] Given that Infosys has a blue-chip client base and was named "India's best managed company" by consultants A.T. Kearney, this is telling. But long hours are not unique to particular companies; they are generalized across the Indian ICT landscape.

The IT magazine *Dataquest* released a study that found that long hours are the leading cause of stress for workers, followed by work timing.[22] As it surveyed workers at some of the largest employers in the outsourcing sector and is largely proindustry in outlook, the findings are worth quoting at length: "Any average agent works for 11–12 hours per day—the number goes up to 14 in case of companies that encourage overtime. The plight of the operational heads is worse—they regularly clock 17–18 hours per day working their shift besides staying back for customer conference calls." In her comparative study of three software firms in China, Hungary, and India, Perlow finds that Indian employees work the longest.[23] The "mandatory" workday is from 9:00 a.m. to 6:30 p.m., but workers regularly end at 7:00 p.m. and sometimes as late as 11:00 p.m. Saturday is also a full workday. Likewise, many workers I interviewed spoke of frequent 12- to 14-hour workdays. Seeing long hours as a positive thing, one executive mused, "Here people are much more willing to sacrifice their time and do things."

Workers at small to midsized companies fare no better. Manoj, a manager at a midsized firm, contrasts Infosys (a "good paymaster") with smaller companies "that exploit their workers too much." Employees routinely work over 60 hours a week, he says, and "too much pressure is given to the developer to complete work." There are also occasional power shortages. When they occur, "Developers have to stay longer and work through the outage. Sometimes people have to work 18–20 hours continuously. It makes me feel like I should leave the industry, but there is satisfaction when I complete the work." There is also the satisfaction of being able to buy his first car, a sand-colored Tata Indica. This and the serenity of domestic life in which the discordant complexity of work is resolved into a harmonious simplicity: salubrious meals cooked by his mother-in-law, a playful child and loving wife, and a meditation alcove from which the sinewy young manager returns with hazy eyes and a light smile that says, "Really, this is all a game, is it not?"

Given these issues, one might wonder about the policy options available to limit the adverse impacts of long and irregular working hours. Mindful of the social consequences of the "24-hour society," the European Union released a "Working Time Directive," which lays out guidelines on the scheduling of shifts, rest periods, and work hours. It is unlikely that such a directive will ever apply to the offshore partners of EU companies. Nor is it likely that Indian companies will welcome the imposition of "foreign" labor standards. The CFO of one of India's largest ICT companies puts the issue of long and busy hours in comparative perspective:

People work very hard. And why do people work hard? They do so because they're a poor country. They're growing up. India's a poor country. So every country has worked hard. Koreans have worked hard; the Japanese have worked hard; the Germans have worked hard. To grow your national economy, a couple generations work extremely hard. People in the U.S. worked hard; people in the U.K. worked hard. Once you become wealthy, you work less, right. A wealthy country cannot dictate to an emerging country and say, "You work less." It's not going to happen because everybody's at a different state of development.

Thus in addition to cost, part of the attractiveness of Indian labor to corporations is its willingness to "work hard." Software developers who visited their U.S. parent office for training said that American employees generally stick to a nine-to-five schedule. They, on the other hand, frequently have to stay into the evening to attend conference calls with "on-site" personnel. They then stay on to fix software glitches, which leads to "more than eight hours of working a day." As an employee who has made frequent visits to the New York office remarked, "People tend to work more here. We work later hours. . . . We accelerate the pace in the evening." A manager in the U.S. office says that the extended hours were unintentional: they simply were not mindful of the time in India. "We have a big clock now that's set to Chennai time on the wall. It's not that big, perhaps it should be bigger, but we are much better about it now," he says.

A BPO worker who previously worked at Reuters's offshore office in Bangalore says that in the United States people are better at meeting deadlines. Indians, by contrast, "are not all that cool with it. We work longer hours to meet their timelines. We're having to raise the working level." She adds that her parents are not very comfortable with her working late. Commutes to suburban work-sites can take up to two hours in company vans and taxis—as workers are picked and dropped in groups—which can extend the "work day" considerably. Says one call center worker of his nightly commute: "It's sightseeing in Bangalore. They should provide a greater number of cabs, but they think to cut costs first. Service is not up to the mark. They put all of Bangalore in one cab."

Long hours and overtime can also negatively affect health. A growing body of research indicates that overtime and extended work schedules increase the risk of hypertension, cardiovascular disease, fatigue, stress, depression, musculoskeletal disorders, chronic infections, and diabetes, among other things.[24] In sum, Indian ICT employees work long hours and are often squeezed on overtime pay. Moreover, simply looking at the length of work hours masks their qualitative density, revealed in infrequent breaks and heightened intensity.

Temporal Displacement

The Night Shift and Health Problems

What is fairly unique to the ITES industry is the permanent night shift. For Indian firms, as a manager puts it, "Working the client's hours at night is often preferable as the client is easier to coordinate with. We can provide real-time updates. Development is available in the same time zone." However preferable the night shift is for businesses, it exacts a social and physical toll and gives rise to serious safety concerns. Coping with this temporal inversion, however, is a necessary condition of employment.

According to the International Labour Organization, "The night shift is the most disruptive of all shifts in terms of physiological adjustment, sleep and well-being."[25] It disturbs sociotemporal patterns and circadian rhythms, leading to stress and sleep disturbances, all of which increase susceptibility to disease. Night shifts have been linked to gastrointestinal disorders, such as constipation, diarrhea, and peptic ulcers, and there is growing evidence tying shift work to coronary heart disease and breast cancer.[26] (Just recently, the government of Denmark began compensating women who developed breast cancer after working the night shift for long stretches.)[27] They may also contribute to miscarriages and low weight and preterm births among pregnant workers.[28]

Of 103 night shift workers I surveyed, 63 reported experiencing job-related health problems. These include but are not limited to loss of appetite, insomnia, eyestrain, fatigue, stomach cramps, acidity and constipation, headaches, and backaches. One worker complained of "acute health loss in 2003 leading to hospitalization." Another said he feels "his memory power reducing." The figures above may underestimate the actual number of people with health problems as many workers, especially men, were reluctant to disclose ailments but later admitted to experiencing problems.[29] A handful of workers said that they acclimate to the night shift after an initial period of adjustment, and research suggests that a permanent night shift may be better than erratic shifts, as it permits some degree of circadian adaptation. However, even this adjustment is ephemeral.[30] Any benefits are lost when workers revert to standard routines, which is inevitable on weekends and days off as workers struggle to make up for lost time with their friends and families. Thus, the ILO concludes, "The body rhythms of permanent nightworkers are constantly in a state of disruption."[31]

The night shift is also linked with behavioral changes like smoking and poor diet. According to one worker, "It's working against the nature. It really impacts the health. It's more of a chip-and-Coke culture, and I've seen a lot of people falling ill. This industry's helping the tobacco industry *a lot*." One former call center worker recalled "falling ill and having headaches, migraines. Intakes of medicine were very high and I started losing weight." Others said that they gained weight because of the sedentary lifestyle the job promotes—working at night and sleeping by day with little exercise in between.[32] The *New York Times* reports on the startlingly high incidence of type 2 diabetes among India's middle class and suggests that keyboard-tapping, junk-food-eating software workers are particularly easy prey for the disease.[33]

Rupa, a doe-eyed, 22-year-old call center worker, says that her firm is a "very nice place to work. But your whole routine changes because of the night shift. If I get a day off, I can't sleep until four or five in the morning. But you get used to it." Wilson, a 24-year-old commerce graduate, interrupts. "But *it is* difficult," he says sharply. "You compromise a lot. You have only Sundays to see family. You lose appetite as you can't eat breakfast at one in the afternoon. For those staying alone, it's very difficult." He adds that making calls is "a major angle of stress. When you start, OK, it's just a new thing. [As] with any new toy, it's easy to play with. But then it becomes very monotonous." Outside, their 26-year-old team leader clenches a plastic cup of coffee in one hand and a cigarette in the other. Asked how many hours she sleeps each day, she says "five or six maximum," and tosses her cigarette butt on the ground in haste, making a proud show of her busyness.

When I take the elevator up to the workspace on the third floor, I see a hulking worker carrying an employee who has just fainted, presumably from fatigue, to a red couch in the lobby. Managers and employees crowd around with concern. The paramedics are called and she is soon taken the hospital. From the dim foyer of a smaller and poorer call center, I watch as two workers slowly descend a winding staircase. One of the women is clutching her stomach and has a pained expression on her face. They walk to the front door and motion to the security guard, who is sitting in the open air, his hat turned dozily to the side, amid a small swarm of mosquitoes. He disappears for a moment and returns with a worn cardboard box full of medicines. The worker takes two white pills, frowns, and climbs back upstairs.

The prolonged combination of stress and fatigue at BPOs now goes by the acronym BOSS—"burn-out stress syndrome." A worker tells of its symptoms: "Since I will have to work the night shift hours, it severely affects our daily lives. I missed most of my family affairs. But the most important thing is that I have suffered a number of diseases like sleeplessness, eyestrain, continuous headache. I couldn't find any time to brace my mind or to take care of my health." Consequently, one manager says that workers cannot stay on the job for more than two or three years. After that, "They burn out. It's very hard on the body and not natural." A 40-year-old former worker says that the combination of health problems and managerial pressure was too much to handle. More than once she had high blood pressure and fell ill. "They said I was dropping my calls. I said, 'I'm dropping the job.'"

As the major factor that sets the body clock is bright light, offices are bathed in artificial luminosity, and blinds are closed to keep the darkness from view. "We can't tell what time of day it is when we're at office," a worker says brightly. Caffeine is another weapon against drowsiness. Workers, however, often find it difficult to sleep after the shift as they return home in broad daylight. "Wearing dark glasses on the way home if we are working the night shift prevents the morning sunlight from activating our internal biological clock," suggests a company flier. A few workers mention using sleeping pills and drinking alcohol to help them fall asleep.[34] Sleep restriction, even at moderate levels, results in increased levels of stress hormones and can "seriously impair waking neurobehavioral functions in healthy adults."[35] Over time, the body's ability to compensate for this sleep deficit wanes, perhaps permanently.[36] Importantly, this "neurobiological 'cost' which accumulates over time" applies to extended shifts as well as night shifts.[37] Yet as job tenure for BPO employees is very short, the health impacts are not as severe as they would be over time. High turnover, somewhat perversely, is good for workers' health.

Social and Family Problems: "We Are Like Owls"

Amartya, 27, is an employee of an ITES firm in New Delhi. Born in Calcutta, he is fluent in Hindi, Bengali, and English and holds a bachelors degree in commerce. He works between 10 and 12 hours a day, six days a week. He travels to work between eight and nine at night through a soft landscape of unfocused forms, dull wind, and intermittent street lamps that produce a crepuscular gloom. In contrast, the morning light is sharp and the air crisp when he returns home, whereupon he breakfasts on a glass of water and a few glucose biscuits.[38] He then sleeps heavily into the afternoon and takes lunch at the "Hotel Kerala," a tiny restaurant tucked into an unpaved alley a short bus ride away. The fare there is "simple and safe." After lunch he takes another nap until evening and then goes back to work. "Eat—sleep— work. Eat—sleep—work. I have become too dull," he says with a laugh that makes his moustache jump.

The second of three children and the son of a retired civil servant, Amartya is the only male child, and this entails a certain financial responsibility. His daily dilemma is like that of many workers in the industry. The job has uprooted him, distancing him from friends and family, but it is comparatively well paying. As he explains, "I'm the lone earner for my family and . . . I can support my family fully with my present job. But socially it's hampered me as we are in night shift and I can't visit Calcutta for receptions and marriages. But I don't have any option because someone has to compromise somewhere."

Of those workers who say that outsourced jobs have improved their lives, their reasons are chiefly economic and secondarily social. One worker stitches these two strands together: "It has increased my social status, a little bit better than being unemployed. Now I have very limited time for family, but the positive effect is that the job has given an economic stability and a little more security." Another employee primly describes his growing professionalism: "The job has brought discipline in my life. I have learnt to appreciate perfection in everything." But even these workers are not likely to stay on for long. Whatever adjustments workers make, job tenure is extremely short and the mountain of mobility is a tough climb. As one manager puts it, "Not everyone can be a team leader."

Compared to other shift systems, fixed night shifts more severely impair personal relationships and mental well-being.[39] A worker at Amartya's firm puts it bluntly: "I feel that my organization's work timings are very odd and that affects my social and family life . . . which demolishes my happiness." And, indeed, camouflaging yourself culturally and temporally can lead to a measure of disorientation. Workers complain that their time with family and friends is curtailed ("My girlfriend has left me since I could not give her enough time"); that they are unable to participate in religious events ("I can't celebrate festivals, as I have to work on those days and that too in shift"); and that they feel cut off from the larger society ("I'm not updated with the current world scenarios"). Nearly half of the overall survey respondents report social or family problems (58 out of 120; 20 nonresponses), and the large majority of them work the night shift. As Mirchandani notes, workers are at a remove "from the spaces of social life such as markets, households, and transportation links, which occur only during the day."[40]

"We are like owls. We're awake when family is asleep," says one former call center employee who now works at an IT start-up, calling to mind Thoreau's reflection in *Walden*, "I rejoice that there are owls. Let them do the idiotic and maniacal hooting for men."[41] And after nights of hooting, workers' diurnal lives can become quite solitary: "We can't socialize because of night work and this leads to depression. [Workers] are willing to spend whatever they can on boozing, shopping, whatever." A shift lead at a BPO who works 12 hours a day, seven days a week, remarks, "My social life has gone for a toss. People at work expect more from you. I desperately need a break." (In some cases this hypertrophied sense of displacement is both cultural and temporal, as with the worker who boasted of taking shots of vodka at 9:00 a.m.) All told, the jobs produce (relatively) high incomes and social estrangement in equal measure.

Safety Issues

The main changes to Indian labor law introduced for the benefit of the industry have had to do specifically with time. These include amendments that allow flexible work timings and shift work, including provisions for work on national holidays and on overtime pay (regulated by the Shops and Establishments Act, 1947); that allow women to work the night shift (prohibited by the Factories Act, 1948); and the designation of ITES and IT companies as "essential services" (as controlled by the Industrial Disputes Act, 1947), a designation that makes strikes very difficult. These changes have the cumulative effect of allowing businesses to function 24 hours a day, 365 days a year. Firms are also exempted from mandatory power outages and are provided with dedicated satellites and power supplies so that their time-sensitive operations are not affected by overtaxed municipal infrastructure. Businesses argue that such changes are necessary to attract foreign investment. And in this they are correct: if offices in the West and India cannot be synched temporally without major disruptions, foreign investment would likely not come. Such concessions, however, are not without their costs.

On the night of December 13, 2005, Pratibha Srikanth Murthy, a 24-year-old Hewlett Packard (HP) Globalsoft Services call center worker in Bangalore, boarded a cab that was to take her to her 2:30 a.m. shift. The following morning, her bloodied body was found in a roadside ditch in the outskirts of the city, and the driver was charged with rape and murder. Although HP has denied responsibility—the 28-year-old driver worked for a company, SRS Services, to which HP outsources its transportation—the Karnataka government has filed a suit against the company under Section 25 of the state's Shops and Commercial Establishments Act (1961), which mandates that employers provide for the safety and security of their employees. If convicted, the company's managing director at the time of the murder, Som Mittal, would face a token fine of 1,000 rupees ($25).[42] The act and another at the central level had been previously amended to allow women to work night shifts in special economic zones.

Would that it were an isolated incident. In November 2007, Jyoti Kumari Choudhary, an employee of a Wipro call center, was found raped and brutally murdered on the Mumbai-Pune Express Highway. In Gurgaon, call center workers have been molested by drivers. Acid was thrown on a female call center employee in Pune by a former driver after she refused his advances.[43] During my short visit to a call center in Bombay, two employees told me of an attempted abduction of their coworker by a driver. Such incidents prompted labor ministries to issue guidelines on transportation safety to ICT firms. A senior executive at one of India's largest IT firms, however, disputes the significance of these events:

> Night shifts are part of a choice that you make, right? You can always get a different job. This is all being blown up for nothing. Yes, it's a heinous crime. It's a chance occurrence that could have happened to anybody. Many people work in the night shifts. It is sad, it shouldn't happen, but it happened. It's not the end of the world, it's not like the industry is evil. The industry has taken care so much. How many industries drop people home in the night? How many people are well paid? How many people have used technology? This is, you know, going overboard.

Globalsoft's Mittal insists that the murder of Murthy was a "stray, one-off incident" that "has nothing to do with the company."[44] He claims that the "element of risk is always there" but denied culpability, musing, "What precautionary measures can be taken against a suicide bomber?"[45] (to which one might reply: many). Likewise, an elfin female call center worker in Bangalore says with a heavy sigh that "these things are blown out of proportion." NASSCOM, the industry association, claims that the industry "is the most responsible employer of women in India." How is it that these abuses are so easily dismissed?

These "episodes," though relatively small in number, bear an uncanny resemblance to the serial murders of young female workers in the Mexican border town of Juarez. Following the passage of the North American Free Trade agreement, tens of thousands of laborers flocked to the city's growing assembly plants, or maquiladoras, "which looked just like the ones constructed by those same companies north of the border."[46] The majority of workers were women. This was new. As Rodriguez writes, "In the past, they rarely would have considered leaving home to work. Now these women were an important part of the workforce."[47] Employers preferred them to men as they cost less and supposedly possessed greater manual dexterity.

As in India, the new industry operated on a 24-hour schedule. Commutes could be long and solitary as workers walked miles to bus stops late at night or in the early morning. And here is where the story turns tragic. Juarez's rise coincided with a dramatic surge in crime and violence, much of it related to battles between drug cartels. Brutalized bodies began appearing in roadside ditches and in the desert. Many of the victims were young women who worked in the maquiladoras. Investigations into the killings were excruciatingly slow, improperly conducted, and inconclusive. Equally galling was the fact that the victims were being held partly responsible for their own grisly deaths. As Rodriguez writes:

> Women's rights activists had begun voicing their outrage that detectives were faulting the victims, implying that they willingly went off with a man or were leading double lives, sneaking off after work to dance at the city's bars and discos. In fact, a majority of the dead girls had disappeared on their way to and from work and were wearing long pants and sneakers, not miniskirts and spiked heels, as police were insinuating.[48]

Similarly, women in the Indian outsourcing industry are rumored to drink and sleep around, and there is also suggestion that the abused women brought the assaults on themselves by their manner of dress. Choudhary, for one, was not dressed provocatively when she was raped and strangled. She was not drunk when her head was bashed in with a heavy rock. In fact, reports suggest that it was her assailants, two drivers who were to take her to her job at the Rajiv Gandhi Infotech Park, that were soused. Yet these myths follow women around like distorted shadows.

An Indian cabbie says that drivers are easily provoked by "flashy dressing": "We think they should wear full dresses instead of short tops and mini skirts. Anyone's mind can get deviated with such dresses." (One would think that this propensity towards quick mental agitation would make one unfit to drive.) Not to be outdone, the president of the Union for Information and Technology Enabled Services in India, P. P. Naidu, invokes pseudoscientific language to rationalize violence against women: "The body chemistry of a human being in the day time and the body chemistry during night are quite different. Keeping this in mind, there should be a small definition of the dress code, not a major one, but a dress code which is well understood is required."[49] (One call center does just this, advising "ladies to avoid skirts with deep slits, deep necked tops, transparent material, tight-fitting/skin-hugging outfits, skirts above knee length.")

In this there is almost a touching admission of weakness. The driver concedes that men are slaves to their carnal impulses. They may know they are doing wrong, but it is in their nature, they cannot control themselves, poor souls. What is not so touching, however, is the brazen displacement of responsibility and the self-victimization. (They seem to say, "Please protect us from these attractive young women who are thrusting their sexuality upon us. We're just humble drivers.") But let us also consider more sensible commentary. Chetan Bhegat, author of a best-selling novel about call centers, glosses the incidents: "Incidents of rape or molestation cannot be predicted and I'm sure that companies try their best to safeguard their employees. I don't mean that people should stop being cautious; it's just that danger cannot be predicted or prevented. Despite the few incidents I would say the BPO sector is still worth nurturing."[50]

More reasonable, certainly, but it partakes of the same naturalizing impulse that treats violence against women as an external force like hurricanes and earthquakes. It is in the order of things; precautions can be taken but it is impossible to protect against an inevitability. The truth, however, is that proper screening could have prevented the Choudhary murder, at least, as the driver had an extensive criminal record. So while globalization produces employment for women, it does so in an unwelcoming patriarchal environment. To be sure, cruelty of this kind is not condoned, but it is trivialized. And although female workers create value, they are routinely devalued by their employers and by much of the society. They are viewed, in Melissa Wright's words, as disposable.[51]

As for the drivers, I wish I had spent more time talking to them as their daily lives are rather poorly understood. According to a former outsourcing consultant turned human rights activist, "they're getting a raw deal." "Rash driving by contracted drivers has led to a lot of accidents," he says. "There is lots of pressure on time, as they have the same timings as BPO employees. They make around 4,500 rupees [$100] a month, they have nice uniforms and haircuts, but at the end of the day they're the worst hit. But on the other hand, they might not have a job otherwise." In Bangalore, frustrated locals refer to the Dell cabs that speed through the streets of India's Silicon Valley as "hell cabs." Not only does night work lead to poorer performance, but it also leads to sleepiness, which, more than alcohol or drugs, is "the greatest identifiable and preventable cause of accidents in all modes of transport."[52]

Exit and Choice

The logic of globalization is unsparing, a point made plain in the preceding discussion on the duration and density of work. But to focus solely on these categories is to overlook time's internal texture, its cadence. As E. P. Thompson argued, what paved the groundwork for the expansion of industrial capitalism was not the length of the working day per se but the very acceptance by workers of the clock as a means of regulating work.[53] Lefebvre, moreover, wrote that the linear, serial, and exogenous rhythms of capitalism and the diverse, cyclical, and irregular rhythms of ordinary life are always in perpetual interaction, producing a struggle over the definition of working time.[54] In this section, I look at the concepts of time imposed by companies and how workers deal with them. I also consider the means available to workers to carve out a space for the emergence of collective rhythms that could counteract the atomizing pressures of a desocialized work environment.

To begin, the mandatory night shift results in the wholesale inversion of night and day. Time is closely regulated and minutely supervised. For non-shift workers, the elasticity of the working day—which expands and contracts like bellows at the whims of the home office—signifies a collapse of the work-life boundary. While the absence of a strong demarcation between work and life could be seen as welcomingly reminiscent of preindustrial work patterns, in the present case, they are not so much intermingled as is life subsumed by work.[55] These tensions are exacerbated by the rote nature of the work, and, consequently, workers complain about the unrelieved monotony of task and pace.

The struggle over working conditions, then, is increasingly about time.[56] Temporal autonomy could mean shortened work hours and rotating shifts; lighter workloads, reduced pressure, and a more relaxed working pace; increased frequency and duration of breaks; a greater appreciation of the unique time-bind faced by Indian workers; and time for unsupervised interaction between workers, thus injecting a social dynamic into the workplace. Only then could workers be said to exercise any meaningful degree of ownership over the labor process. It is thus not merely a fight of securing more "leisure time" but of integrating collective rhythms into the workplace setting.

The balance of forces between capital and labor in the offshore ICT industry is reflected in the ability of workers to wrest concessions from employers (job mobility, breaks, pay raises, etc.) and vice versa (temporal inversion, long hours, flexibility, etc.). Hirschman argues that there are two main ways to express your discontent in an organization.[57] You can *voice* your complaints through the appropriate channel and hope that the grievance will be addressed. Or you can *exit* from the organization and ply your trade elsewhere. Importantly, for the latter to be a meaningful option, you must have a measure of social or economic security: either the skills to acquire another job or some private or family wealth to fall back on. Otherwise, even voice becomes a perilous option. The issue becomes one of workers' bargaining power.

Wright distinguishes between the *associational* and *structural* power of workers.[58] The former concerns the power created by the formation of collective organizations like unions and political parties. Structural power, by contrast, accrues to workers "simply from their location . . . in the economic system" and can be broken down into two parts. What Silver calls *marketplace bargaining power* "results directly from tight labor markets."[59] *Workplace bargaining power* derives, by contrast, "from the strategic location of a particular group of workers within a key industrial sector." Marketplace bargaining power could mean possessing scarce skills that are in high demand. It could also refer to a situation of low unemployment or to the workers' ability to withdraw from the "labor market entirely and survive on nonwage sources of income." Workplace bargaining power could mean occupying a critical node in a complex, tightly integrated production network, where a work stoppage in one place could bring the entire network to a halt.

Indian ICT workers have very little associational power. The major unions have expressed interest in organizing workers but have made no real effort. In terms of marketplace bargaining power, workers seemingly have it in abundance. They know English and have specialized skills generally available only to the middle class. Furthermore, demand is fast outpacing supply such that companies have to raise salaries significantly each year.[60] Another critical thing workers have in their favor is that many are middle class and can depend on the family if they want to quit.

As far as workplace bargaining power goes, being a link in the global service chain gives them the ability to disrupt the network through a work stoppage. As offshoring has matured, companies have developed deep linkages between their various offices around the world, so much so that many are directly dependent on their offshore subsidiaries. Krishna, the jaunty senior executive with the Roman nose, makes this point plain:

We operate in the extended team model. Almost 100 percent, 99 percent of the development process happens here. . . . Only the requirements, business problem definition, and the production support is done in the U.S. As far as the development at [the financial services firm], it's happening here. If [the subsidiary] is not operational or cannot deliver, [the parent] will have to stop. As far as [the parent], we are the heart, or the brains. . . . We drive it.

A work disruption, he says, could prove disastrous for the U.S. operation. Events in the outside world, such as social unrest, can also have ramifications. A strike in Bangalore following the death of the celebrated South Indian actor Rajkumar disrupted work for two days. As companies like Microsoft and Sun refused to shut down operations—legally they are considered "public utilities" and do not have to honor strikes—they were directly attacked by mourners and were not able to keep production online. While such difficulties may lead companies to reconsider their offshoring plans, the competitive nature of the global economy ensures that when a few major players make the transition, such as General Electric or IBM, others have to follow suit. As a U.S.-based manager puts it, "We have to make it work. We have little choice."

To recapitulate, the main factors that alleviate the pressures of long work hours, a stressful work pace, and the night shift are (1) the demand-supply imbalance, (2) the possession of scarce skills, and (3) workers' ability to withdraw from the labor market. This power has enabled workers to exercise *voice* in some seemingly trivial matters. More importantly, the fluidity of the labor market has allowed many to move horizontally from company to company in search of the best compensation package. As an official of the Indian National Trade Union Congress, which is affiliated with the Congress Party, put it:

There have been some attempts to organize but they have been met with resistance by employers and the workers themselves. Employment opportunities are shrinking. Educated people are increasingly unemployed. BPO and IT are offering good opportunities. In a bank, you make six to seven thousand rupees starting. In IT/BPO you make fourteen to fifteen thousand rupees to start with. You may say anything about health hazards and long work hours to which workers are exposed. But considering the compensation package, these are not hazards. Promotions are quick. They have sort of an open-door policy. In a factory, you can't meet the proprietor. [In BPO/IT] you can send an email to your employer. Interaction is more free. Grievances are addressed through companies.

In comparison with other sectors of the Indian economy, the union official argues, ICT workers do quite well. Although the pressures on them may be intense, they can work two years make a tidy sum and quit. For the CFO of a major IT company, the main criteria that should be used to evaluate the decency of working conditions are choice and the possibility of exit.

You must remember that this industry is resource-constrained; you can't force people to do anything you want. If you force people to do something, they walk away. It's a hot market for employees. Look, you unionize people when workers are exploited, there's surplus labor and . . . the pay is less. You have a situation where the pay goes up 15–20 percent a year. It is a sellers' market, so what is the need? People are making choices. Today you don't have to work in a call center, you've got other jobs. You choose to work in a call center, you get money. We are a democracy; let the people decide. If it's that there are no jobs and call centers are the only work, there's a point. There are so many jobs available. Attrition in call centers is 45 percent. Forty-five percent that join leave within a year, so what are we talking about?

It is indeed difficult to argue that workers are "trapped" in these positions. However, withdrawing from the industry deprives people of a means to improve their life-chances. As Castells writes: "Be in the network . . . and, over time, increase your chances. Be out of the network, or become switched off, and your chances vanish since everything that counts is organized around a world wide web of interacting networks."[61] For many, exit becomes difficult because of the accumulating possibilities they are passing up. The compensation packet is attractive enough, says one worker, that few leave the industry for good.

So despite the aforementioned sources of structural leverage, one must not mistake potential power for its realization. It is "a perpetual possibility only in a world of speculation," to quote T. S. Eliot.[62] And there are also a variety of sources of workers' *insecurity* that reduce their leverage. Workers' complaints of unfair practices are often ignored. As one worker comments, "If you speak up, you'll become a bad person. People are very scared to go and speak." Labor laws provide little protection, and the lack of collective representation also restricts workers' voice. In a changed labor market, an atmosphere of generalized insecurity could develop and be used to bargain down wages and working conditions. And, indeed, as a result of the global economic crisis, many workers face significant salary freezes and benefit cuts. Reports suggest that they are spending longer hours at work and reducing leave requests in order to save their jobs. Discriminating employers like Infosys are adopting "zero-tolerance" policies toward "nonperformers," while unions have begun a "stop the pink slip" campaign to encourage companies to explore alternatives to layoffs.[63]

Coda

On the heels of the 1929 stock market crash, John Maynard Keynes sought to allay the "economic pessimism" of the day. "We are suffering, not from the rheumatics of old age," he wrote, "but from the growing pains of over-rapid changes, from the painful adjustment between one economic period and another."[64] Scientific and technological advances would "within a hundred years" usher in an "age of leisure and abundance" and "economic bliss." Later technological optimists envisioned such a reduction of toil in the transition to "postindustrialism." As the prevailing work pattern prior to the Industrial Revolution, according to Thompson, "was one of alternate bouts of intense labor and of idleness, whenever men were control of their working lives," one is tempted to ask whether the irregular working rhythm of the preindustrial era been recaptured in the flexibility of postindustrial period.[65]

Such dreams have not come to fruition. In fact, the trend is in the other direction, toward longer and busier hours. The workplaces of "new economy" are traversed by novel and retrograde modes of work pace, rhythm, and time-discipline. What is at stake, Basso writes, "is *a return to the past*, to hours that are not only long but extremely intense and variable, autocratically established by companies and by the state."[66] Time should therefore be brought to the forefront of discussions about working conditions. And as the livelihoods of workers in global north and global south are inextricably linked through international trade, a transnational perspective is increasingly important.

Some forty years ago, Thompson observed (rather belatedly) that "without time-discipline we could not have the insistent energies of the industrial man; and whether this discipline comes in the form of Methodism, or of Stalinism, or of nationalism, it will come to the developing world."[67] Not only has time-discipline come to the Third World, but work-time pressures have been intensified by globalization. As offshoring gains momentum, not only may costs be driven down, but so may working conditions, particularly as they relate to time. While firms do not go offshore for the benefits of time arbitrage alone, it can become of an element of concession bargaining: "Work longer or faster or we can go offshore where workers are more willing." Globalization therefore does not entail the loosening of temporal chains, but their reconfiguration: a combination both rigid and flexible that binds even as it liberates.

CHAPTER FIVE

The Rules of the Game

In 2005, Ravi Aron, a professor at the Wharton School of Business, interviewed Vivek Paul, then vice chairman and CEO of Wipro Technologies, one of India's most successful service companies. Paul had been named by *Business Week*, *Barron's*, and *Time*/CNN as one of the most respected managers and CEOs in the world, and during the public debate on outsourcing he was its amiable Indian face. ("I was brave to take the arrows on my chest," he says.) He exudes confidence and calm and speaks soothingly about the merits of offshoring for sending and receiving country alike. In addition to a cozy, knowing smile and a breezy, tie-less informality, Paul has all the right credentials. He was recruited by and reported directly to Jack Welch, former CEO of General Electric, as head of a joint venture in India. Welch at the time had drawn his share of praise and criticism for his unequivocal stance on mass layoffs, winning him the sobriquet "Neutron Jack." In an email to GE employees, Welch announced his "70:70:70" rule whereby 70 percent of the business had to be outsourced, 70 percent of the outsourced business had to offshored and 70 percent of the offshored business had to be in India.[1] The company's core activities would remain at home.[2]

A former water polo captain at the University of Massachusetts, where he earned both his B.A. and M.B.A., Paul, in a sense, embodies Welch's rule. He is of Indian extraction and his speech retains a subcontinental lilt (Welch's 30 percent), but his basic outlook and core beliefs are those of a global executive. He says that Indians are "great individual contributors, not great managers"; that Indian managers "have grown up in a cocooned world" and that "this has to change." He is credited not only with boosting efficiency and profits at Wipro, but with taking a company that was Indian "to the bone" and making its employees "think big and global."[3] He prefers the term *global collaboration* to *outsourcing* and says that the backlash is "gone, it's over." While Paul had always been rather candid, when asked whether there is "a profitable and robust revenue stream" for Indian service companies, his answer was surprising:

> If you look at the service business, absolutely. But if you look at that service business as leading to innovation and product outcomes, the answer is absolutely not. Frankly, I feel that when people work in a service business like ours, it's almost like we give them a lobotomy. I don't think, and I hope I'm wrong, you will see a single successful product startup coming out of people who were working at Wipro or any other similar companies. . . . Why that is, God knows. But I truly believe that there is some sort of inadvertent lobotomy that we give people.[4]

While he maintained that "it's not just 'brainless' blue-collar workers who are working for you, they have to be adept at some pretty advanced skills," the matter hinges on a distinction between intuitively knowing what to do and having to be told what to do. As he told me, "There is an incredible amount of innovation going on in India. In terms of R&D, we had 7,000 engineers innovating for U.S. engineers. We were the fourth most prolific chip designer in the world. The problem is that engineers don't know what to do. They have to be told what to do next. If you're asking about leaps of knowledge, that knowledge resides here." He put it similarly to Aron:

> The stuff that's been done in India is staggering in terms of range and depth. I don't think that anyone can say that the work we're doing is trivial. But the work we're doing is under somebody else's direction. . . . For an engineer, there's a big difference between discovering something, versus discovering something that you know somebody else says can be done. . . . And there's a second quality I didn't mention: knowing what you want, or what the market wants, versus being told what to do. . . . A service business is really individuals working for someone else. . . . So unless you have a very clear view of your corporation's value added, you have no entitlement to an enterprise value.[5]

There are two points to be taken from Paul's remarks. The first is that the Indian outsourcing industry is not terribly innovative. The second is that Indian workers are innocent of the knowledge of what to do and must be told. You might conclude, as many managers are wont to, that certain (Indian) character traits inhibit innovation and discovery. But while the much lamented "culture of deference" in Indian workplaces may have something to do with this, workers do not take "ownership" of their work for a variety of reasons, not simply an ingrained lack of initiative. The international division of IT-based service labor is such that "creative" work is concentrated mostly in the global north and low-skill, replicable tasks in the global south.

Individual responsibility becomes a fuzzy notion where skill development is limited, career paths inertial, and work fragmented and piecemeal. Furthermore, Indian companies rely heavily on standardized processes, making it difficult for workers to invest themselves in the rote task at hand. Even where workers receive considerable on-the-job training, a *skills ceiling* remains in place. Workers know that there are only so many team leader posts, only so much room for growth within any one company. Yet the aspiration lingers. The task for managers is to get them to lower their sights, to bow their heads ever so slightly.

Lobotomies and Cheerful Robots

Thinkers as far back as at least Adam Smith and Marx have written about the destructive effects of too fine a division of labor on the minds and bodies of workers. In modern parlance, extreme rationalization increases productivity but "deskills" workers and renders them unthinking cogs in the machine. This line of thought enjoyed a vogue in the late 1970s when labor-intensive manufacturing jobs started to be moved offshore in large numbers. The focus then switched, at least in the advanced industrial world, to the prospects of information-based service work. Scholars were divided about whether the march of technological modernization would be liberatory, leading to upskilling and overall improvements in job quality, or the opposite, degrading skills by relegating workers to mundane tasks and subjecting them to greater managerial control.[6] In both scenarios, "creative" work, which involves the manipulation of symbols and not the production of things, was to be concentrated in the global north, while labor-intensive work was to slowly trickle south. Then, suddenly it seemed, global corporations began looking to the Third World for the provision of seemingly complex services.

Technological advancements have made it possible to automate some of the more rote aspects of service work. Globalization means that those banal tasks that cannot be automated can at least be sent offshore. Paul's distinction between intuition and command then has implications for both workers' morale and the niche that developing countries occupy in the international division of labor. The employees of the Indian outsourcing industry are white-collar proletarians—they work with information technologies yet perform the rote work, or as one executive put it, the "dog work." The condition of this class fragment is paradoxical. In India, they are arrivistes, but globally, the workers are the cyber scriveners of the information age, and the managers and employers, the new compradors.[7] The same could be said for the industry writ large: to all outward appearances, these offshore offices look like twinkling towers of innovation. But, like plastic fruit, they are imitations. (Yet, as in trompe-l'oeil art, they are imitations with a fantastic life of their own: Indian offices under a long Western shadow.)

The scholarly literature confirms this view. Prasad, for example, argued a decade back that Taylorist production dynamics have resurfaced in the Indian computer industry and that an "invisible de-skilling" stymies career development.[8] More recently, Aneesh described software development in India in terms of high and low "skill saturation," and argued that, by and large, outsourcing involves the latter.[9] While there are few technological barriers preventing the offshoring of highly sophisticated work, the skills ceiling is determined largely by the role played by developing countries in the global service supply chain. As Taylor and Bain argue, this is a consequence of the way that companies have made their offshoring decisions:

Organizational restructuring and strategic review in UK companies tends to precede the horizontal segmentation of services, leading to the most standardized and least risk-laden processes being sliced-off and offshored. Fundamentally, then, and expressing the importance of the cost-reduction logic, India largely hosts an extreme version of the mass production model.[10]

This tropism toward cost-reduction has consequences for workers' satisfaction. Call center employees, for example, are roused by expectations of "stimulating work and prestigious careers promised by employers" but "the mundane nature of incessant call-handling can cause disenchantment and disengagement from job and organization."[11] The IT magazine *Dataquest* sounds a similar note:

> When a fun loving city graduate joins a call center in India, in addition to commendable command over the English language, the employer sees a lot of enthusiasm and positive attitude in him or her while hiring. However, the new call center employee's zeal dies in the first few weeks. Despair and disillusion set in and the final outcome is that he or she quits the job. Little do these call center employees realize while they are being hired that, instead of fun, what lies ahead of them is much hard work and long, stressful days. The unrelieved monotony of their jobs and the repeated rejections from sometimes abusive clients ensures that their cup of woes brimmeth all night long.[12]

The unlikely combination of stress *and* monotony is particularly grating, especially when it occurs during the graveyard shift and in a context of unstable employment. Indeed, the strains resulting from this temporal dislocation are one of the leading causes of the industry's high turnover. But for all its drawbacks, routinization has certain benefits. For one, it renders outcomes more predictable and frees firms from dependence on the skills of particular workers.[13] Standardization also reduces sociocultural differences as companies now rely on fixed standards for governing and overseeing quality. This reduces the space for "play" and consequently innovation and creative thinking.[14] Executives I spoke with foresee continued employment growth in the industry but admit that it will likely be concentrated at the bottom of the company pyramid. Knowledge process outsourcing (KPO), the appellation for complex, "judgment-dependent" services, can be a risky gambit and does not supply as dependable a revenue stream as its duller, dumber, older brother, BPO. It would be better if firms employed an army of industrious automata. And to some extent this is what is occurring with the prevailing emphasis on standardization, that is, Paul's "inadvertent lobotomy." In this context, as Mills once wrote, "human relations" is largely about increasing the "morale of cheerful robots."[15]

According to a BPO executive, the best way to reduce costs is not offshoring, but automation, a goal that can only be approximated in service work. But if easily replicable work cannot be automated, the next best solution is to send it offshore where it can be performed for less. One study argues that for developed countries, "IT offshoring risks are limited to low-end occupations (such as programmers, coders and support specialists) that are labor intensive, easy to codify, or require little face-to-face contact."[16] Moreover, the industry magazine *Global Services* reports that "the traditional cost centers such as HR, finance and accounting and some low-value, high-volume customer-facing functions have been the most frequently outsourced activities. In such services, reducing cost has been the objective."[17] According to a survey by the consultancy EquaTerra, "Most companies are not looking for transformational outsourcing. Only one in five respondents said it was a priority to transform or optimize service." A venture capitalist says that Indian suppliers "are heavily dependent on process. This takes away individual responsibility and thoughtfulness. It's a double-edged sword because process-level guarantees are also what enable them to get the work." And even offshored work is vulnerable to automation. According to one BPO executive, "What threatens the low end is automation, definitely transactions."[18]

The uncertain trajectory of the ICT industry is well explained by Manoj Khanna, the COO of a leading KPO, a term that he says he coined. Khanna is well-spoken and well-dressed and wears his hair in a subdued pompadour. He says that the importance of offshoring resides in the fact that over a very short period of time, Indians have realized they can be a world leader in something. It's a booster to confidence and pride. We're not just following but actually leading. The younger generation is extremely confident. Our generation, we had a high level of nervousness and fear.

Nonetheless, he says that when he first used the term *KPO* he was under no illusions about India's place in the global service market. The neologism was in many ways aspirational; it suggested a possibility. "I'm not saying that we're doing things that are absolutely critical," he says, adjusting his tie. While offshoring involves a spatial shift of capital to the developing world, he concedes that American companies own intellectual property and thus call the shots in the "flat" world.

During the 2004 U.S. presidential campaign Khanna was at a meeting with members of NASSCOM, the Indian industry group, and a number of Western executives who were concerned about the outsourcing backlash. To allay their fears, the foppish Khanna made a facetious proposal. "OK. We don't want any more of your jobs. We're fine with that. But in exchange, let's have the ownership of intellectual property revert to Indian companies. How many of you would go for that? Everyone in the room was silent," he says with a satisfied smile. Intellectual property is warp and woof of the home office, while "commodity technology" can be subcontracted.[19] Offshoring-related growth, in other words, cannot widen beyond frontiers determined by multinationals.

An executive at a BPO specializing in legal services says that the quality of work "is often better in India because Indian employees are more qualified than their U.S. counterparts." Ph.D.s, for example, perform the work of American paralegals. (While salaries are comparable to a midsize law firm in India, the pay rate is 10–15 percent that of U.S. lawyers.) "You are putting a higher skill level to the task," he explains. While the life of a junior Indian law clerk is hardly to be envied, an M.B.A. at a legal outsourcing firm in India performs work that a similarly credentialed person in the developed world "would never do." Moreover, there is a structural disincentive to moving up the value chain. Another executive explains that sophisticated work has lower margins:

In terms of value, you can look at it two ways: one is high profitability and the other is a higher dollar value. For high profitability, you'll want to do stuff that is lower in terms of intellectual value. Higher dollar value would be something like consulting. For BPO you're maybe making $16 and your paying $8. For consulting services, it's $120 to $100. Margins, in other words, shrink as you go up the chain.

Higher-value projects are also risky. "KPO has a potential downside. If companies mess up, then there are fees and penalties that can go into the millions," says a venture capitalist. These are not unalterable laws, however. Multinationals like Microsoft, Honeywell, and Cisco have invested considerable sums in research and development in India. Infosys supposedly makes it a point to develop the skills of its workforce, and the *New York Times* reports that Hewlett Packard is planning "software universities" in eight Indian cities to train software testers—although testing is hardly the most innovative of activities.[20] And companies will no doubt find ways to hedge risks over time. But for the large majority of Indians employed by the industry, the geography of service work is such that they will continue to perform standardized work for the foreseeable future.[21] The current global recession has only dimmed the prospects for "risk-reward" outsourcing in which companies forge long-term relationships with subcontractors with a view to shifting complex activities to the supplier. The momentum for these "higher level" deals has appreciably slowed as companies are choosing to keep certain outsourceable activities in-house and to pare down projects.[22]

Employers and managers are locked in a contradiction. On the one hand, they want workers to mature into responsible professionals who take initiative and "ownership." On the other, the structural conditions of the global market favor the migration of easily replicable tasks, and their standardization is critical in generating a revenue stream for Indian suppliers. The relationship between turnover and standardization, however, is cyclical: high turnover and absenteeism produce a need for a standardized process so that operations can continue undisturbed when workers do not turn up. Standardization in turn results in dissatisfaction, in alienated labor, and thus more attrition. Managers are left with the delicate task of intimating upward career paths where they do not exist.[23] The following case study illustrates this paradox and illuminates the delicate relationship between onshore and off-shore work-sites.

"Client First"

The antechamber of Praxis, the Chennai-based subsidiary of an American investment bank, is tiled in multicolored marble. To one side of the reception desk, behind which sit a gentle, mustachioed man and a gruff, well-dressed woman, is a track-lit Kandinsky-esque painting. To the other is a 50-inch flat screen television. Today's feature is a two-minute promotional video in which executives and managers from the United States and Western Europe comfortably extol the bank's virtues. It runs continuously, day and night. (Today's feature was also yesterday's; the same video was playing when I visited 10 months earlier, and, on a conservative estimate, it has been screened at least 200,000 times.) What is remarkable about the video is that no Indian faces appear. Nor is any mention made in its hushed soundtrack of the subsidiary's existence, which, according to one executive, is the infrastructural backbone of the home office's operations. It is a none-too-subtle reminder to employees of their place in the command-and-supply chain. (The phrase "Client First," flashes repeatedly.) It stands as an illustration of the front office / back office distinction, as well as a representation of the international division of service labor.

Praxis got its start in 2001 as an affiliate of Synergy, a financial services subsidiary of a large investment bank.[24] In the late 1990s, Synergy had sought to cut labor costs by moving some of its work upstate from Manhattan. Additionally, some 150 consultants were hired on contract. While they were based as far apart as Ireland, Ohio, Connecticut, Phoenix, and Bangalore and received few of the benefits of full-time employees, the consultants were quickly integrated into Synergy's daily operations. In 1999, for example, the workers in Phoenix covered daytime production support, while those in Bangalore worked the second and third shifts.

As competitive pressures increased (do they ever ease?), it was decided that the company should be even leaner, and the first fat to be trimmed was the ring of contractors. "People were very nervous. I was crushed. I built this from nothing," says Paul, a friendly, bearded manager in shirtsleeves who worked closely with the contractors. The contractors, he says nostalgically as if recalling a motley set of high school chums, were a "very diverse group"—variously, Scottish, Mexican, Hawaiian, Iraqi, and Irani—with whom they had developed a special rapport. (Because of their lack of job security, they could be ingratiating. "They were a lot friendlier than working with in-house employees," he says.) Whereas Paul's team "talked to India" once a month, they spoke with the contractors in Phoenix once a day. When the latter were let go, a few more were hired in Bangalore. From there the dominos fell quickly. Next in line were the contractors in Connecticut and Ohio, then Ireland, and last, following the logic of cost-cutting, were those in Bangalore. It should be noted that, as with temporary workers, consultants who are let go, even after several years with the same company, are not recorded in government statistics as layoffs, which is "a classification reserved for normal employees who lose their jobs."[25]

Short of automation, however, you cannot just keep cutting.[26] After hiring and then eliminating contractors, Synergy went forward with a plan to incrementally offload its IT functions to an Indian subsidiary in the coastal city of Chennai. This did not sit well with its U.S. employees, especially when management slashed a small percentage of its own workforce. Dave, a U.S.-based manager who works on the company's mutual fund trading system, says of the layoffs:

When we started building up India, we had three rounds of layoffs. We lost programmers who were making $80,000. Now they're Indian. I lost friends I used to work with. I've been laid off. I know what it's like. I have a sensitivity. They have families, mortgages to worry about. It was tense for everyone. I never feel secure. But it's just the way companies do it. All Wall Street cares about is that you cut payroll by 10 percent.

While the staff in India expanded from an initial workforce of 50 to 1,600 today, Synergy instituted a hiring freeze in its IT department in the United States. This strategy of "natural attrition," in contrast to mass layoffs, relieved the company of the burden and guilt of firing its own, while at the same signaling its intention not to hire high-priced U.S. workers in the future.[27] "Even before 9/11 things were tightening. Within contracts they had the ability to cut X amount of people. I understood why they did it but it killed me. These were my friends. Why upset the apple cart? There was tension in room. It wasn't animosity but unfamiliarity," Paul recounts carefully.

Moreover, offshoring suggested to U.S. employees their impending professional obsolescence. "From the tech perspective," Paul says, "people are afraid of job loss." If their colleagues' jobs could be moved 8,000 miles away because of the plenitude of inexpensive labor, their own position seemed all the more precarious, their own skills that much less valued. Seated in a vast sea of anonymous cubicles, Dave is alive to the potential for scapegoating and discusses what Sennett refers to as "skills extinction"[28]: "Indians are the new minority. They have smelly food, dark skin, accents, and so on. The reality is that some skills may be outdated. You basically become overpaid and price yourself out of the market. You can't expect to spend the next 10 years as a programmer, it'll go offshore. You have to move to a manager, to analytical work." As is the case with professional identity in general, the structural shifts in the economy are understood in terms of individual responsibility.

"Too Many Chiefs and Not Enough Indians"

Employee misgivings aside, offshoring had achieved a certain momentum at Synergy. As the work moved to India grew in scope from basic IT maintenance to software development, the U.S. office became more managerial in complexion. That is, while U.S. employees were not promoted or given pay raises, they essentially filled the role of managers, coordinating with the Indian workforce by phone, email, and Black-berry. The idea was to maintain a relative parity in employees between the two offices. It was essentially a core-periphery model, which mir-rored the geography of developed and developing countries. What is more, it posited a distinction between planning and execution, which was based on a division of labor between manager and worker.

Synergy envisioned a "fifty-fifty model" whereby the Connecticut office would be replicated in Chennai. Aspirations aside, this does not mean that the offices are mirror images of each other. Form must be distinguished from content. An Indian worker explains: "Our role is developing and maintaining software. The business group is in the U.S. We don't have a business team here, just a replica." Dave puts it more directly: "It breaks down as programming and low-level work on the Indian end; business analysis, system design, and management on the U.S. end."

Raza Qamer, a U.S.-based manager, says that the organization is becoming older and "top heavy. If there are 500 here and 500 there, there they have younger, newer people." According to Dave, no one has left at the U.S. office, but they have not hired anyone either: "We used to hire computer graduates locally, but we haven't done that in six or seven years." He says that the average age is 26 at Praxis, while it is at least 10 years higher in the United States. "There are too many chiefs and not enough Indians," Qamer observes with a small laugh.[29]

Many U.S. workers remained deeply skeptical about offshoring. This skepticism took two forms, neither of which was very disruptive, as the generalized anxiety that had been created within the company left workers insecure about their own jobs. The first was buried resent-ment toward management for letting perfectly capable people go. The second response was a passive-aggressive posture in which they would do the least possible to advance the process without undermining it. This meant that undesirable work was moved over and that U.S. man-agers would invest precious little by way of training in the Indian staff. (The lack of trust would not go unrequited. Indian workers, for their part, returned the favor by jumping ship when they received a better job offer.) According to Dave,

There was a lot of resistance, just kind of an "us-them" mentality. U.S. managers weren't sending them work. We had to add a category on the time sheet called "waiting for work." Someone spent 20 hours one week waiting for work. People were trying to keep everything close to their chests. It was a step-by-step progression. They [Indians] were spoon-fed. First, you have business requirements; second, tech design; and third, low-level specs and pseudo-code. They were giving these guys almost prewritten code! They should give them work from the lowest level and have them work through it. Otherwise, they won't come up in skill level.

The disparity in work experience also rankled. Paul explains that "the main problem was that you lost six people who had five years of experience and their seven replacements would have less than six months of experience. You won't find a lot of people there with 10 years experience. We lost people with good experience and now we get trainees." In the beginning, only a few (around 5 percent) were "laterals" (i.e., from other companies), while 95 percent were "freshers." These young workers, he says with knitted brow, "don't know anything about what Synergy does." Nor do they "have as much dedication because everything is already in place, like the IT architecture." And, finally, words that seem to echo throughout every offshore office: "The majority of people are not taking responsibility and ownership of the project."

At the same time, Paul notes, the Indian workers were only getting portions of work, discrete tasks, so in a sense, there is no project for them to own. One Indian worker reflects warmly on the days when things were catch-as-catch-can:

Initially, we didn't have many managers, only one or two. We struggled, took ownership. We did it. Now, project architecture is there. Before, if there was a problem, something's going down—oh no! They worried about it. Now people don't care. Intuition is missing. It's a human tendency. If we don't have any information, we'll struggle to get it. If we do, we take it for granted.

And another expresses his frustrations:

Sometimes the jobs are monotonous. You're working for the same team for a long time. The product is in place and we are just maintaining it. We don't have the opportunity to design. Most of the high-level development happens in the U.S. We only get to do the low-level design. We also don't get the chance to talk to customers. This goes through on-site clients. Most of the work starts from low-level design and then coding.[30]

Importantly, this restricts Indian workers' skill development. "The only way we can grow is by doing high-level design," opines an Indian manager. "For any issue, we have to call so many people." Workers find this particularly frustrating given that they have an expertise in design and development and have even obtained higher software certifications than the U.S. office. With some pride, one worker says, "They haven't reached the same level. They are more of a bank than a software company, so we can't expect them to." In this regard at least, the tutee had outclassed the tutor, making the limitations all the more exasperating.

Granular Grunt Work

The word *job*, in its Middle English origins, meant "lump" (*gobbe*) or "piece" (*jobbe*). In the eighteenth century, Samuel Johnson defined *job* "as petty, piddling work; a piece of chance work." Flexibility restores the "arcane sense of the job, as people do lumps of labor, pieces of work, over the course of a lifetime."[31] Global sourcing further fragments work and disperses it across electronic channels. As the business magazine *CIO* reports, "Today, IT services companies take work, break it down into pieces, and perform each piece in the location that offers the best combination of skill, cost, quality and manageability. . . . 'This is he future,' says [Infosys CEO] Nilekani. 'IT is being disaggregated. Slice by slice, the whole model is changing.'" The article advises CIOs to "[break] down the work into the most granular pieces possible . . . into discrete processes, and each process into tasks," and to analyze "which ones you can or should do and which ones" should be sent offshore. The author does, however, caution that if tasks are spread out too broadly, workers become "less motivated because they feel as though they have less invested in the final product."[32]

Yet the banality of the work is in striking contrast to its importance. One Indian worker reflects on the volume of work that has been moved to Chennai. He says that earlier everything was done in the United States, but, slowly, work was moved to India. "In Chennai, things are cheap. You get bits and pieces of work. We were on the learning curve. In 2001, we reached a stage where we were really doing things, adding value." The Indian office is now vital to the daily operations of Synergy. One Indian executive says that 99 percent of the "development process"—which is used internally in such things as financial trading applications—takes place in Chennai. But, critically, Praxis has reached its apex. The executive reflects on limits:

> What we are doing is about the optimum. Because given that all of our hardware and users are in the U.S., real-time production support cannot be done from here. We can only do part of it. If you have to meet the users on a regular basis and get the requirements, it has to be done on-site. What we are doing today is about what we can do. . . . What can't really chip any more out of what they do. We can't carve out anymore.

"Oh, it was excellent," says Paul enthusiastically when asked about the quality of work in India. "They did work no one wanted to do." Even before Praxis was founded, "Bangalore was doing the grunt work all along." The rub is the lack of business knowledge. What happens is that a "bright, fresh Indian recruit goes out on the floor straight from one of the best engineering schools. We kind of expect the knowledge to filter in." This proves unrealistic. As Paul reflects, with a measure of empathy:

> You can't expect someone with six months' experience to write a business report as thorough as someone with 10 years experience. You can't expect them to assimilate this information. You need to give them help. You're taking someone who's done this for 20 years and replace him with two new people from India without much experience. The industry itself is younger than 12 years there.

To Dave, the quality of work is only "acceptable." U.S. employees, he says, carp about kinks in the code, about having to undo and redo work. But the fault is not only India's. In an exasperated voice, he rehearses conversations he has had with employees: "They complain that the Indians don't know how to test. I tell them, 'It's because you didn't give them the business requirement. I need to test against my requirement, not the code. What stage are you giving them? Specs? At that level you can't write a test plan. Did you teach them how to test it?'" The regimented and piecemeal nature of the work precludes a proper understanding of what it is to be done. In other words, there is a structural reason for Indians' not "knowing what to do next."

The partitioning of knowledge, moreover, is critical in legitimating hierarchies. The notion of expertise, for example, is used to exclude workers from knowledge of the production process.[33] Educational attainment and what is called the "achievement principle" also help determine who makes the decisions and who is left to carry them out.[34] Such educational sorting, of course, applies in this case as well, but there is another means of determining the division of labor *within* offshore workplaces like Praxis. What can be called the "Western principle" justifies the chain of command between offices, provides informal sanction to the distinctions between management and labor, and helps determine one's position in the organization. As Chopra observes, "An overseas education in independent India promises a kind of cultural capital that an education from even a top-quality Indian institute cannot provide."[35] Familiarity with Western business justifies differences in rank and salary. Only certain people occupy positions of authority. Only certain people are given access to the company's remote and secure servers. Only certain people deal directly with onshore managers. What these people have in common is that they were trained or have studied in Western Europe or the United States.

The result is that many workers I spoke with complain repeatedly about not understanding the company's business plan, of performing piecemeal work whose importance in the overall scheme of things is elusive. The best way to get a sense of the broader business picture, incidentally, is to visit the U.S. office. After only a three-month visit to the onshore office, one bright Indian worker says she developed a better understanding of the company's operations than in her two years in Chennai. Those fortunate enough to be selected for these treks, moreover, find them not only intriguing but lucrative as they are remunerated in dollars.

Paul reflects on the discrepancies between work visits to Chennai and New York. He says that when they go to India, they are put up in five-star hotels. They have cell phones handed to them as soon as they walk through the office door. A car and driver is also on call. When Praxis workers visit the United States, however,

> They get a $150 stipend a day. You take care of your own lodging. They don't even pick them up at the airport. It's disgusting, really. They rent out room, a private room. A guy lives with his wife and kid and rents out one room. The Indians eat meals with the family. They have drop and pickups [to and from the office]. They pay $700 month [in rent], which we might say, hey that's a lot, but they're getting $150 a day. It's big money. That's a lot of rupees. It's a financial windfall.

According to the human resources manager, one of the major reasons employees leave Praxis is that they do not provide enough opportunities for U.S. visits. Even the U.S. staff is reluctant to let Indian workers leave as it is impossible to reproduce the intimate texture of personal interaction through email, phone calls, and instant messages. Paul explains: "When Indians come here, [the U.S. staff] doesn't want them to go back. You can't replicate that overseas." Or as one consultant put it, offshoring involves the substitution of "process for personality." As a result, Indian workers have rather impersonal personalities, or so it seems to U.S. employees.

Mister 25/8

The institutions of work, to borrow Mills's terms, are shaped by "drift—many little schemes adding up to unexpected results—and by plan—efforts paying off as expected."[36] While the transition to India was carefully planned, its implementation required discrete and drifting steps taken in a hectically competitive atmosphere. In addition to discrepancies in age and experience, what the Synergy brass did not count on was an overheated labor market. According to Dave, the transition "was such a challenge because turnover was so bad. You can't keep throwing money at it." When two of the more senior staff left for more lucrative jobs, Paul says, "It really got to me," pressing his hand over his heart. "I called them the core." But as Dave explains, the attitude of U.S. employees exacerbates the situation: "Across the whole spectrum, people were holding back. They don't want to teach them because they'll leave in six months. Training is an investment."

According to Qamer, who makes frequent visits to Chennai, there is a lack of informal trust between offices. U.S. employees "feel like they're training people who are then leaving. Why bother if they're just going to leave? Managers in the U.S. still don't trust them. The majority, I should say, don't trust. They feel like they're doing double work. When there are split teams, Chennai gets the grunt work." But whatever the difficulties, they have little choice: "Its $100 million in cost savings. Even if we're only getting 80 percent correct, at high quality, at 1/5 the cost, it's worth it. Even if not 100 percent accurate, it's worth it."

Despite such solicitation, junior employees at Synergy persisted in failing to understand the "business side," that is, the "benefits of offshoring." "They feel like they're getting less than their money's worth. They'll give requirements to Chennai office and say, 'What came back wasn't what we wanted,'" almost hoping the work does not pass muster. In response, Dave appealed to their self-interest. As he asked one bothersome employee, "Do you want to get a call in the middle of the night [for maintenance problems]?" The person responded quickly, "No, no, they can do it." For those who manage to keep their jobs, offshoring can make things easier.

Moreover, the resentment was also manifested in the cavalier, if not hostile, attitude of U.S. employees toward their Indian counterparts. Dave, who served as a "relationship manager" during the migration, says that some of the staff had a "sweatshop mentality":

> If [an Indian employee] doesn't work or perform, they thought, "Just throw them back" [into the labor market]. People here are coming in at nine to nine-thirty and want a meeting with the Indian office. It shows a real insensitivity. There are so many morale problems, turnover. I basically had to tell them that these people are people, that they have families. Let's use it to our advantage. [Instead of having them work the night shift], let's have 16 hours where work can be done rather than doubling up on eight. [The time issues have] been corrected, but it's hard to let go of the eight-hour mentality. I talked to them about doing your work, going home, and that the next morning, an email will be on your desktop. However, the lack of response on the Indian end complicated things. I told managers in India that you have to respond.

They would ask too much of Indian workers, he says. And what the Indian staff lacked in business knowledge they made up for by working late. "I asked them, when are they going to sleep? It's grunt work. It's not fun. It's technical," Dave says. He mentioned one especially industrious worker named Girish. Girish works very hard and "can sleep standing up. We may be 24/7 but he's 25/8. Mr. 25/8 is what we call him. He liked working at night and didn't stop working at breaks."

Paul says that by and large the U.S. staff has overcome their "biases" and that resistance to offshoring has started to wane. (As Uchitelle writes, "The permanent separation of people from their jobs, abruptly and against their wishes has become standard management practice.")[37] Dave, who has a copy of the conservative tabloid *Newsmax* on his desk, went from closet protectionist to free trade advocate:

> I was one of those people that was against it. I'd like to see jobs stay here. I'm very conservative but I have a protectionist streak. Now I've become a proponent. It's very ironic that I was chosen to be relationship manager. There's a place in my heart for a nationalist view: keep jobs in America, an American view. Once you take a global view . . . God bless America, but it's not God's country. People have it much worse than we do. In India, tech has really given an opportunity to the country. Really, they're people like us. It's not like it is here. I don't know if there was anything else be-

fore IT. Here we can find a living. I think they need the jobs more than we do.

While the *idea* of offshoring may be objectionable to U.S. workers, the practice of working with Indians is less so. Workers at the World Bank office in Chennai, for example, were trained by the very personnel they would soon be replacing. Yet the novitiates claim that their U.S. counterparts were not too bitter about losing their jobs. I'm told that they often worked overtime and the shift of 100 or so jobs was punctuated with an exchange of gifts between both sets of workers.

The War for Talent: Between Scarcity and Plenty

The Indian outsourcing story as told by its boosters has a certain heartwarming appeal: a former colony rising to global eminence by dint of hard work and comparative advantage. Moreover, like the East Asian tigers, the Indian elephant has become the "world's back office" by collaborating with rather than turning its back on the West. So promising is its future that India "could drive down the global costs in services, just as China drove down global costs in manufacturing," the authors of a World Bank report conclude.[38] (Indeed, there is already talk about a "Chindia price" for goods and services.)[39] Another Bank report limns an optimistic scenario:

> Given the enormous size and rapid growth of the BPO market, the economic implications for developing countries could be enormous. For example, if half of India's 50 million English-speakers were to eventually earn $10,000 per year in IT-related services, this would more than double India's current GDP of $450 billion. Given that IT-enabled exports tend to be associated with high levels of foreign direct investments, human capital formation, demonstration effects, and knowledge-spillovers, the indirect benefits might also be substantial.[40]

But there is to be no fairy-tale ending just yet. Such rosy prognoses must be tempered by the reality that there is no guarantee the Indian industry will continue to grow at the current pace. Nor is it certain that companies will continue to leverage the Indian option in the long term. The *Deccan Herald* sounds the alarm: "The spectre of a severe shortage of knowledge workers in the IT/ITES sectors by 2010, is hanging over the country like the sword of Damocles. While demographics clearly weigh in the country's favour, quality of the workforce does not."[41] The problem is that while some companies would like to scale up their operations in India, they find that it does not have the capacity. "There is a shortage of employable people," says an executive. "Only a handful is actually worth taking on." Likewise, NASSCOM claims that the ICT industry will soon face a deficit of 500,000 "knowledge workers." The head of Infosys warns of "an acute shortage of manpower."[42]

Nonetheless, India remains the most viable option. As a panelist at an industry conference in New York City explains:

> Right now, we are frustrated in India. We have high attrition, a lot of things going on, and we are looking at Latin America and others. But at the end of the day, we do not have a choice. The scale at which we need people, the only country that can provide it is India. I can't go to Austria and hire the amount of people I need, looking at my 10-year expansion plan. And when I put the marketing opportunities that we have to tap in India, we don't have a choice. The issue is how do we address the issue of shortage in the short run? In the short run, it's really a war for talent. In the long run, I think there's a lot of work at the governmental level, interventions required and structural changes.

"Fifty million English-speakers" may sound enticing to the cost-minded executive, but many have already learned the hard lesson that only a narrow segment is readily employable. For both low- and high-skill work, English facility is a necessary but by no means sufficient condition of employment. As one executive explains, "The issue is not the availability of highly skilled workers. It's training." The head of a firm that screens call center applicants for multinational companies says that out of every 10 people that apply, only three to four have the language and conversational skills necessary to get placed. As another executive says,

The shortage of talent in the service provider community, it's not the actual numbers. . . . [I]f you want a thousand people with a college degree, you can get a thousand people. The question is: what is the level of investment you need to do in those people to make them into productive resources for your client? And that right now is a huge challenge.

So severe was the talent squeeze for engineers that a major IT services company began hiring people with a masters in other disciplines and then gave them six months of training, plus on-the-job and night training. As the former CEO says proudly, "We were the first to do that. In three years, this would give them [an equivalent of] an M.A. in engineering. I would say that they are at least as productive as others, and they don't come in with a sense of entitlement." But even if the talent problem is solved in the near term, the Irish CEO of a Bombay-based BPO firm wonders, "What will happen when the upper layer, the cream of the crop, is picked clean, when the middle-class tranche is exhausted?" And what will the state do for those Indians "currently not employable by the offshoring industry?" The longevity of the industry depends, in other words, on the depth and breadth of Indian "talent," by which I mean the possession of specific skills useful to multinationals. The two major consequences of the talent scarcity are high turnover and rising wages.[43]

"The Curse of the Industry"

There is a shared jargon among HR managers and, perhaps second only to *skill set*, the term bandied about most frequently is *attrition*. While they may have a shaky grasp on its pronunciation ("*i*-tration"), there is no mistaking the anxiety it provokes. This "curse of the industry"—which can reach 45–50 percent in voice-based processes such as customer care and 15–20 percent in nonvoice processes—is analyzed from every possible angle, its causes dissected, its consequences monetized.[44] It is the product of a tight labor market and the cause of poaching among rival firms.[45] (Says a labor lawyer, "There are no ethics in the industry. It's based on stealing employees, on poaching.") It makes the work of management tiresome, and, what is more, it spoils relations with the "home office" as the Indian workers they come to depend on leave with little prior notice.[46] At Praxis, for example, turnover was a major reason why U.S. managers did not invest much time in the training of Indian staff or give them larger projects to work on.

The attrition rate at Praxis hovers around 17–20 percent annually and is subject to an intricate dissection. As the HR manager explains, "We do various drilling down. Right from the overall to department-wise, band-wise, manager-wise, which is project-wise, almost. We do it experience-wise. We do it reason-why. It's a very detailed analysis that we do." Almost 30 percent of the people, he says, state compensation as the reason for leaving. Similarly, a survey of the major players in the industry finds that salary is the "chief reason for leaving and one out of every two employees cite it as their reason for making that jump."[47] The COO of a high-paying KPO in Gurgaon says that while a small percentage of workers are fired and an even smaller percentage leave to pursue education, most of the turnover is "undesired." Of these latter, half have been with the company for less than a year. They provide benefits like stock options to retain people, but it not always enough. As one call center manager reflects:

> People come and they work for two months. You give them the training and just for 500 bucks or 1,000 bucks, they want to change their job. In that case, you feel that, oh my God, now we have given full training, now he's an agent that can take out the good number of results for the company, now he wants to leave the job. In that case, you become very helpless. . . . Again, we have to take the interviews, again we have to train agents. People come, they complete their three months, they find another job, a little bit of a higher salary. Then there is no stability actually.

A worker will tell you that he likes his job and is grateful to have it. He will also tell you he likes his coworkers and even his manager. He may even ride to work with his supervisor. Then, without notice, he will switch jobs. Because it pays better. Because the facilities are nicer. Because the manager seems nicer. In a social world in which prestige is highly unstable, status competition and panic are often the result.

This fixation is only amplified by the aura of uncertainty that surrounds the new industry. Unsure that they are receiving the highest salary their labor can command, they move frenetically from job to job. Paradoxically, underlying this status insecurity is a new confidence in personal worth, for you cannot feel that you are being taken advantage of unless you possess something worth having. Outsourced jobs, then, fulfill social as well as pecuniary needs. When workers feel they are not getting their fair share, they display a deep sense of aggrievement.

Ashok, an HR manager at a call center specializing in debt collection, comments on how the labor market "imbalance" affects workplace relations. He says that in Indian companies "the feudal relationship is still involved," meaning managers feel that they "can treat employees any way. But, suddenly, this changes. Now you have to make an effort to keep them. This is the first time in India that there are more jobs than workers. There's a reluctance to admit this is a reality." Solipsism and servility are not the most compatible of attitudes. Once the culture of deference and conspicuous hierarchy was shaken, the rational pursuit of material advantage was given free reign. The problem is exacerbated by the lack of vertical mobility. Ashok's ideal employee, therefore, is someone who is *singularly unambitious*." Someone who "sticks around for three years" and does not "jump" to another company. "The problem," however, "is that you can't find a singularly unambitious person."

Likewise, the COO of a call center says that he wants "people who are bright to an extent, not distinction holders. In the last three years, the labor queue is tightening. I never worked in this sort of environment when I started my career." Attrition is a "continuous challenge." Profile matters, so they do "pyschometric tests" and "nine out of ten times" this works fine as a vetting process. Nonetheless, even the undistinguished worker wants to "see some movement in his career path, though it may not be in the same company. . . . If someone stays two years, I'm happy." The technology used in the center allows "zero downtime," he says, leaning back in his chair, his chest puffed out with pride. This, I think, may have more than a little to do with turnover.

While many in the media and business are impressed by the steady stream of students issuing from Indian universities each year, Ashok directs attention to the *quality* of education.[48] Government schools, he says, are "pathetic." Betraying a touch of class privilege (belied by a weathered dun windbreaker) he says that "a college education means nothing. Educational norms are not strong." Inside the company, English skills "determine where employees go." Those with weaker skills are put on nonvoice processes and draw a lower salary. There is a "lower talent pool with good English skills; the availability is lesser." For these workers, "Salaries get pushed upwards." Narrowing his eyes as if to say, "How silly, this talk of attrition," Ashok notes that people are still waiting expectantly for "that eureka moment." They engage in wishful thinking. "The job candidate has been with three companies in the last two years," Ashok mimics the musings of a hypothetical HR manager. "This would be his fourth job in the industry. He may make a good employee because he is now probably ready to settle down." And they must pay heed to workers' concerns, however trivial they seem.

Many companies provide meals and snacks for their employees, especially for those on the night shift. And as if they are unable to find a substantive reason for leaving, many workers mention poor food. This, at least, is what they report in exit interviews. Studies and my interviews indicate that compensation, the night shift and long hours, and poor management are the leading reasons why people leave. Food is one complaint among many, and even these concerns should not be dismissed. At three different companies I visited, workers complained that they had gotten sick after eating in the company canteen.

But at least one call center manager takes the complaint very seriously, so much so that she switches caterers every three months. "The only food one doesn't get sick of his mother's. We do a round robin . . . Teeerrrack!" she says loudly, taking an imaginary wheel in her hands and jerking it clockwise. It is a matter of business sense and culinary aesthetics: "We've been strategic about it. It starts from the plate, the infrastructure of the plate. Whether its round, rectangle, et cetera, we try different things. We provide banana leaves for every plate."

Ashok believes that neither food nor stress is the underlying cause of turnover. For one, most employees are between 23 and 27 years of age, a time when "you have maximum ambition and the most confidence in yourself." A second more pivotal factor has to do with management. Ashok says that when the vice president of the company visits from the United States,

> He asks the uncomfortable questions like "Are they really leaving because of the food? Would it really reduce attrition if they changed caterers?" You see, the internal pulls have to be stronger than external pulls in the market. . . . If you ask people the top reason for attrition, they'll say stress, a hiring defect, or a profile mismatch. But what they won't list is the boss-subordinate relationship. They're not satisfied with the way the boss operates and they leave.

In a moment of candor, Ashok says the "HR infrastructure is lacking." The best performers are often promoted to leadership positions for which they are unprepared. "Just because he performs well on calls doesn't mean he'll make a good manager," he says. "He doesn't know anything about management." According to a former American employee of Infosys, there is a "dearth of managerial talent" and as a consequence India lacks a "culture of mentoring." Consultants McKinsey & Co. elaborate:

> In the country as a whole, middle managers are also becoming scarce. Although India has more of them than other offshoring destinations do, the country also has higher demand because the offshoring sector has grown so fast: over the past decade, the number of middle managers it employs has expanded by more than 20 percent a year, and even more briskly in some cities. New entrants often lure qualified managers from existing businesses instead of training their own. Sometimes they poach across borders as well— Russian entrepreneurs, for example, have hired middle managers from India. Rapidly rising remuneration is evidence of their scarcity. Annual wages for project managers in India's export-oriented IT sector, for instance, have increased, on average, by 23 percent annually over the past four years.[49]

Apropos of this dearth, the COO of an IT company remarks, "In the U.S., you generally have good management structure. You have all the developers and engineers working, then you have middle-level management. In India, I think there's still a big gap in middle-level management." This deficit is also reflected in exit interviews, where, he says, workers frequently complain, "I didn't have the proper training, there was too much pressure on me, my manager wasn't empathetic, all those. It goes back to the shortage of management talent that you see when any economy rapidly grows." So while they are quick to point the finger at workers, executives and managers grudgingly concede that the root of the problem may lie further up the hierarchy.

Flattened Pyramids

The end result is that workers' commitment to companies is often superficial, like a passing, neighborly acquaintance. But the companies, too, play a role.[50] Hire-and-fire policies in a demand-saturated market produce reciprocal mistrust between workers and employers. Yet in the absence of a binding social contract, the labor market situation provides a modicum of job security. One can say that the supply-demand gap is a source of *structural featherbedding*, forcing employers to hire extra employees to make up for high turnover and absenteeism, to offer bonuses and pay raises, and to throw parties and indulge the whims of workers. It prevents employers from hiring and firing indiscriminately (although employees do complain about unfair labor practices, arbitrary promotions, and dismissals). It also allows employees, especially experienced personnel, to call their employer's bluff, so to speak, and to move from job to job with relative ease.

Yet there are limits to these concessions. Things also look much different at the bottom of the employment pyramid, which, incidentally, is where future employment growth is expected to be concentrated. Here mobility is limited and liberal labor policies prevent employees from asserting themselves for fear of being dismissed. This can dampen wage pressures, as there is always a fresh recruit around the corner, at least for entry-level positions. Workers make no unified demands and there is little collective resistance to a regime of long and busy hours. (The threat of one worker quitting is much different than an organized slowdown or strike.) Moreover, the workers, like their U.S. counterparts, measure their performance in terms of personal mistakes and achievements.

The fear that wage inflation will undermine India's cost advantage, I shall argue, is exaggerated. Much is made of *average* salary increases each year, on the order of 10 percent for BPO and 15 percent for IT. (Still, India offers a wage differential of around 85 percent to the United States).[51] But when you look at how the increases are distributed among different positions, the picture that emerges is much more complicated. In 2004, for example, salaries for those in IT with less than 2 years of experience dropped 12 percent; individuals with 2–5 years of experience increased 11 percent; those with 5–10 years increased 24 percent; while the few with over 10 years rose 26 percent. Additionally, the same survey finds that the top IT companies increased their headcount by 35 percent in 2004, but "a large part this recruitment happened for entry-level positions."[52]

Attrition is most pronounced at the midmanagement level and up the hierarchy. A union official disputes the claim of across-the-board pay raises:

> I would strongly refute the 10 percent to 15 percent increase because overall the industry has not seen a major change in entry-level salary for the last three years going. By the NASSCOM logic, if in 2003 an entry-level CSR [customer service representative] got 8,000 rupees per month ($182), now for the same post a new joinee should get 10,000 rupees ($228), but it has not happened. So that means the spiraling effect . . . has not been felt [at the entry level]. Yes, the top performers or those who want quit an ITES firm are given these kinds of raises, so this applies only to particular individuals and thus cannot be generalized across the sector. I would love to call for an investigation on how these random numbers are generated by NASSCOM, which are sold to all and sundry.

Employers can afford to be somewhat discriminating in hiring for junior positions. Vivek Paul, for example, refers to call center workers as "replaceable," in contrast to someone with experience who is "immediate fodder for somebody else. Every unit of experience drags along five units of inexperience." And, moreover, offshoring to India stands to be cost-effective for the foreseeable future, though this does not mean that companies will not move to even cheaper shores. As an industry magazine reports,

Wage inflation will seriously challenge the economics of offshoring: India's attrition level and rising wages were corporate America's problem for a good part of 2005. But as recent studies . . . have shown, it will take offshore destinations like India close to 25 years to reach America's wage levels. Even if you add other costs that come with offshoring, even a serious debate on whether the costs are comparable is still a decade and a half away.[53]

While HR managers are hard pressed to find workers with scarce "skill sets," employers are generally optimistic about wage levels and labor supply. According to the dapper executive Khanna, who employs M.B.A.s and lawyers, "We don't see any problems for 10 years. As we keep scaling, we add more to the bottom of the pyramid. That's how a growing business works." Another says that while there was a dip in engineering enrollment following the "tech wreck" between 2001 and 2003, the situation had steadied by 2005, when I interviewed him:

A lot of people—parents who had heard stories of someone who had bad experience in engineering—looked at [computer] engineering as not a future career. Enrollments dropped. But in 2004 the market was back and in 2005 it's really back. In India, we have a privatized academic infrastructure. There is scaling in engineering, but there's a latency period: it takes four years to make an engineer. As we see it, by 2008, the supply and demand gap gets fixed.

What emerges, then, is an employment hierarchy where the base is growing exponentially and where those at the bottom are viewed as more or less expendable. According to one former Indian executive, "Indian companies have been able to retain profit margins despite having to pay higher wage rates. They've done this by flattening the pyramid. But the center of gravity has stayed the same." The government-funded V.V. Giri Labor Institute describes this as a "dual labor regime."[54] In this model, there is a core group of permanent employees—managers and team leaders—and a peripheral group that consists of lower-level workers who are replaceable. Additionally, because of the high levels of turnover, companies routinely overstaff. Such practices are a drag on employee morale and increase the sense of insecurity. At the lower rungs, surveillance is also stricter. Slacken labor demand or increase supply and the reins tighten.[55]

One senior BPO employee reflects on the climate of insecurity. His company has a number of clients, he says, some of whom "pressurize you":

> They say you should do it, not knowing the situation here. There are times we have done a double shift during peaks: 10, 14, 16 hours. Twelve hours is regular, very often. If the client wants something by a certain time, we have no choice. They can go to someone else to get it done. They may go to another vendor. Internally, you don't get much positive feedback.

The burden weighs heavily on managers as well: "We're not used to having to have the pink slip in India. Sometimes it's your duty to tell them that they're no more."[56]

So while job-hopping can be seen as positive from labor's perspective, the unstable work environment that underpins it has profound consequences for workers' morale. The wage competition and anxiety that pollutes relations between workers, the constantly changing workforce, and the high pressure associated with deadlines and productivity targets, each pose specific problems. But taken together, they undermine the quality of social relationships and the informal trust that are the foundation of a stable workplace setting. For their part, HR managers are left vainly clutching at straws.

There is no easy solution to the problem of worker dissatisfaction. The emphasis on replicable process helps deal with high turnover in that, if someone leaves, work will not grind to a halt. But it also becomes a cause of turnover, as workers become frustrated with rote work and inertial career paths. To keep Indian workers happy, it would seem, companies should invest more confidence in them and entrust them with more complex work. However, this also means that more responsibility and work then migrate to supplier countries—more offshoring, in other words—creating problems at home.

CHAPTER SIX

The Infantilizing Gaze, or Schmidt Revisited

> The office is not a stupid institution; it belongs more to the realm of the fantastical than the stupid.
>
> —*Franz Kafka*[1]

In his famous 1911 essay, *The Principles of Scientific Management*, Frederick Winslow Taylor claimed to have discovered a method to optimize labor efficiency. His system would generate greater productivity with only a marginal increase in wages. To illustrate this possibility, he tells the story of "Schmidt," a "little Pennsylvania Dutchman" who worked at a company called Bethlehem Steel. Taylor's task was to get Schmidt to perform "impossibly hard work"—handling 471 tons of pig iron per day—and make "him glad to do it." The strategy was to get him to focus on comparatively high wages. Writes Taylor:

> Schmidt was called out from among the gang of pig-iron handlers and talked to somewhat in this way:
>
> "Schmidt, are you a high-priced man?"
>
> "Vell, I don't know vat you mean." . . .
>
> "Oh, come now, you answer my questions. What I want to find out is whether you are a high-priced man or one of these cheap fellows here. What I want to find out is whether you want to earn $1.85 a day or whether you are satisfied with $1.15, just the same as all those cheap fellows are getting."
>
> "Did I vant $1.85 a day? Vas dot a high-priced man? Vell, yes, I vas a high-priced man" . . .
>
> "Well, if you are a high-priced man, you will do exactly as this man tells you to-morrow, from morning till night. When he tells you

to pick up a pig and walk, you pick it up and you walk, and when he tells you to sit down and rest, you sit down. You do that right straight through the day. And what's more, no back talk. . . . Do you understand that? . . . Now you come on to work here to-morrow morning and I'll know before night whether you are really a high-priced man or not."[2]

It turns out that Schmidt is a high-priced man. He works steadily throughout the day under the benevolent if exacting eyes of his supervisor. He lifts the 471 tons and receives $1.85 per day. But on his own, and this is Taylor's point, Schmidt could not understand the "scientific principles" whereby both he and the company would benefit. He needed to be told how to labor and what was in his interest. Otherwise, he would have dissipated his energy in frenzied bouts of labor and would fail to load the required tons: "This science amounts to so much that the man who is suited to handle pig iron cannot possibly understand it, nor even work in accordance with the laws of this science, without the help of those who are over him."

Taylor's contempt is obvious; he viewed Schmidt as "so stupid and so phlegmatic that he more nearly resembles in his mental make-up the ox than any other type."[3] Needless to say, such open condescension is no longer tolerated and Taylor has been raked over the coals for viewing the worker as a brute who needs to be tamed and prodded. But his views are not so easily dismissed. He readily conceded that such "rough talk" was only appropriate for workers as bovine and "mentally sluggish" as Schmidt. For more intelligent workers, a language of "initiative and incentive" would do the trick. And in this regard, there is a homology between his thought and today's worker-friendly "human resource management" (HRM). Taylor focused primarily on the relationship between wages and effort. The "enlightened managerialism" of HRM is viewed as a more comprehensive, not to say holistic, managerial art:

HRM aspires to synergistically combine a number of old techniques, re-titled as human resource practices, into a more comprehensive labor management strategy addressing all aspects of the employment relationship. . . . Conflict around the wage bargain is minimized by pay above the norm or through profit and gain sharing schemes. . . . Quality circles, consultation, a participative management style, and minimal status differentiation are used to increase employee commitment and managerial legitimacy. The commodity status of labor is denied by relative employment security and claims to treat the employee as a valuable resource rather than as a cost to be minimized.[4]

Allied to this approach is the notion of "flexible professionalism," a favored trope of what is called the knowledge economy. In contrast to the worker who indolently waits for orders, the professional knows what to do and moves quickly and discretely from task to task. Yet, as was discussed in the previous chapter, there are inherent difficulties in enjoining workers to take ownership of work that is banal and fragmented. This chapter explores the contradiction of commanding responsibility itself. As Schneider writes, "How can you command someone to be independent or to take initiative? The very act of saying it undoes it."[5]

While this attempt to professionalize workers by belittling them is not new, it is especially prevalent in the sunrise sectors of developing countries where the "moral economy" of workplaces is inchoate.[6] Ross, for example, registers frustrations with the "Chinese mind," which employers and managers say is too "process-driven and lacking in creativity."[7] The situation is similar in India, where they carp about worker servility and immaturity, but is rendered more acute by the youth of the workforce. According to one estimate over 90 percent of BPO employees are under 30.[8] In the eyes of many managers, they *are* children. Incentive schemes and small bonuses are introduced to get employees to work longer and harder. The husky voiced human resource manager with the special sensitivity for workers' dietary needs (who we met last chapter) explains:

> We provide a night shift allowance—150 rupees for every night you walk into the office, because it's certainly difficult. If you had clubbed that into the salary, they wouldn't come. You need to understand their psyche. We have a performer's league award. . . . Recognition, certificates, money, that's all. If a guy gets a platinum award, he has dinner with the CEO.

The "high-priced man" has been replaced by the green "customer care *executive*."

The chapter proceeds as follows. First, I briefly discuss the balance of control and consent in the workplace. I then explore managerial views of Indian employees. This is followed by an analysis of how professionalism plays itself out in the lives of workers. Next, I look at some of the less than salutary effects of this push for moral reform. The chapter concludes with some suggestions on how the situation might be improved.

Consent and Control

> We cannot assume today that men must in the last resort be governed by their own consent. Among the means of power that now prevail is the power to manage and manipulate the consent of men.
>
> —*C. Wright Mills*[9]

To bring professionalism into intelligible focus it is necessary to consider the balance of consent and control in the workplace, the relational parameters in which the ethos is manifested. As the rhetoric of contemporary capitalism attests, autocratic management styles have long gone out of fashion.[10] Bendix, Burawoy, and others have observed that coercion alone is not enough to secure workers' consent; they must be granted a measure of discretion.[11] Yet this is merely to displace the problem, which is that the unwieldy elements of personality must somehow be checked. Berger and his coauthors write that the

> production process necessitates "human engineering," that is, the technological management of social relations. Although this management may involve attention to highly personal idiosyncrasies of individual workers and may even contain a positively therapeutic dimension, its fundamental purpose is to control the unfortunate intrusions of concrete humanity into the anonymous work process.[12]

Mills put it similarly: "For in so far as human factors are involved in efficient and untroubled production, the managerial demiurge must bring them under control."[13] Thus the use of human labor involves a seemingly irreconcilable difficulty. Castoriadis states the paradox of human relations plainly:

> A factory in which the workers were really and totally mere cogs in the machine, blindly executing the orders of management, would come to a stop in a quarter of an hour. Capitalism can function only by drawing upon the genuinely human activity of those subject to it, while at the same time trying to level and dehumanize them as much as possible.[14]

That is to say, production depends on intelligence and resourcefulness and ingenuity, on *conscious* human activity. But at the same time it is stalled by certain stubbornly inefficient human qualities. The voice and quick thinking of the call center worker, for example, is necessary to handle an inquiry successfully. But certain markers of Indian identity are considered problematic, such as accents, names, idioms, and tacit understandings. The same holds true for the IT worker. She is valued as the embodiment of skills that can be put to a particular task but is criticized for not showing conspicuous signs of spontaneity and intuition. Nor does she have the indefatigability or regularity of a machine. She requires rest and leisure as well as motivation and incentive. How then do managers attempt to manage our humanity?

In addition to surveillance, management applies a softer moral pressure to inculcate notions of responsibility and accountability. Workplace studies since at least Foucault, who conceived of power as something exercised rather than possessed, have focused increasingly on the latter—the ideological and normative methods of control that supplement more traditional modes—and on the subtle negotiation between "empowerment and entrapment" forced upon workers.[15] Mir and Mir, for example, describe the "empowerment" techniques that go into "producing the governable employee."[16] To summarize these views crudely: Empowerment is basically a ruse, but there are rare instances within this framework where workers can find some measure of autonomy.

This hardly means that strict surveillance is somehow passé. Computer technologies represented a considerable advance on barrack-room discipline, making the Benthamite panopticon—where authority is everywhere present, but nowhere visible—a very real possibility. As Zuboff writes:

> Information systems that translate, record, and display human behavior can provide the computer age version of universal transparency with a degree of illumination that would have exceeded even Bentham's most outlandish fantasies. . . . Information systems can automatically and continuously record almost anything their designers want to capture. . . . They can transmit the presence of the omniscient observer and so induce compliance without the messy conflict-prone exertions of reciprocal relations.[17]

There are therefore two levels of surveillance: "the deep layer of computer monitoring and the surface, and more quixotic layer of human supervision."[18] The relationship is symbiotic. Ideologies like professionalism "pave the way for the acceptance of strict technocratic forms of control."[19] Together, the internalized self-discipline of the electronic panopticon and the moralizing pressure of the manager penetrate into the domains of the self.[20] The worker is both the subject and object of professionalism: the active agent of change and the site upon which such designs are exercised.

Offshoring complicates matters. Management practices are imported from abroad and redefined locally.[21] Workplace conventions and tacit expectations between employer and worker are unstable. For companies, the transition is said to be so large, the gulf in work culture so vast, that it resembles a merger and acquisition. The Indian outsourcing industry is young and so are its workers. There is also a crucial sociocultural component: Indian society and its workplace structures are said to be more rigidly hierarchical than in the West.[22]

The managerial gaze in the Indian outsourcing industry, I shall argue, is infantilizing. That is, Indian workers are constructed as professionally and culturally underdeveloped by managers and employers. Development, in this view, is conceived of as a teleology proceeding along Western lines, while offshoring is a motor of change, a fillip on the well-traveled but pitted path from tradition to modernity. (It is to take the term *developing country* very literally.) Yet so long as the modern is understood as "as a *known* history, something which has *already happened elsewhere*, and which is to be reproduced, mechanically or otherwise, with a local content," postcolonial societies will always be seen as incomplete and of secondary importance.[23] Chakrabarty writes that historically in this "transition narrative," "the 'Indian' was always a figure of lack. There was always, in other words, room in this story for characters who embodied, on behalf of the native, the theme of 'inadequacy' or 'failure.'"[24]

Likewise in the minds of executives and managers who juxtapose the Western *homo economicus* with the Indian *homo hierarchicus*[25]—a contrast rendered more acute by the post-Fordist emphasis on teamwork and flexibility.[26] Many scholars have sketched the contours of the new personality type demanded by globalization.[27] The notion of imitative counterpoint allows us to show how it is constructed on the ground and how it diverges from the mold. In its Indian instantiation the defining poles of professional life are brio and timidity, impetuosity and meekness. The result is a subject that oscillates between an obedient servant-bureaucrat and a self-policing professional. This chapter illustrates how the infantilizing gaze, the ethos of professionalism, and structural flexibility are mutually supportive. Importantly, what troubles this constellation is a tight labor market, the structural condition that allows professionalism to be interpreted as individualism by employees.

"You Have to Push Them Sometimes"

> Nothing in India is identifiable, the mere asking of a question causes it to disappear or to merge in something else.
>
> —*E. M. Forster*[28]

For companies moving work to India in the late 1990s, one of their first major surprises was a puzzling difference in work culture. Western or Western-trained executives and managers noticed that, in their speech and bearing, Indian workers observed a different propriety, a meekness of disposition. In addition to "language barriers," says Gary, an American manager, there are "just different ways of doing business." "Culturally, they're very into hierarchy" and this "culture of deference" arises from a fear of displeasing superiors. Divining why workers appear diffident, just this side of servile, is an exercise in cultural diagnostics. The Hindi term for job, *naukri*, derives from *naukar*, a Persian loanword meaning "servant, attendant, retainer," and as an HR manager at a call center observes, "The feudal relation is still involved." In the era of statist dirigisme, it also came to denote a government servant, while retaining certain unflattering connotations. Today, naukri.com is self-described as "India's most popular job site." An executive reflects on what he sees as workers' docility:

> They certainly need to learn some communication, etiquette. One of the problems—most people here don't like it when I say this—[is that] the Indians by nature are kind of submissive, particularly when people travel there. You can hardly hear them when they talk. It's not that they cannot talk, it's just that out of respect, that's how they talk. You don't raise your voice in front of adults, elders, teacher. So this gets into their system right from the beginning. In school, never say anything against teacher. At home, don't talk to your parents like that, don't talk to your grandmother . . . just do it. They've always been taught to be submissive. So that also shows up here.

While there may be some truth here—the past is of course the source of present expectations—the concept of *naukar* does not adequately explain why workers behave so sheepishly at times. That is to say, while it may help explain some part of the subservient attitude, the term can only be stretched so far. For many if not most workers, the job is their first experience in the labor market, or at least an initial step at the beginning of their careers. They are often "fresh" out of school. It is thus not surprising that they lack the confidence in their own abilities that characterizes seasoned professionals. In this context, we can interpret their behavior as the product of age and of an organizational structure that places the contradictory demands of routinized piecework and innovation on them. Circumstances, not cultural traits, are decisive here. As we shall see, when workers realize that they have some bargaining power because of high labor demand, they become more forthright and demanding. This does not mean that culture and custom do not matter but simply that they are not as static or timeless as one might suppose.

Nevertheless, *naukar*, or something like it, is the category that managers and executives use to describe workers. In the Connecticut offices of Synergy, the manager-worker distinction between U.S. and Indian employees was reinforced by cultural traits suggestive of the frozen legacy of feudalism. Thomas, a U.S.-based manager, says that "they have an inability to say no. I've been to India twice and met with leads and asked for feedback and complaints. You have to push them sometimes." Prior to offshoring, "Work could be very stressful, but they always knew where they stood with me. Guys out there appreciated it. Phoenix tended to push back a little, Bangalore and Chennai tended not to. Sometimes I needed it, the pushing back." (Thomas once pushed so hard that a valuable employee resigned. He eventually returned but only after Thomas pledged to change "the way he says things.")

Feedback is given only when pressed and even then the answers are ambiguous, as if any response will do. Indians are "vague" and as a consequence Thomas would tell them to just "say something, anything, even 'I don't know; I'll get back to you.' It's very hard for them to admit and say, 'I don't understand this requirement.' They're working 12 to 16 hours a day because they can't say no," he says. (Note how he shifts the responsibility for long hours onto the workers themselves.) Anything to maintain harmony, to keep feathers unruffled. Gary was once so vexed that on a visit to the Indian office he presented a group of managers with a blank sheet of paper upon which he had scrawled NO in large black letters. Moreover, this disinclination to "give bad news can put one in a very bad position" and result in mistakes and missed deadlines.[29] "They'll say, yeah I'm working on it," remarks an Indian manager. "Yeah, it's done. I'll send it to you right now. And then the right now will come three days later. So as I tell them, these [responses] maybe okay here, but these are not okay generally in a professional environment, where you're expected to say it as it is." There was "never this urgency over there," the Synergy manager Thomas says. His "jaw would drop sometimes on realizing that the culture thing was still there."

Themes of immaturity recur in discussions of workers' character. The subject triggered a sudden volubility in Atul Gupta, the otherwise gloomy COO of the IT subsidiary of Synergy, Praxis:

> The way I look at it, the maturity level is slightly lower here than in the U.S. Maturity could mean taking your work seriously, taking ownership; it could mean how you work with others in a team; it could mean how you respect others. So all those are slightly lower here than there. Yeah, in terms of respect, no one will beat people here, you'll always be respectful to anybody. Even the guy who wants to kill you, you'll be respectful, you know. But overall, the professionalism and that maturity of being able to do what you need to do, I think it still needs to improve.

Additionally, he believes worker grievances can be petty. Small issues balloon into big problems, as workers are unable to put things in proper perspective, or so says Gupta:

> In the U.S., when you manage people, mostly you deal with real issues, real problems, you know at a higher level. Where in India, there are still a lot of little, little problems. People's needs are small, people's problems are small. So the little things become problems. Like, "Hey, do I get this snack in the evening or this benefit?" A lot of these little, little things you don't care about in the U.S. anymore because they don't matter. But here a lot those things still matter to people. So they have lot more small concerns that you work with.

In this view, the competition over salaries and perks, this "narcissism of minor differences," betrays workers' childishness.[30] Immaturity means one is not fit for the responsibility of making big decisions, and according to Gupta, it signifies the lack of an ethical compass:

> If you screw up, just say "I screwed up" rather than making somebody else go in circles. No company always penalizes people for screwing up unless you do it every day. They need to be a little bit more mature in terms of being able to distinguish between what is

right and what is wrong in terms of behavior, in terms of ethics. People are still so worried about little things that sometimes they are driven by money. So the bar—what is right and what is wrong—is not that high here; it's very blurry. I actually sometimes give people an example that you need to be honest and integrity is very important. I tell them that if you're going to reach here only in 45 minutes, don't say two.

Responsibility is an index of maturity and the beginning of all virtue. Indian social structure is culpable for workers' underdevelopment, Gupta claims, as it diffuses responsibility throughout the extended family. "There's a lack of ownership culture," he says, "maybe because of cultural and social reasons. In the family, at the home life, the culture is still more like a united family, joint families. There are very few opportunities where people have to hold themselves accountable. There are always your father, your grandfather, your mother, your grandmother, they're always around to make those decisions." The rational self is unable to shatter the integument of familial dependence. The individual is not given "the exposure to being able to take that ownership. Saying, hey, this is my problem. Take simple things. There's a problem in plumbing at home. Generally, somebody at home will get it done, because there are so many people around that you don't really care about it. I do find that gap, the accountability and ownership culture is still not there." He gives a long sigh. Adopting a tone of paternal tolerance, he goes on:

> I'm constantly telling them to take the ownership. If you have a problem and you say it's my problem, take the ownership. Even during the inductions, when new joinees come, I tell them that one of the most important qualit[ies] for you to succeed is for you to take ownership of what you do. . . . Don't just think, I have to do this and I'm done. Make sure it actually gets done, it actually works. It's changing slowly. But you really need to be very patient. . . . Having been exposed to [the Western] work environment, you don't have that much patience. You say, I told you to get this done, but now you want to talk about it? So come and talk, what are you waiting for?

In an interlinked world of firm and snap decisions, Gupta feels that Indian work norms are stubbornly inefficient. Workers' patience and their stutters and equivocations make Gupta impatient. The need for self-discipline and self-direction is all the more pressing, as work-place flexibility entails a loosening of direct surveillance. He contin-ues, his voice taking on a rather batrachian undertone:

> We have a very free working environment where we don't restrict people to certain hours. You work late, you come late the next day, that's okay. But then sometimes people make it a habit to just show up late every day. Or if you're going to be late, it's okay to say, "You know what, I'm going to be late today." Don't hide it. You see in the West if someone's going to be late, they'll say it, they don't feel shy about it. Here, they'll hide it. They'll try to quietly sneak into the workplace, which is not necessary.

The professional occupies an uncertain place in the historical arc of Indian occupational character types. Even when India embarked upon a path of state-led modernization after independence, the personalized obedience of the *naukar* was merely supplanted by the impersonal obedience of the bureaucratic functionary to rules and orders.[31] The chain remained unbroken:

> In India, historically, most of the jobs were government jobs. And in government jobs you never had any accountability. You can just do whatever, you never get fired. You always get your raises, every four years you get promotions. You know, there was no driver for people to excel or to take the responsibility.

Submissiveness, lack of ownership, an inability to express one's opinion—unkinder things have been said. But while such frustrations would be expected of any manager, what is remarkable is how probing the criticisms are. Many of these managers and executives began their careers in an environment of hierarchy and sinecure and social con-nection. But now these children of bureaucracy and extended family are themselves passing into middle age, and the old values that held the society together sting like a rebuke from an unaccountable supe-rior. And although accustomed to the deference of servants, the sight of a worker idly waiting for marching orders chafes like a request for money by a dissolute cousin. They deplore the workforce's lack of "professional" and individualistic qualities.

It is a ponderous search for faults as criticism of Indian culture is at least indirectly a criticism of the innumerable traces that make up one's self. (It is worth mentioning that I could not find one manager or executive who was unable to supply a catalog of workers' shortcomings.) Their aversion to the features of their own culture, indeed, to their own pasts, recalls Adorno and Horkheimer's description of the overly rationalized individual's discomfort in the presence of child-like, noninstrumental elements of social life:

> Those blinded by civilization experience their own tabooed mimetic features only in certain gestures and behavior patterns which they encounter in others and which strike them as isolated remnants, as embarrassing rudimentary elements that survive in the rationalized environment. What seems repellently alien is in fact all too familiar: the infectious gestures of direct contacts suppressed by civilization, for instance, touch, soothing, snuggling up, coaxing.[32]

What is especially interesting is finding Indians recycling colonial-era tropes of cultural underdevelopment.[33] This holds both for managers and executives who have lived in India all their lives and for those who have returned after some time in the United States or Europe. As for the latter, they do not return out of nostalgia or any special fondness for their country of birth. They miss not the culture but the privileges they enjoyed. I was told that the cost of living is less and they can thus enjoy a higher standard of living: cheap servants, deferent drivers, loyal gardeners, palatial homes, private schools for their children, higher status, and so forth. In a word, nabobism.

Reacculturation

Mark Scheyer is the founder of an outsourcing company that specializes in legal services. Seated at an oaken desk, he is the very image of connectivity. A cell phone is clipped to pleated brown slacks. A landline telephone and a PDA gasp for air upon the cluttered desk. A wireless headset and an open email inbox complete the picture. Adept a multitasking, he types furiously while responding to my questions and occasionally interrupts our conversation to take calls. He says that Indians communicate differently than Americans. I say I know what he means.

"They're bright and articulate, but—sorry if this sounds racist—they have a tendency to say yes a lot, which can mean 'Yes, I understand' or 'No, but I acknowledge.' It's a culture of inappropriately saying yes which manifests itself as lying," he says. He thinks that this meekness stems from a fear of looking bad and making mistakes. This is a problem because the key to business is the "absolute elimination of ambiguity," and as a lawyer, he knows to be very specific. Indians are far less confrontational, and in this they need to be "reacculturated." "Some of it entails changing our behavior, but some of it has to be reacculturation. It's all in here," he says, holding up a dog-eared copy of a book by management guru Peter Drucker.

Yet while they shy away from friction, Scheyer says that workers are "always defensive" when questioned and adopt a "condescending because direct tone." As an example of this lack of tact he shows me an email from an employee to a client that was "too blunt and direct," that "wasn't soft enough." Moreover, according to another executive at the firm, Vikram, "timeliness" and "promptness" are "completely foreign concepts in India." But while it takes some time to teach employees how to deliver services to clients, "ultimately it gets ingrained in the organization. If you tell someone that you've sent something to them 10 minutes ago, you better have sent it." Or what? Or you will be asked to leave, and that very politely. Workers are "asked to resign; they're not terminated." If the firm fires a few workers, "the others tend to think the ship is sinking and that the next day the windows will be boarded up." Beneath the new confidence is an anxious feeling that the promise is somehow precarious.

While Gupta emphasizes ownership, Scheyer tries to foster a "culture of empowerment." This is achieved, in part, by not over- or underworking employees and by providing incentives and benefits like stock options. He also encourages workers to "get dirty and mess it up." If they make a mistake and admit it, his response is to say, "Good, tell me. What do you think we should do to remedy this?" In recruiting, they look for someone "who's self-starting, inquisitive, someone who asks questions. Someone that's not looking to be an employee."

One such person is Dev, a 26-year-old at the company who describes himself as an "entrepreneur *and* professional," laying heavy stress on the conjunction, as if to say two is better than one. Dev is a votary of Michael Dell and Thomas Friedman, whose hyperbolic *The World Is Flat* is one of his favorite books. Whatever his aspirations, Dev is a trainee and is treated as such by his tetchy manager Vikram. "I'm not pissed that you didn't know. I'm pissed that you didn't ask. The next time you come across something you don't understand, ask someone. This is how addresses are written in the U.S. . . . There are commas after every three numbers. *No lakhs*," Vikram tells Dev with rehearsed frustration. And like a naughty child who has been caught scrawling on the bedroom wall, Dev flashes me a guilty smile.

Across the hall sits Deepa, a wan woman from Himalchal Pradesh with heavy, kohl-lined eyes, a silver nose ring, and short black hair. Her voice is soft and low; she speaks almost in a whisper. She lives by herself in a women's hostel but her thoughts are of her family back home, with whom she makes joint decisions about spending her income. Thirty-one years of age, Deepa describes herself as a "fresher," a term normally applied to "fresh" college graduates. Although she holds a doctorate in engineering, what counts in her diminutive estimation of self is not what she has accomplished but what she lacks. With little work experience, she is a professional manqué. But for every demure Deepa there is a boisterous Bhuvan who craves celebrity. What she lacks in confidence is amply compensated for by the élan of a prospective employee who during an interview announced that he did not want to be an employee. Asked what he did want, the young man responded with vim, "Fame!"

There are two kinds of Indians, according to Scheyer, those with an "ownership mentality" and those with an "employee mentality." If the latter predominate, he says with some gravity, "it will be the death of many companies." Similarly, an American venture capitalist says that the maturity of the Indian workforce is "way down" and that it "wouldn't be a stretch to compare an early 20-year-old in India with a 14- or 16-year-old in the U.S." The workforce is primarily Indian and so too the work culture. "They aren't adopting business culture fast enough," he says, plainly identifying Indian culture as an impediment to success.

There is a large map of India on the wall of Scheyer's Manhattan office and a miniature statue of Ganesh on the window sill. He says he has a "love-hate" relationship with the subcontinent and describes the widespread poverty there as "appalling," so much so that he once returned to the United States in tears. Although most of his employees hold professional degrees, Scheyer is alert to the philanthropic potential of offshoring. "We're hiring people for 50 bucks a month. They're dying for that job. We treat them with more dignity than they've been treated with before," he says with emotion. But there can be no question of saving them from poverty or indignity; if his workers knew the term *bourgeois*, they would no doubt use it to describe themselves. More than the employees needing the jobs, Scheyer needs them to need the jobs. When asked about the impact of job migration on U.S. workers, he goes apoplectic: "I don't give a shit if Americans lose jobs! These people need jobs and they often do it better." He constructs Indian employees in the image of an industrious and skillful beggar despite their relative class privilege.

Sweet and Sour Work Environments

Workplace environments also illustrate the infantilizing gaze. While architecturally of the modern institutional style, BPO environments often resemble nurseries more than spaces of serious work. Walls are candy-colored and some companies appoint "employee care executives." One company has a contingent of "fun officers." Workers are rewarded for good performance with monetary incentives and also with certificates and awards. (One motivational strategy is based on cricket. If one does very well, the worker's name is broadcast on a large screen with a score of six-runs—the cricket equivalent of a home run.) Larger companies have on-site gyms, nutrition experts, game rooms with carom boards, darts, punching bags, and table tennis tables, and Internet kiosks (as web traffic at workstations is controlled by management). On the ground floor of one call center is a 10,000-square-foot cafeteria, where you can get dishes like chicken hariyali and butter chicken "for only 15 bucks" [meaning 15 rupees, which is about 32 cents]. Bunk beds and bean bags are available "where you can crash after working overtime."

Why go home at all? The charm fades, however; the machinery shows signs of wear. Some companies do not provide Internet access because of "security issues." The e-kiosks at one company "never work at any given time." Employees stop patronizing canteens for a variety of reasons: because they "saw rats," because of the "tasteless food," because "the sweet dishes leave a sour taste."

In one call center I visited, the manager introduces me to the employees en masse. "This is Mr. Nadeem. He's a researcher from America. You will answer any questions he asks you," she commands flatly. (I am embarrassed and flattered). A hush follows. Though unintimidated, the workers seem to shrink in her presence. Like students desultorily scanning pages in study hall to give the impression of activity, the workers swivel around and face their desks, pick up headsets and stare vaguely at their computer screens. "This younger generation, they lack patience," the manager says with a click of her tongue. "So you have to be quite mature to understand things with them. Thanks to God all my agents are very nice, very cooperative. Whatever I tell them they take that as an order and 'OK, ma'am, we will do that.'" Given that coordination in the center has been delegated to shift leads and that workers know how to perform their jobs, the manager's supervisory function is hard to discern. Her watchful eye is a lingering accusation of guilt: if workers were not naturally wayward or lazy, she would not be necessary.

Moreover, the freedom and individualism enshrined in the absence of a dress code was taken away at one call center where workers came to work with tousled hair, bead necklaces, torn jeans, plunging necklines, and shortish skirts. An employee manual illustrates the shift in company thinking:

We would like to showcase professionalism in our behavior and in the way we dress. . . . Casuals may be worn ONLY on Friday, Saturday and Sunday. Closed shoes at all times through the week. Sandals, Slippers/Floaters, round neck t-shirts NOT permitted. Ladies to avoid skirts with deep slits, deep necked tops, transparent material, tight fitting/skin hugging outfits, skirts above knee length. . . . Remember how we look is how people outside will perceive of BPO.

Whereas as the BPO environment screams child, Praxis, the IT subsidiary, politely enunciates professional. While the offshoring of jobs is veiled by a smokescreen of corporate-speak and confidentiality agreements, transparency *within* the workplace is one of the principal attractions of offshored jobs. Praxis's sunlit "coffee corridor" commands a fine view of a truncated but lushly verdant scrub forest. The uncluttered offices and conference rooms are fronted with glass walls and doors, an architectural accent on the company's ethos of transparency. The walls are traversed by a horizontal band of frosted glass bearing the names of prominent scientists, intellectuals, inventors, and other luminaries. "Make a right at the Homi Bhabha room, then a sharp left at Marie Curie, and you will see us seated in Benjamin Franklin," an employee might direct a visitor. Bhabha was the father of India's nuclear power program; Curie was a Polish chemist who discovered radium and polonium; Franklin was a founding father, inventor, and diplomat. Thus while BPO architecture panders to workers' perceived instincts for fun, IT environments express their desire for professional probity. The latter sees them as capable of growth, while the other consigns them to a state of perpetual adolescence. But behind these surface differences is a common attitude.[34]

Service and Servility

The notion of domestic service, where one tends to the needs of others, is not readily amenable to modern ideas of democratic equality. In the household, the scope of service is often unbounded: the servant must be at the beck and call of the employer. Employers, according to Muir-

head, often feel that they are "worthy of service even at the cost of dis-
placing the independent needs of those performing the service."[35] No
one willingly devotes their lives to the service of others, we tend to
think, unless under some form of compulsion. But while an individual
may be forced to knuckle under, she may also do so of her own accord;
that is, she may freely choose a life "composed entirely of service to
others" if she thinks it proper or her duty.[36] Indian culture and social
structure are said to supply such a rationale through mutually binding
relationships of paternalism and deference.

In the charged atmosphere of flat organization and cellular enterprise, shadows are cast by the past: status distinctions of an earlier era
are said to persist and to intrude upon the present day. The *naukar*
does not transpose well to the corporate work environment, nor does
the servant's approach square well with the contractual and volunta-
ristic norms upon which it is predicated. As Roland writes of cultural
differences:

> In contrast to Western hierarchical relationships—which tend to be
> based on a fixed status and power relationship, governed by con-
> tractual agreements and an ideology of essential equality—Indian
> hierarchical relationships are oriented toward firmly internalized
> expectations in both superior and subordinate for reciprocity and
> mutual obligations in a more closely emotionally connected rela-
> tionship. Where traditionally there are few if any contractual agree-
> ments, the superior in particular is profoundly assumed to be con-
> cerned, giving, and responsible for his or her subordinates, and the
> subordinate to be loyal and deferential to the superior.[37]

Others argue that because of the prevalence of hierarchy in other
spheres of life, Indians expect the same at work.[38] Consequently, they
tend to be more "submissive" and evince a desire to please. In other
walks of life such behavior might simply be described as polite. It is in
the radical culture of contemporary capitalism that it appears mani-
festly backward. So, despite the mod interiors, an air of antiquity pervades workplaces. (At one company, tunes from Bollywood's golden
era wafted softly in the background, literally lingering in the air.) One
HR manager says that Indian culture is "a culture that respects au-

thority." It is "slightly feudalistic." But the flip side of obsequious manners is broad employer prerogative. Former Proctor & Gamble India CEO Gurcharan Das argues that a central reason that young Indians prefer to work at foreign firms

> is that the Indian business world is still largely feudal with the owner centralizing decisions. Some owners treat their employees no better than they treat domestics. In fact, once I heard an industrialist refer to his finance manager as a "servant" within earshot of his foreign collaborator. Employees feel more respected in the professional environment of a foreign company. Therefore, even when Indian companies are able to hire a good manager, they are not able to retain him.[39]

Das then quotes Amiya Kumar Bagchi, director of the Centre for Studies in Social Science, Calcutta, on the same point:

> As a result, the owners are arrogant and the managers are servile. . . . In East Asia, the owner will happily sit down with an employee for a meal. It is this attitude which has helped them to succeed, create universal education, and wipe out poverty. India, in contrast, is like the Philippines, which is a relative failure in East Asia because it shares our social structure.[40]

To an extent, firms stand to gain by a work ethic that counsels quiet diligence, a willingness and expectation to work long hours. While its influence has certainly waned, Sahay and Walsham argue that "the presence of caste is still felt in virtually all domains of Indian economic activity."[41] Hinduism, after all, is a religion in which occupational stratification is divinely ordained. It supplied transcendental supports for work and rendered the intolerable tolerable.[42] But caste may not be the most convincing explanation. As the Bagchi quote reveals, the reason that workers appear duty-bound to be tireless and obedient has more to do with the social organization of production, with the "arrogance" of executives and the "servility" of managers. The workers I spoke with who put in long hours did so because they feared losing bonuses, promotions, or being fired, not because their religion counseled them to do so. And given the absence of independent collective representation, they have little choice.[43] It is difficult to be self-starting, moreover, in an environment where workers "generally have very low levels of discretion" over daily tasks, work procedures, the scheduling of breaks, and the pace of work.[44] But while companies may have benefited from obedience in the short term, it is generally agreed that the inability of workers to take ownership of projects and responsibility for their actions is bad for business, especially if there is any hope of moving up the value chain.

Interpretations of Professionalism

The stage is set for the creation of cultural norms more in keeping with the demands of the new economy. As we have seen, executives and managers argue that workers are unachieved, submissive, and immature. (Americans, by contrast, are the opposite, but they are also spoiled.) What is needed is a substitute ethic, one that empowers the individual within the framework of the organization. Professionalism bridges the distance and is a premonitory sign of the country's development. The ethos, built on the idea of individual moral responsibility, converts the old blind deference toward authority into a sparkling reverence of it. Positions of authority are awarded on the basis of achievement rather than social connections. IT executives are admired for their self-made success and regarded with wondering esteem by their employees. The young professionals, in turn, are rewarded for taking responsibility, even risks within certain limits, and having the courage to make and learn from their mistakes.

Thus companies committed themselves to deposing the servant and exalting the professional, with managers seeking to fashion employees in their own image. But the progenitor's wish must remain unfulfilled. The worker is still a subordinate, at best, a manager-in-training. Superiors must be regarded with the respect due to an equal *and* with muted deference. This is the meaning of professionalism: a worker who thinks like a manager but knows her place. (What troubles managers is that workers are increasingly unmindful of the latter.)

Professionalism is more than a posture (bolt upright) or a matter of sartorial choice (ironed slacks and dress shirt). For many, it is a way of being. Take Kumar, for example. Kumar has a slight build, a thick head of hair set off by a thin moustache, and a mild disposition. His posture is impeccable, as is his English, which is marked by a precise economy of words and colorless tones. He graduated from the Bengal campus of the famed Indian Institute of Technology, has eight years of work experience, and has thrice traveled to the United States on business. At Praxis, he helps maintain an online cash management application, which allows banks and financial institutions to transfer money to different countries. He is unmarried and lives with his parents—the father, a retired Hindu priest, the mother, a homemaker. At the time he got his start in the industry, his family's combined monthly income was well under 20,000 rupees ($450). "That's Indian rupees," he stresses. Now he is the "breadwinner" of his family. Unlike in America, where one leaves home after college, in India the "dependency's there," he says. This is his first time working for an American multinational and he is proud of the fact.

Kumar's voice is impersonal and detached, his gaze steady but oddly vacant. A commodity, his value can appreciate or fall. "This job has increased my value both personally and officially," Kumar declares, enunciating. "People I've been working with have gotten a good impression of me. It has improved my image and my reputation. I've been more cooperative with everyone. The company is taking care of employees, so the employees can take care of the company," he continues in a spirit of goodwill, a statement fit for the company's website. He says generously that "everyone is a professional," not a worker or "cyber-coolie," as critics allege. As if giving a speech at a self-help seminar or, conversely, as if a student reciting a lesson or dutifully answering a question, he tells me that the "key to a high-performance team is *personal accountability*." It is this mixture of contrary qualities—of self-help and docility, of lecturer and student, of consent and submission—that is most baffling. He is giving me an interview because his immediate boss told him to. "We work for the person also and ask for requirements. For me, I can say you're also a client. I need to understand your requirements."

Among employees, there is a slight, if unconsidered, antipathy to trade unions. They look instead to the handful of IT billionaires, the folk heroes of "Shining India." Not content with mere professional status, many harbor entrepreneurial desires. Vijay, a former General Electric–India employee, acted on this impulse and founded a number of small call centers. I had arranged to meet him at Barista, an upscale coffeeshop in Delhi's Defence Colony. Ten minutes before we were scheduled to meet, I received a call on my mobile from Vijay. His first words were an apology. "I'm very sorry. I will be about 10 to 15 minutes late," he said in a restrained but agitated voice. He asked me to hold, but the piped music that filled the intervening moments was not the gentle if banal pop instrumentals you normally hear on the line but the jarring, plangent strains of car horns. Someone had rear-ended him in traffic and had badly dented his new car, the now blighted fruit of offshored labor. As if his discomfort were a sign of immaturity, he explained that car insurance is not the same in India as in the United States: although he was not to blame, he would have to pay for the repairs out-of-pocket. He apologized again and then hung up.

When Vijay walked into the café some 15 minutes later, he immediately proffered a rationale for the courtesy call. "If I was a typical businessman in India, I would not have called. I would have apologized for the delay only when I got here, 30 or 40 minutes later," he said, his voice now as unruffled as his crisply ironed imperial purple shirt. His experience in the outsourcing industry has altered his business sense and endowed him with a new way of looking at life: "I called because in America you call as a courtesy if something happens. You have to be punctual. *I have to think like an American businessman.*"

A few themes predominate in workers' definitions of professionalism. A professional is diligent and time-conscious, yet works at an unhurried pace. She is serious yet amiable, has a core specialty but is flexible, and excels in a competitive environment. Kumar says that, as professionals, "everyone wants to be the best." For one BPO trainer it means that "you don't drop an appointment, even in going to the movies. You stick by your word." Professionals are "more of a specialized kind of people. They are not many, only very few." When asked what skills they had acquired on the job, a few workers mentioned "personality development."

Just as workplace identities and relations are composed of a variety of influences—not mere Indian clay that is easily pressed into Western shape by the firm fingers of management—the labor process is a mixture of assembly line and flexible modes of production.[45] The worker is therefore compounded of professional probity and standardized parts. In interactive work, this can amount to a form of emotional mechanization. The *Washington Post* reports on a pretty call center secretary named Musa who, like a Stepford wife, says via televised conference call that "a smile can be heard" and that "posture can make a difference. A dress code makes a difference."[46] Tight monitoring, emotion detection software, and adherence to a thicket of quality parameters also make a difference.

As Noronha and Cruz explain in painstaking detail:

> The agents were marked on phone etiquette, average handling time, adherence to the script, documentation, knowledge of the process and product, display of cordiality or warmth, clarity in the message transmitted, fluency in the English language, mother tongue influence, errors in speaking, pacification of irate customers, opening and closing, apologies, and other parameters specified by the client. . . . The breaks were monitored, and insufficient login hours on outbound calls required working on holidays. Monitoring was essential to decide on the continuation of the services of employees. Inability to perform resulted in the employee being sent for retraining, which essentially meant notice before dismissal.[47]

Somewhat surprisingly, workers often accept call monitoring, seeing it as a chance to distinguish oneself from other agents. It is a means of separating the wheat from the chaff. The ambivalence is well illustrated by a call center worker who fumed that management records every call, "every damn thing," and in the next breath said that such vigilance is necessary as it prevents workers from "playing around" and shirking their duties. This oscillation between cursing your boss and whistling while you work is evidence of consciousness of oneself as a worker and as a professional. The worker likes to "play around" when pressures are relaxed, while the professional accepts strict oversight as a means of keeping undeserved respite at bay. Neither modality is necessarily "false" in the Marxian sense. Worker consciousness allows the worker to slip out from under the control of management, while professional consciousness allows one to get ahead by playing by the rules. The former is generic and collective, whereas the latter is individualized and personal.

The Servant, the Bureaucrat, and the Professional

In management's narrative, workers played the respectful *naukar* in a context in which it had little use, much as Don Quixote's romantic ethic of chivalry seemed absurd in a world that had changed. Thus they retooled and learned new lines and, with the help of management, became professionals and knowledge workers like Kumar and Ajay. In traditional modernizing narratives, runaway specialization introduces a disjuncture between one's work identity and one's "real" private self, what Berger and his coauthors describe as "double consciousness."[48] The work-defined self can be reluctantly accepted as a necessity, coolly managed from without, or hotly embraced. Crucially, it is objectified, looked upon from the outside, as the individual tries to maintain a distance between the two identities; the core of identity remaining in the private realm. As a consequence, there is sometimes an impersonal and benumbed quality to the way employees describe their working lives.

The problem is not that managerial designs missed the mark; rather, they penetrated too closely to the center: the public self and private self became conflated. The worker adopts the role as the true self and in dialectical fashion the true self pervades the role. Once the needs of the interiorized private self are acknowledged by management through teachings about accountability and responsibility, they are transformed by employees into the demands of the "professional." The result is a professional of a sort. While employees are now speaking up and taking "ownership," they also act singularly out of self-interest when the prospect of improving one's lot arrives.

In describing the microsocial practices that generate professionalism—the exhortation, the training, the surveillance—one distinction, I think, is critical. Whereas the *naukar* depends on an outside power to govern her conduct, the professional must internalize that power, police herself, and deliberate on courses of action. And it's precisely in the protean, open-ended, and creative nature of this power that it differs from that which exacts the obeisance of the bureaucratic functionary who exists in a world where "there is no initiative, no invention, no freedom of action; there are only orders and rules."[49] Under flexible capitalism, the individual actively shapes its operations. Individual initiative and freedom and the responsibility that necessarily underpins their exercise are the hallmarks of the new ethos. It is very literally a "culture of *empower*ment."

Children are naturally impetuous; servants follow orders, not reason; bureaucratic time-servers cannot help but be lazy. It is difficult to assign blame, as it is presumed that they cannot act otherwise. We may chastise a wayward child, but we do so as a means of teaching a lesson, recognizing all along that she is not entirely at fault. Similarly, a servant may make a mistake, but she is not normally fired unless her actions undermine the informal trust upon which employment relationship is built. Professionalism is the instillation of individual moral responsibility, the maturation of the adolescent into adult. It also means that praise and blame can be assigned more readily as the professional is ostensibly free to deliberate between courses of action: to take risks or play it safe, to be diligent or lazy, to follow orders or take initiative. The structural analogue to this character-type is the flexible labor regime where it is easier to both hire and to fire and where labor laws are weak or are not enforced. But where labor demand outpaces supply, blame and responsibility work both ways: if an employee feels that her merit goes unrewarded and her potential unrecognized, she is free to move to another company. A power that individualizes therefore gives vent to individualism.

Once management introduced individualism into in the workplace,

the term's various connotations came crowding in like frenzied pas-
sengers boarding a Bombay train. Workers become more assertive and
mindful of the salary their skills can command in the market. They are
very status-conscious and want promotions frequently. They are mindful of each other's pay, rank, and title. In IT, development projects are
coveted and maintenance projects seen as a sign of mediocrity, and
their apportioning becomes a matter of dispute. Some have little loyalty to their particular employer. The ambitions of the previous generations appear claustral by contrast and suggestive of a closed horizon.
It is hardly one's duty to get rich, but it is not proscribed either. (That
is to say, religious justifications for work have long been replaced by
secular motivations of lucre and status.)[50]

Big-name companies, like brand-name goods, are status symbols.
Just as a green card can improve one's marital prospects dramatically,
making one a person of consequence, so too can working for a well-
known company.[51] As one executive remarks, "In India today, brand
name is of value. If you ask a 25-year-old man, he probably needs a
brand-name job so that his father is able to pressurize to get him the
right kind of bride." Ever mindful of familial and societal perceptions,
work becomes a means to a social end. As one worker comments stiffly,
"I am at the start of [my] career and I feel proud to work in such a company, which gives lots of exposure of various technologies and business. I am from a higher middle class of India, and working in such an
environment is graded highly in Indian society."[52]

Status concerns can take many forms. Even religious hierarchy—
seemingly antithetical to modern pursuits—is symbolically grafted
onto occupational stratification. At one firm an experienced Indian
software developer was asked at the last minute to perform quality assessment on a project. The proud worker refused on the grounds that
the work was beneath him. "He said he was from the priestly caste and
that he couldn't do that kind of work," his American employer remarked with feigned amusement. Just as handling leather is deemed
unfit for an upper-caste Hindu, quality assessment is somehow pollut-
ing and poisonous to one's self-image.

A classified in the "matrimonials" section of the *India Times* combines the threads of software, status, and romance. A "29/5'4" BE MS(US), good looking Software Eng working with MNC wants v. b'ful, slim, gori [fair-skinned], very homely girl. All Brahmin accepted." Another seeks a "b'ful, cultd & well Edu Brah girl for May '08 divorcee (nonconsummation of marriage) N. Indian Brahmin Boy 34/5'10" MBA working IT MNC Mumbai/Gurgaon based." A less caste-conscious Tamil father seeks only a "good looking" and "god feared" bride for his five-foot, four-inch, 27-year-old software-engineering son, whose yearly income is also included in the posting.

The coding of ICT work as white collar and knowledge-based by virtue of the instruments by which it is performed gives it a certain prestige. Contractual equality, nominal promotions, and glorified job titles, however, can mask very real inequalities in social status. (HSBC's Calcutta office is referred to as "The Center for Excellence.") When call center agents are given titles like "customer care executives," the name obscures the reality of the role. As one former call center worker complains, only after becoming a "team leader" do you have "the complete freedom to take a leak when you want and for however long you want." Moreover, two legal cases in the Bombay Industrial Court have established that a call center employee is actually a "workman" rather than professional, as the role entails no managerial or supervisory duties. Crucially, this means that workers are entitled to labor protections. (In both cases, the companies argued that employees were supervisors so as to put them outside the ambit of labor laws.)

Moreover, many workers lay great stress on dignity of being, for they are "from the upper middle classes of India," as a worker at a legal services firm put it. One BPO worker who says she has progressed from being a worker to a knowledge worker to a professional explains why she prefers working for a multinational firm:

It's great to work here, much better than an Indian company. The BPO environment is better. You can wear jeans on Saturdays. It's better than normal private firms. There are good incentives: cash, certificates. The BPO work environment is good. You get to meet a lot of young people and work on a team. Everywhere else you're on your own. Over here it's complete teamwork. It's like a family.

Nevertheless, the professional sense of fraternity rests on a mostly cultural and altruistic base. It has no social or economic character. Since workers are competing for a limited number of lead positions and since performance is evaluated on an individual basis, it makes little sense to assist a coworker. While distrust between management and workers is often mutual (hire-and-fire policies and job-hopping are flip sides of the same coin), the tendency among workers is toward invidious distinction. In the absence of a strong esprit de corps, many workers identify with superiors. That is, they aspire towards upward mobility rather than a collective solidarity of workers. (In a survey of 150 ICT workers, 109 self-identified as "professional," 15 as "knowledge worker," and only three as "worker," with the remainder undecided.) Resistance would thus seem more likely to take place where supervision is tight, such as at call centers. A recent effort by the Union Network International to organize workers targets just this sector, the blue-collar strand of the digital workforce. To date, the union's success has been limited, although officials claim that membership has shot up from 5,000 to 18,000 in a year as a result of the economic crisis.[53]

The youth of the workforce is also supportive of the new ethos. For many workers, this is their first labor market experience and they have scant memory of the modern social contract. Nestled in the IT-equivalents of free trade zones, the industry is an example of Ong's notion of "exceptional" spaces of neoliberalism that stand apart from other sectors of the economy.[54] In these spectral sites, Brenner and Theodore write, unionization and collective bargaining give way to the "atomistic renegotiation of wage levels and working conditions combined with expanded managerial discretion."[55] The infantilizing gaze is thus conjoined to "reformed" labor laws. As a labor lawyer remarks, "They can't carry on with this hire-and-fire policy much longer. Either they should abide by the existing labor laws, or evolve new Model Standing Orders for them. They can't carry on treating them like schoolkids under the monitor's watchful eye." But to young workers, the environment seems as natural or inevitable as anything else.

Taking Privileges

> We must be aware of the dangers which lie in our most generous wishes.
> Some paradox of our nature leads us, once we have made our fellow men the
> objects of our enlightened interest, to go on to make them the objects of our
> pity, then of our wisdom, ultimately of our coercion.
>
> —*Lionel Trilling*[56]

That the new managerial ethos can shade into an excruciating didacticism should not obscure the fact that it is animated at least in part by goodwill: a sense that firms are instilling values that will help the company and its employees succeed. And the emphasis on ownership undoubtedly has certain merits when compared to the condescension that went before it.[57] The infantilizing gaze conjoined with a reformist impulse, however, can be far from edifying. This is especially so where there is a lack of expertise at the middle-management level and where labor laws offer few protections. In these cases, the seemingly anachronistic elements of workplace relations—deferent *naukar*, autocratic manager—linger like scattered clouds on a sunny day.

It is important to distinguish between what Boltanski and Chappelle call the "spirit of capitalism," its guiding ideology and normative supports, from its substance and practice. While global capitalism privileges things like transparency and flexibility, these categories often mask other modes of workplace relations. Paternalism, in contrast also to impersonal bureaucratic authority, has not been abolished; rather, it is transmuted into a project of moral reform. The idea is to get workers to *own* their responsibilities. Recall, for instance, the female call center worker who was not allowed to transfer an exceedingly long call despite needing to visit the bathroom. It was a matter of forming her professional character. Employers and managers seem to think that they have an ex cathedra privilege to mold workers' characters for their own good, which at times can mean bending rules and playing favorites.

Recall also Deepak, the junior call center manager who mentioned his VP's "philosophy" ("women, wine, and water") for reducing attrition. Another means of slowing down turnover that his company has been experimenting with is supporting workers' higher education. This initiative came as a response to workers' dissatisfaction with career immobility. But even something so undeniably positive as subsidized education can have a perplexing underside. The real intention, according to Deepak, is to give employees the illusion of upward mobility, an intimation of a stable career path. "It's a trap," he said glibly. "They do encourage them to take correspondence courses but they don't allow them time off to complete them, to finish the exams. It's a trap," he repeated with a sardonic grin. (I have heard repeatedly from managers that such courses are quite worthless educationally and only marginally less so professionally.) But Deepak did not think the company was in the wrong. He was contemptuous of his peers and had fully absorbed the managerial thinking: the obsession with high attrition as an ill so grave that it had to be extirpated by any means necessary. As Jackall writes of managerial motivations: "The principal goal of each group is its own survival, of each person his own advancement."[58]

Some employers attempt to have open-door policies with their employees. Consequently, workers have a high regard for them, as I discuss in the next chapter. In less positive cases, there is a tendency to treat workers as children in need of instruction and discipline. And like all projects of uplift and engineering, it can end badly. What makes such things possible are authority relationships in which managerial prerogative is largely unchecked, allowing superiors to operate in a sort of ethical suspension. The following cases—examples of managerial moral hazard—occurred at the Bombay call center division of one of the largest BPOs in the world. They are reminders that beneath the smooth, elegant ethos of the new economy there lurks the potential for emotional violence, sometimes overtly acted out on others, but most often subtly and administered with careful deliberation.

An attractive female call center worker has performed well and is awarded a bonus. Of generous disposition, she uses part of it to buy chocolates for her coworkers. Weaving through the company canteen, she happens upon a bounderish manager who she knows has taken a fancy to her. When she asks him politely, "Would you like a Cadbury or a Toblerone?" he responds pruriently, "Treats aren't just taken in the canteen, you know." Embarrassed, she walks away, hoping the matter would subside. The lascivious manager, however, persists. Seeing her alone one day at work, he walks up to her and asks if she is free the coming Sunday. He parries the inevitable excuse—that she is working—with a show of managerial bravado, "Don't worry, I can always schedule an off." Reluctant but tired of his amorous advances, she relents:

"Where?"

"How about we go to a guest house?"

When the incident is brought to the attention of her superiors, she is put through a series of interviews. She is questioned by the human resource manager, by the head of operations, and by another manager, all of whom are men. They ask suggestive questions: "How did you feel in his presence? Where did he touch you? What did you feel?" Not wanting to "be the source of these cheap thrills," she feels that she has no choice but to resign, if only to preserve her dignity. In the words of a sympathetic coworker, "She didn't want to rehearse her humiliation over and over again."

At the same call center, a female worker had been harassed repeatedly by a team leader. In a comment that should be noted for its cynical vulgarity if nothing else, he tells her that she looks pretty, and when she flashes him a disgusted look, he retorts: "Come and lick my ass and tell me what flavor it is." Though an employee relations "executive" overheard the offensive comment, little disciplinary action was taken; the team leader was mildly rebuked and moved to another project. Insulted by this weak pretence of accountability, she quit a week later, after three years of call center experience, officially for "health reasons." She says she does not want to work in a call center again.

Four workers consequently wrote a letter to their employer titled "Matters of Conscience," in which they detail managerial mischievousness. The charges cluster around four themes: unprofessionalism, partiality, ineptitude, and fraud. Regarding the first, they accuse managers of using "foul" and "abusive" language, of disrespecting employees, and of being "loud, indecent and crude" in their behavior. One senior manager, they write, is "blatantly aggressive and intimidates CSPs [call center professionals] so that they would not go to the higher authorities." Another "sexually harassed a teenager to the point of her resignation." They are "unprofessional on the floor," and one manager "does not follow the dress code and cannot curb her romantic desires while on duty. . . . She must understand that each employee works for [the company] not for her."

With respect to favoritism, the workers say that management employed a divide-and-rule policy and created a "mafia" of select team leaders. Among other things, favored employees would be allowed to drop calls and Quality Assurance would look the other way. Certain workers were told when they were being monitored so that they would be extra careful in handling those calls. Of one manager they write, "Favouritism and partiality is his outstanding quality"; another is "partial to the core and forever seeking attention." The managers cover up "unethical practices by some of the CSPs" and allow "some to earn their laurels by unfair means." One uses "her official position to settle personal scores." As for ineptitude, managers lack product knowledge and language and motivational skills. They "can survive only in an unethical atmosphere."

As for fraud, managers are "scheming, coercive, and unscrupulous" and "illegal unethical practices are a habit." Managers are accused of not paying workers "their rightful emoluments on time." One allegedly fines her team monetarily for not "achieving quality parameters" and then "pockets these fines that she arbitrarily levys on CSPs." Another "builds false reports against the honest and principled workers." Another "illegally entered conversions to his favourite CSPs account thus depriving the honest CSPs of his rightful rewards."

Higher up the ladder, a senior manager is said to be insensitive to workers' concerns. He "never interacts with CSPs . . . avoids understanding their problems . . . is totally inhuman . . . [and] only believes in getting the figures balanced by the end of the day (any which way). . . . Due to his ineptitude, lack of analytical discernment and negligence he has put the process at stake and threatened the employment of over a 100 CSPs." Overall, the workers write that "management is selectively open to issues which could affect them but conveniently closed to matters which are detrimental to the reputation and image of the company and could lead to huge losses. They join hands in character assassination and slandering an honest worker's name."

Worthy of note is the articulation of a collective identity: "On behalf of the loyal workers of this organization we the undersigned have gone forward with voicing what we are compelled to do . . . follow our conscience." The workers "threaten to take up the issue outside of the organization" if the letter "goes unheeded." Against "we" stands "they": "erring officials" they want "brought to book." In an access of Jacobin vengefulness (or perhaps something was merely lost in cultural translation), they recommend that the "senior corrupt management should be *eradicated* [my italics] in time to save the company from losing valuable business and be replaced by honest and efficient personnel." Finally, the workers tactfully identify with the company: "This letter is written with utmost sincerity and loyalty towards the company with the belief that necessary action will be taken." Not surprisingly, the company's management denies these charges. The four workers have either since quit or been fired. One case is currently pending in court.

Management repeatedly refused my requests to discuss the charges so I can neither confirm nor deny them. I cite them as instances in which workers reject the ideology of professionalism promulgated by management. Instead, they believed that they were responsible professionals to begin with and that management was wrong in treating them like unruly children in need of direction. (Even union members prefer to be called professionals rather than workers.) There are thus many different interpretations of professionalism. And while one cannot generalize from these examples, I found complaints about managerial favoritism and disputes over pay to be fairly common. Such practices exemplify what Jackall calls "patrimonial bureaucracy," where success is less contingent upon hard work or merit than on personal loyalty.[59]

There comes the question: What are the causes of these lapses in managerial propriety? Certainly, a dearth of middle-management expertise, a discrete lack of scruples and accountability, and a climate of disrespect where employees are treated as expendable, and in some cases, as sex objects. How, then, can the industry claim that its labor practices are among the best in the country? This returns us to the paradox of the electronic sweatshop. Like inexpensive suits tailored to look like those from Savile Row, these workplaces in all their high-tech finery are beginning to fray. At bottom, outsourcing is about labor costs, about doing certain things on the cheap. This does not mean that services are necessarily of poor quality but simply that, in some cases, ethical problems are allowed to slide so long as the balance sheet remains untroubled.

Conclusion: Fixing Broken Windows

Management's infantilizing gaze, its project of moral reform, and the "flexible" labor regime, then, are mutually supportive. What immediately unsettles this neat arrangement is the tight labor market. It allows certain workers to give vent to their individualistic aspirations and produces a mutual disregard between worker and employer. But if the young industry's workers are in a state of protracted adolescence, then so too are many of its managers. In addition to abusing their authority, they poach workers from rival firms, a practice they know is mutually disadvantageous in the long run, but they continue to go at it like obstreperous children.

Over the past few years there has been a spate of security violations and fraud committed by BPO workers, which has threatened India's reputation as the ideal place to relocate back-office services. Some workers have also been caught fabricating their résumés, and others have forged positive customer feedback to win promotions and bonuses. While I do not mean to condone such behavior, there are a few mitigating factors. Call it a broken windows theory of management. With lax ethical standards at the managerial and executive levels, it is little wonder that workers act in morally dubious ways themselves. In fact, such behavior is somewhat predictable. They are young and sharp; the work they do is often mind-numbing and stressful. Managers and executives, on the other hand, are charged with the responsibility of upholding the moral and social order of the workplace. Impartiality and fairness are what legitimate their authority. If managers continually flout the rules, workers will likely do the same.

What is more, they will see it as unjust when they are caught and punished. Managers are often role models to young workers. They set expectations for proper behavior. Yet, their amour propre does not forbid their indulging in favoritism, their subsidizing trips to nightclubs, their contravention of hourly limits on work, their creation a climate hostile to female employees. In short, it is a culture of impunity. In this light, workers cheating on feedback scores, drinking and sleeping around, and stealing credit card data seems in retrospect like the inevitable denouement to which every other plot development was leading.

More generally, rule-bending undermines the meritocratic aspirations of the contemporary workplace. As Jackall asks, "What rules do people fashion to interact with one another when they feel that, instead of ability, talent, and dedicated service to an organization, politics, adroit talk, luck, connections, and self-promotion are the real sorters of people into sheep and goats?"[60] While the relative inexpensiveness of Indian labor made offshoring viable in the first place, poor managerial practices may ensure that labor is not only cut-rate but also catchpenny. And, as we saw in the case of Deepak and his VP, the same could be said for those workers who are later promoted to management. An ethically challenged management reproduces itself, as superiors tend to promote the very people who think and act like they do. There is a simple test to this broken windows theory: If management's behavior is cleaned up, workers' behavior should follow a similar upward ethical trajectory.

The British banks HSBC and Barclays, which are cooperating with the global union, Union Network International (UNI), are positive examples. They have maintained relative transparency in moving work from the United Kingdom to India and have made provisions for job security, including retraining and redeployment policies. Globally, they have agreed to respect international labor and "human rights" standards, including freedom of association and the right to collective bargaining. ("Barclays work does not exploit labour abroad and adheres to freedom of association," reads a press release.) While such statements do not solve the structural problems posed by offshoring— such as the downward pressure on wages and job losses—cooperating with unions such as UNI goes some way to ensuring that living wages are paid, working hours are not excessive, and that unfair practices are checked in "onshore" and "offshore" offices alike.

I spoke with a pensive HSBC call center employee in Bangalore. With four years of experience in the industry, he has observed differences in working conditions among firms. HSBC, he says, "cares about employees and has their own values." In "99 percent of companies," by contrast, "there are only problems. Each and everything is a problem. You don't get proper breaks. You don't get welcome from HR. There are politics in the team you're working for. There are a lots of restrictions." He says that at HSBC "you can take a break," while at other companies, "If you're on call when break time comes, you lose your break." He believes that the union's code of conduct and the company's "10 core values" produce an open atmosphere. While he has some complaints—his contract was temporary at the time I spoke with him and he still had to work on national holidays—he makes 22,000 rupees ($550) a month, more than double the sum at many other companies. "I've struggled for that," he says with averted eyes. The company also provides good benefits and overtime pay. "It all depends on salary structure and whether you're satisfied at the end of the day. You motivate yourself to go to job and work toward the future," he says.

CHAPTER SEVEN

The Juggernaut of Global Capitalism

Where, not the person's own character, but the traditions and customs of
other people are the rule of conduct, there is wanting one of the principal
ingredients of human happiness.

—*John Stuart Mill*[1]

What is it like for an American to manage Indian workers? After
five years with the company he cofounded, Tyler Pfeifer, an ear-
nest man in his early thirties with gimlet eyes, closely cropped blonde
hair, and some ability as a pop psychologist, has decided to quit. "The
business world is depressing. That's why I'm leaving," he says mood-
ily. Tyler plans to return to school and study mental health. He is particularly interested in the question of happiness. "Happy people are
less likely to hurt others and be destructive," he says by way of explanation, as the cold rays of the declining sun glitter on the Arabian Sea.
We are seated at a café on the upscale Juhu Beach in Bombay and I
cannot help thinking that the moment is both touching and cloying in
its sentimentality, as if out of a Bollywood script.

Offshoring has many merits for the receiving country. In a narrowly
economic sense, it provides employment and contributes to rising living standards and economic growth. It also increases women's mobility
and bargaining power and contributes to workers' self-confidence and
a growing sense of the country's potential. Of course, there are also de-
merits. The lack of mobility, investment in skills, and stimulating work
frustrates workers. They complain of managerial favoritism, health
problems, and difficulties in striking a work-life balance. Culturally,
workers become individualistic, even crudely materialistic.

Tyler Pfeifer had come to India believing firmly in the promises of globalization and found a hopelessly muddled reality instead. This chapter traces his movement from intense optimism about offshoring to searching doubt—an arc that is echoed in the energy and ennui of workers and managers, the histrionics and sobriety of the media, and the official optimism and pragmatism of the state. It also provides a valuable glimpse into how globalization is experienced by one of its former proselytizers. Today, Tyler is hardly an angry apostate, but neither is he a firm believer. What eventually doomed his mission were the impossible expectations he had for workers, the outsourcing industry, and Indians more generally. He wanted not merely that Western patterns be replicated, though he did want that, but that they be surpassed: Western entrepreneurialism with Eastern spirituality, a land of economically prosperous yogis. The fault lies in a desire to civilize and a desire for salvation, and it is not his alone.[2]

Tyler's aspirations have a well-worn provenance. In them, you hear the mingled echoes of crusading colonists calling to shore, faithful missionaries reciting the Lord's Prayer in newly built schools, boisterous businessmen counting their change, and hippies chanting in ascetic ashrams, among others. They serve as a reminder that the transregional movement of capital and culture is not new. Nor is the traffic only one-way.[3] Colonizer and colonized, American executive and Indian worker alike are intimately affected by these processes. (As Cooper writes, "The struggles were unequal, but they were not one-sided.")[4] Gauging Tyler's reactions to, say, the shifting comportment of his employees allows us to see both sides of the snaking street paved by offshoring. Such a dialectical understanding is crucial if we are to arrive at a fuller appreciation of our increasing interdependence.

The Indian Option

Tyler's passage to India, to use the time-worn phrase, was a unique one. In the late 1990s, he had spent some time working as a "Power-Point production associate," a job as titillating as the title implies. As these were the heady days of the dot-com boom, of exuberant ideas and instant if illusory success, he and an Indian-American friend, then a secretary at an investment bank, quit their jobs and set up shop as a vendor in Manhattan providing production graphics. While they were able to gain some clients through word of mouth, they were in need of a larger business plan. Then inspiration struck: Tyler's former employer had an office in Chennai, and he decided to approach venture capitalists (VCs) about the "Indian option." "I guess we were a bit overconfident. We had the graphics knowledge. Those days it was relatively easy to get funded. We were the first to do this sort of stuff," Tyler says somewhat self-critically. A VC fund provided $2 million and bought half the company. "Their idea was that we would just set it up, transfer knowledge, move out, and the customers would line up. They thought we would be able to deliver services easily as it was just stupid, easy work. VCs are arrogant," he says.

In 1999, Tyler and his business partner arrived in Bombay with only the name and address of a real estate agent. But however "stupid" the work, the initial years were far from frictionless. Soon after operations were up and running, Tyler called the Los Angeles–based CEO, Ryan O'Shea, to tell him that the office had to be shut down for the day. A gaggle of hired goons had congregated outside and were demanding protection money or else they would smash up the new company's computers. Tyler was crouched under an office desk. "Capital does not flow to where things are easy," O'Shea explains, laughing. "It just doesn't happen."

The water was choppy but Tyler got his sea legs in a hurry. The company's initial clientele consisted of a bevy of medium-sized firms and one large company. They moved over the work with the slowest turnaround first, that which required overnight delivery. Business picked up when the company began providing EDGAR (Electronic Data-Gathering, Analysis, and Retrieval system) services, the portal through which companies file documents and reports with the Securities and Exchange Commission. Five years in, Dynovate had expanded from a staff of 50 to well over 1,000 and in industry jargon was moving up from the relatively low-skilled business process outsourcing to the judgment-dependent knowledge process outsourcing. Its customers now include global investment banks, blue-chip law firms, and management-consulting and publishing companies.

Impunity and Deference

Despite their seeming remoteness, the northern suburbs of Bombay are where the life of the metastasizing city is reputed to be. They are where the young rent "flats," where IT companies cluster, and increasingly where the rich reside. Dynovate is located near the international airport and a few long miles from the railway station. For some employees, it can take up to two hours to reach the office. The area is congested, noisy, and heavily polluted. When crossing the street, you have to just go; there is no letup in the general flow of auto-rickshaws, cars, scooters, bicycles, and trucks. The sun is scalding; dust and dirt swirl in the air, prompting people to cover their faces with handkerchiefs and scarves. But a different order obtains in the company's sixth-floor office. Six sheepish young people are seated quietly on cramped leather couches in the lobby busily filling out job applications. Insecure security guards at the front desk check bags for hammers, screwdrivers, cameras, recorders, and computer hardware—anything that can be used to smash, record, or steal. Passage into individual offices is restricted as the company has confidentiality agreements with its clients, such that visitors should not be allowed to espy a client's name on letterhead or computer screen. It is as if their work is somehow illicit; that, if found out, the game would be up.

The atmosphere was hardly this cold or formal in the initial days when Tyler tried to foster a "culture of openness and ownership in the company." He spent his first two weeks interviewing 150 people, of whom they hired 35. With the fondness of a schoolteacher for her students, Tyler attached passport photos of each new recruit to his or her application, the better to associate names and faces. In time, he knew most everyone's names, including the service and security workers. But what is proper in one environment can be a solecism in another.

While Tyler encouraged employees to address him by his first name, only two had the confidence to do so. This attempt at egalitarianism was met by incredulous and embarrassed smiles. "Workers were blown away. They had certain expectations as to how you should be treated by an MD [managing director]," Tyler says.

Tyler ascribes the grateful attitude of prospective employees to limited economic opportunities. He is sometimes regarded with a reverence bordering on adulation. Recently Tyler was approached in the hallway by one of his first hires who said by way of thanks, "Sir, when you interviewed me, the first thing you did was stand up and shake my hand." "And all of this . . . because of *him*," says another employee dreamily, waving her arm broadly in the air to indicate the sleek climate-controlled workspace, the black modernist pile, in which we were seated.

Early on, Tyler says he could tell who would make a good worker, as "there's something familiar between Indians and Americans." Personality matters. Women are better workers and an office with mostly males in their early twenties "sucks." Goan Christians and dark-skinned southerners, "those who Indians call blacks," carry themselves "like people who've worked in a corporation." But despite the familiarity, he identifies some critical differences. Because of certain "forms of respect and ways of working with colleagues, they won't raise issues that might cause conflict," Tyler says. They are reluctant to give bad news and to displease clients or superiors. This is related to the notorious "yes" culture, wherein short-term harmony is preferred even if it means trouble in the long run. "Some say it's to avoid conflict, but they're fearful of being chided or disappointing," he explains. "They know that they'll eventually have to say no, but they'd prefer to do it later."

For managers, there is mixture of impunity and deference. "Young managers offer sharp criticism [to subordinates] and people are being hurt. If they have something to say, they just offer it bluntly," Tyler says. Consequently, workers perceive them as "rude, duplicitous, and autocratic." Managers in their forties who join the nascent industry with a background in manufacturing, for example, "suck," as "they don't know how to work with knowledge workers." Tyler fired one of the "traditional guys" because he was "completely ineffective." He says that "minimizing the subjective element as much as possible [is a] big challenge for a 24-year-old team leader," and that many young managers and team leaders do not even realize that they are being partial. "Their judgment is terrible," he says wearily. The lack of experience at the middle-management position cuts not only at service quality and the bottom line but also saps morale and loyalty. Workers' deference and an autocratic management are mutually reinforcing. He says with an uncomprehending laugh that he even has a peon, a proper *naukar*. There is a buzzer in his office, which when pressed sends in a sallow-faced boy with an uncertain smile and what little English he knows. "What do you want, *sir*?"

Like Dostoyevskian characters, managers and team leaders display a perplexing mixture of haughtiness and humility. That is, while they can be highhanded with subordinates, they assume a different attitude toward *their* superiors. Tyler says he is sometimes absurdly brazen with managers when they make mistakes. "Bad, bad. You did bad, you," he says wagging his forefinger ironically at an imaginary manager. A sharp tongue is sometimes necessary in getting managers to appreciate the urgency of deadlines.[5] (He directed my attention to a neat stack of holiday cards that were to be mailed to American and British clients. Someone had forgotten to send them, and they now sat uselessly in the corner of his spare office, as the festive season had long since passed.) Bemused, he says that managers get a thrill out of it, that they delight in their own abasement. What is more, it creates a leadership vacuum that inhibits workers' professional development: "You can't get them to mentor when they're posturing for the boss."

By contrast, managers of a Western cultural disposition tend to the needs of employees and clients more effectively. "They understand what you're experiencing and that your role is part of a larger picture," he says. In the main, however, employees have "no clue about the boss's reality." That is, they fail to take the perspective of other people into consideration. This lack of imaginative sympathy is reflected in seemingly insignificant matters like emails, where few take time to consider how the recipient will read it.[6] "They don't have self-awareness,"

Tyler says and adds that they have a basic "incapacity" to empathize, not a mere unwillingness. He believes it "goes to the home."

"It's Premodern Here"

> A number of porcupines huddled together for warmth on a cold day in winter; but, as they began to prick one another with their quills, they were obliged to disperse. However the cold drove them together again, when just the same thing happened. . . . In the same way the need of society drives the human porcupines together, only to be mutually repelled by the many prickly and disagreeable qualities of their nature.
>
> —*Arthur Schopenhauer*[7]

Thus did Schopenhauer describe the twin and contradictory pressures of individualism and sociality, the need to be alone and the need to belong. Tyler feels that the latter predominates in India and that the country is the worse for it. The subcontinent was home to the Indus Valley civilization, the birthplace of four major world religions, and the staging ground for a remarkable nonviolent anticolonial movement. But instead of exploring and enlarging the riches of this shared history, Indians today prefer the easy satisfactions of consumer society. Hallowed traditions have been hollowed and cultural treasures traded for the latest fashions. Remarking on his workers' bottomless fascination with things American, with scooters, sunglasses, and blue jeans, he says in an exasperated voice, "This is supposed to be the civilization that explored the depths of the mind. Some say that the Christian tradition put compassion for others at the center. This may have caused a stronger awareness of the self." Such awareness is critical in any definition of personal responsibility. It is also a necessary condition of empathy, which, Tyler says, is largely inaccessible for middle-class Indians.

In the gloaming, the beach is a soft taupe hue. Tyler contemplates the silhouetted crowds. "When they see me at the beach alone, at first they feel sorry for me. But then they see that I have equanimity. . . . They feel like I'm a more powerful person," he says. Individualism, he thinks, is an almost a foreign notion in India, something that filtered in from outside like ideas of nationalism and parliamentary democracy. Like V. S. Naipaul, whose oeuvre served him as a guide in navigating Indian culture, Tyler is unforgiving of India's faults. "It's premodern here," he says in a self-possessed voice. However jarring to the postmodern ear (or, for that matter, to anyone outside of Lévi-Strauss or Rousseau, who found romantic nobility in savagery), Tyler had chosen his words carefully. But he did not mean to convey that he finds Indians somehow barbarous. Rather, he feels that the thigmophilic tendency of Indian males to publicly hold hands and walk with their arms around each other shoulders, for example, is evidence of a stunted individuality. The need to touch, to be close, is a "physical representation of this desire" for companionship. I ask if he thinks that the Indian ego is underdeveloped, a reference to the work of Indian psychoanalyst Sudhir Kakar. "Yes, if the continuum is individuation," Tyler responds without hesitation.

Kakar argued that the "underdeveloped ego" in India is produced by a strong mother-child bond and is further encouraged by the extended family model. A child's "differentiation of himself from his mother . . . is structurally weaker . . . than in the West," Kakar claimed, and he suggested that the strong maternal bond is "manifested and symbolized by physical proximity."[8] The hand-holding Tyler observed could be interpreted as the extension of the weak ego into adult life. Moreover, as "the individual functions as a member of a group rather than on his own," a lasting dependence on authority figures for guidance develops.[9] Where such bonds form the basis of the social structure, the self-reflexive individual is yet to be cut loose from its moorings.

The dependence on authority is reflected in workers' submissive attitudes toward managers and also in managerial deference toward superiors. The lack of individualism is betrayed by worker's reluctance to take initiative. As you will recall from previous chapters, this trope of a premodern cast of mind shaped managers' recurring complaints about the immaturity of workers. So it is with Tyler, who thinks that India has not been witness to as many "iterations of individualism" as the West.

Tyler's minor musings join a long line of Western thinking that denies non-Europeans discrete selfhood simply because it is constructed differently.[10] As Mbembe writes of the limits of empathy in the Western tradition:

> Each time it came to peoples different in race, language, and culture, the idea that we have, concretely and typically, the same flesh, or that, in Husserl's words, "My flesh already has the meaning of being a flesh typical in general for us all," became problematic.[11]

Moreover, how does one reconcile Tyler's claims with the somewhat Janus-faced character of employees? On the one hand, they are tireless workers and can be counted on to put in extended hours. But on the other, they are restless with intensely personal aspirations and are willing to hop jobs at a moment's notice. The answer may have to do with the special character of individualism in urban India.

In his observations of early democratic life in America, Tocqueville celebrated the citizenry's capacity to practice "self-interest rightly understood."[12] What he meant was a form of individualism that was intensely other-regarding. While scarcely compatible with grand gestures of self-sacrifice, this doctrine of numerous, "small" sacrifices enabled Americans to forego "some of their own well-being for the prosperity of their fellow man."[13] Key here is the ability to empathize, which, for Adam Smith, formed the basis of the moral order. "How selfish soever man may be supposed to be," he writes, "there are evidently some principles in his nature, which interest him in the fortune of others, and render their happiness necessary to him, though he derives nothing from it, except the pleasure of seeing it."[14] Without empathy, the richness of interpersonal interaction is reduced to instrumental encounters between subject and object. The pressing question, then, is how upwardly mobile Indians will interpret individualism. Will they interpret it broadly to include shared sacrifice, or will they prefer a self-interest ill-defined and narrowly understood?

Like so much of this country, Bombay is a place where vast inequalities in wealth and power are not just objective facts, but cultural norms. The city may be India's richest, but it is also the world capital of slums, hosting some 10 to 12 million squatters and shanty dwellers.[15] But while the poor crowd into slums like Dharavi, Asia's largest, along the Mahim River and the elite repair to the forbidden bunga-lows of Malabar Hill, it is never entirely possible to extricate oneself from the human crush nor from the fact of human suffering. The latter makes itself most immediately felt in the legless body of the leprous beggar, the prematurely wizened faces of slum children, and the ago-nized song and gouged eyes of the blind street musician—nothing but the darkest night in those plunging sockets. Yet you cannot even give charity with a clear conscience as the beggar who approaches you may be part of a racket—a network that ruthlessly exploits the most des-perately poor. This at least is why Tyler refrains from giving money. As Adorno once put it, "Wrong life cannot be lived rightly."[16]

It is understandable, then, that people have tried to distance them-selves psychologically and emotionally and, as much as possible, physically from these unsightly sights. This distancing act may also have something to do with the residue of the caste system by which compassion for others is demarcated by distinctions of purity and pol-lution.[17] While you might give to a beggar out of a genuine sense of charity, it is also believed that you can earn some sort of divine credit (*punya*) by doing so. Just as, in Tyler's view, workers were not able to see things from the perspective of colleagues, so are Indians unable to empathize with the beggar. The destitute are viewed as objects and not as individuals deserving of moral sympathy. They "think thing," Tyler says, pointing to an imaginary mendicant on the sun-dappled ground. Their suffering is not real. "It doesn't have to be like this," he says, agitated.

(Again, Tyler's perspective is ambitious but blinkered. Simply be-cause the affluent in the West have been more successful in separating themselves from the poor by means of less viscerally objectionable forms segregation does not mean they are somehow more virtuous or morally expansive. Fortified enclaves and gated communities and the vast inequalities that underpin them are becoming common features of urban landscapes in global north and south alike.)[18]

Tyler does, however, think that "modernization" along Western lines is possible. While Ameriphilia and materialism may be by-prod-ucts of globalization and the expansion of the middle class, Tyler says that they are not the only or even most important consequences. Ben-

jamin Friedman, for example, argues that economic growth is corre-
lated with enlightened social policies and attitudes.[19] Likewise, Tyler
notices a subtle but unmistakable shift in the ways young Indians are
beginning to self-identify. He says that some of his colleagues think
that India will swallow up Western white-collar jobs and are almost
"gleeful" about it. He believes their schadenfreude, however off-putting, to be healthy, as its implicit nationalism cuts away at the caste
and class divisions that still have an undeniable relevance.

"This is the first generation not to say, 'I'm Keralese, Gujrati, or
Marathi,' but that they're Indian first," Tyler says. (Fractious though
India may be, he overlooks the sense of shared purpose that characterized the independence struggle and parts of the postindependence
period.) He adds, somewhat ruefully, that "less than half think this
way." Juhu, with its trendy shops and restaurants, business class hotels, strolling couples, and ice cream stands, he observes, was cleaned
up only recently and that probably because people were embarrassed
that this could not be the impressive India of Bollywood and information technology.

Still, there are hints of a broadening civic sensibility among the
young, a movement from local identifications such as family, caste,
and kin to the city and the national polity as modes of affiliation.
This shift away from inherited solidarities to chosen ones, combined
with the increasing complexity of the division of labor, recalls the famous dualisms of sociology. Ferdinand Tönnies contrasted the paro-
chialism of gemeinschaft (community) with the cosmopolitanism of
gesellschaft (society).[20] Durkheim observed a shift from mechanical
to organic solidarity, from uniformity to diversity, from the sacred to
the secular.[21] But although Durkheim viewed this transition as largely
positive, he had misgivings about the fragmentation and anomie that
resulted.

Similarly, while holding that modernization is a force for national
unity, Tyler understands that rapid growth can precipitate large dis-
parities in income and the attendant social problems. "The U.S. is
founded on this wonderful ideal of multiracial social harmony," he says
in a worried voice, "but there are all these things we have to deal with
like rape, depression, suicide, and murder. What's going to happen
when they go through their 1970s New York, when everybody's mur-

dering each other?" The transition is already occurring to some extent in India's major cities. The crime rate in Bangalore, India's IT hub, climbed almost 75 percent in one year, from 16,002 in 2004 to 28,000 crime cases in 2005. Delhi had 47,404 crime cases in 2003 and 53,623 cases in 2004, a 13 percent increase in one year.[22] IT workers, with their conspicuous identity tags, are particularly ripe candidates for petty crime. In Bangalore, they are told to keep tags hidden.

Moreover, rising incomes do not automatically enlarge the scope and depth of our sympathy. According to an editorial in the *Times of India*, "The current wave of liberalization has deepened the tendency which the wealthy Indian already had to ignore the poor. . . . Once it becomes legitimate to ignore poverty, the sense of community ceases to have a place in social life."[23] Absent a socially binding vision of the public good, an imperative to promote growth *and* equity, uneven development may provoke new divisions.

Just as some think that "parts of the Indian economy . . . are skipping right over the 'second' industrial age, and straight into the information era," BPO workers, if we extend Tyler's observations, are jumping from premodernity to postmodernity and bypassing the prefix-less intermediate stage.[24] With the fading of stable career paths, the paternalistic state, and the social contract, workers find themselves very much in a postmodern context, in its uncertainty and essential ambiguity. Class privilege and insecurity are the defining features of their working lives.

"The idea of a job for life, like 1950s America, has been shot for this generation of BPO workers," Tyler says. Lost is the sense of a career, which "in its English origins meant a road for carriages, and as eventually applied to labor meant a lifelong channel for one's economic pursuits."[25] Yet in place of this lost continuity rise more equalized life chances. Individuals are defined more by personal achievement than accidents of birth. (Though it seems that most workers have chosen their parents wisely, as the middle class is the principal beneficiary of liberalization.) With globalization, individuals may experience the lack of a moral and professional compass, but the appeal of the new India lies precisely in the possibilities it presents to create oneself anew; the belief that privilege and pedigree matter little.

Posed the question, "Who are you?" Bell writes, "a traditional man would say 'I am the son of my father.'"[26] The modern person, by contrast, would reply, "I am I, I come out of myself, and in choice and action I make myself." This distinction, Bell argues, is the "hallmark" of modernity. An Indian call center worker might respond, and indeed did respond, that she is Britney Gupta, combining her infatuation with the celebrity Spears and her given surname. In this wrestling between anchored regional identities and the floating, astral identities of the new globalism, the ICT workforce is suspended between the poles of imagined (Western) modernity and imagined (Indian) tradition, the synthesis of which produces a postmodern fugue. They are restless with desire to disencumber themselves of familial and societal constraints but reluctant to fully do so. They are pressing forward and holding back, by turns self-confident and anxious, and in this respect they resemble Schopenhauer's porcupines. There is an economic rationale for this aborted liberation: the middle-class family serves as a buffer against anomie and financial insecurity, whereas the poor experience globalization's rawer forms.

"This Juggernaut of Job Creation"

> Passage to India!
> Lo, soul! seest thou not God's purpose from the first?
> The earth to be spann'd, connected by net-work,
> The people to become brothers and sisters,
> The races, neighbors, to marry and be given in marriage,
> The oceans to be cross'd, the distant brought near,
> The lands to be welded together.
>
> (A worship new, I sing;
> You captains, voyagers, explorers, yours!
> You engineers! you architects, machinists, yours!
> You, not for trade or transportation only,
> But in God's name, and for thy sake, O soul.)
>
> —"Passage to India," Walt Whitman, 1871

Tyler was drawn to India by more than wanderlust. His decision to out-source, however materially based at the outset, acquired an extra-rational, even ethical dimension. He went not only "for trade"; he came to view his work as a religiously informed vocation. As Weber famously argued, the idea of a calling provides a psychological moti-vation to work. One, as the saying goes, does not live by bread alone and absent an overarching, powerful ethic, neither duress nor the in-trinsic merits of work are enough to inspire people daily and "elicit engagement."[27] Weber viewed the extramundane sources of motivation that animate temporal activities as central to the Protestant work ethic, providing otherworldly reasons for worldly economic pursuits. The fierce certainty that one is of God's elect is reflected in the industrious-ness of one's labor. It is to forget one's mortal coil while plunging all the more deeply into the mundane world of labor.

In many cases, meaning is extrinsic to work, such as when people derive satisfaction from supporting their family. Seeking work that is intrinsically meaningful, however, is hardly to gild the lily. Tyler had been brought up a Mennonite in Pennsylvania. He attended a confes-sional high school and college, where he was taught the hidden truths of American history like the extermination of Native Americans and the brutalities of slavery. Tyler, however, grew tired of the student body's dogmatism, its embarrassing moral clarity, and became "very cynical." In this light, his decision to go into the corporate world can be seen as a departure from the faith's commitment to social justice. His own politics are hard to place. He ascribes his modest success to a mixture of good fortune and merit. He thinks that unions are like cartels and that liberals are more hypocritical than conservatives, though his sympathies tend toward the former. His wife, a grade school teacher, is a "recovering activist."

In his Smithian view, the amoral machinations of capitalism, rather than the good works of a committed few, ultimately redound to human-ity's benefit. Business for him is philanthropy continued by other means. Tyler says Mennonites "talk a lot about sustainable develop-ment." Some of his relatives work for Ten Thousand Villages, "one of the most respected nonprofits." By practicing fair trade, "It's helping 20 to 30 villagers in Tanzania, and increased their income by 40 percent." This is hardly to be scoffed at, he says, but globalization provides enormous employment opportunities.[28] This was evidenced by the grateful, almost supplicatory attitude of workers and prospective employees. Dynovate, he says, has created careers "for a thousand people. It's a growing profit center. It's integrated into the world economy and has doubled some people's income." (The vice president of human resources, he notes, makes 18 lakhs ($40,565) annually.) "I've given three years of my life to creating employment in India," he says with some force.

When asked if he sees his efforts as good works, Tyler enthusiastically agrees: "The standards are pretty low here. It's not hard to improve on them." Western companies have a "dramatic impact" on Indian working conditions. Better jobs also bring stability and have "tremendous" spillover effects, such as the diffusion of management knowledge.[29] Taken together, these beliefs lend his endeavor a missionary aspect. Despite the fact that his employees are privileged enough to find jobs outside the outsourcing industry, Tyler, like Mark Scheyer, constructs them as needy. (It is as though an employee should go to work with a begging bowl in one hand and a Palm Pilot in the other.) Consider it a postmodern twist on the "white man's burden": the view that under the tutelage of multinational corporations Indians can develop into mature and responsible selves; that the adoption Western ways will lead to cultural development.[30] Not one for false humility, Tyler says he has "created this juggernaut of job creation."

The word *juggernaut* is a corruption of the Sanskrit *Jagannātha*, meaning "Lord of the universe." More specifically, it is a title of Krishna, the eighth avatar of Vishnu, and the presiding deity of a twelfth-century temple at Puri. Each year an image of the god is placed in a "chariot" so unwieldy and cumbrous that it requires the exertions of many to wheel it to the temple on the outskirts of the city. Once started, the idol-bearing cart's momentum is such that it crushes anything in its path, including people. According to legend, devotees would throw themselves under its wheels, like so many desperate Anna Kareninas, for reasons of self-sacrifice and salvation. To missionaries, the sumptuous and fatal chariot processions came to symbolize the material and spiritual decadence, even sadomasochism, of

Hinduism.[31] The term *juggernaut* has thus come to mean "a belief or an institution that elicits blind and destructive devotion to which people are ruthlessly sacrificed; an overwhelming advancing force that crushes or seems to crush everything in its path."[32]

There is a rhetoric of inevitability that buttresses global capitalism.[33] Its proponents refer to it with ritual frequency as an inexorable force. An Indian-American executive says with apodictic certainty that "globalization is completely irreversible. It would be foolish to try to do so." To modern day capitalist-missionaries, the procession of jobs from West to East is virtuous, a "great, great thing," according to the CEO O'Shea. Capitalism, he says, is a "powerful economic engine that has generated great success stories."[34] Like a juggernaut, "it is unstoppable."[35]

It is easy to write Tyler off as a cocksure young executive, so critical is he of a culture that he admittedly does not understand, so readily does he congratulate himself on creating jobs and improving it. But you must give him some credit for speaking without embarrassment about things that are not easily spoken of. His observations on how Indian society works are as perspicacious as they are ill informed. And next to many managers Tyler is a paragon of probity. Moreover, a bit like Weber's laboring Protestants, he sees himself as a vessel serving a broader purpose. Similarly, Lloyd Blankfein, CEO of Goldman Sachs, told the *Times of London* after the financial collapse, "We help companies to grow by helping them to raise capital. Companies that grow create wealth. This, in turn, allows people to have jobs that create more growth and more wealth. It's a virtuous cycle. We have a social purpose." While the company received $12 billion in bailout money from the U.S. government, he said that he was "doing God's work," recalling the motto that Francesco di Marco Datini, the fourteenth-century Italian merchant of Prato, had inscribed on his ledgers: "In the name of God and profit."[36]

Tyler is not so grandiose, but the salient point is that capitalism is frequently justified by reference to the common good. By the alchemy of the invisible hand, self-interest comes to coincide with the general good. Trade is also said to exert a civilizing influence, thereby balancing the more malignant passions.[37] In this regard, Tyler says outsourcing fosters self-confidence among workers and softens prejudice. By way of illustration, he tells me the story of a female employee. One of the most technically skilled workers, she has met the Dynovate team in New York City, and speaks regularly with U.S. and U.K. customers, a privilege granted to a small minority of workers. Her manager was a Christian who speaks mainly English at home, while she is dark-skinned and from a poor family. "I guarantee her parents don't speak English," Tyler says emphatically. Somewhat shy, she "doesn't hang out" with workers after hours at nightclubs. Yet she commands respect and her colleagues speak of her with "words of reverence." When the young manager passed her up for a promotion, she was deeply hurt.

Dismayed by the manager's prejudice, Tyler decided to promote her to a shift leader, which he says is like the "holy grail for an entry-level employee." To his surprise, she demurred. "She said, 'Thank you for this honor but I can't accept.' In her heart she decided she could not," Tyler recalls. With 80 percent of employees at the associate or entry level, there are very few shift leader jobs, and thus, "Saying no to it is like saying no to a whole world of possibilities, like saying good-bye to her dreams for the three years." Tyler had an extended conversation with her about "bias and emotions." He tried to "address her hurt" and to "rebuild her sense of self." After three days of discussion and deliberation, she eventually agreed to take the position and "she's just radiant" every time he sees her. She does not speak badly of the manager, who was mildly reprimanded, but simply does not want to deal with him.

Materialism and Dashed Hopes

> Along with air, earth, water, and fire, money is the fifth natural force a
> human being has to reckon with most often.
>
> —*Joseph Brodsky*[38]

Tyler wants his employees to treat the firm as a "team, as a special company." He says that training and skill development "never stop" and that customer requirements become increasingly complex. Working with Americans has a "dramatic impact on how people see themselves as individuals." What matters is not where you are from, but what "hub that you're in." Workers are happy for friends that do well, and this fellow-feeling "cuts across caste." Early on, workers felt a palpable loyalty to the company, as only 1 out of 50 employees left Dynovate for other jobs. (Two others left for family reasons, and this over two years.) Attrition began to rise steadily as the outsourcing industry grew. There was and remains a sentiment among workers' families "that foreigners [are] just using you for a few years. They feared that the jobs would move to Philippines." At the time of writing, the company's annual attrition rate was around 15 percent, which is good by industry standards and has probably dipped further because of the slowed economy. Tyler says that some workers leave for money, while others, especially women, want day jobs.[39] Turnover is highest "where managers are bad, where they're rough with people or seen as secretive." It also tends to be high when there is no work because "if there's no work they know that their career is going nowhere." Ever concerned with his employees' well-being, he writes in a technology magazine that "lifestyle disorders, stress, unfair treatment, and the repetitive nature of the job often keep employees away from work. However, team leaders can play a vital role in curing many of these . . . problems by giving [employees] challenging and accomplishable goals."

In the beginning, employees used to say meekly, "Sir, I just want a good job." Now they have other choices. Before they "wouldn't give any hint of a doubt. They wouldn't ask anything." Now they want to know about career path progression and income prospects. For most of its BPO processes, the company has a six-month training cycle, but, within four months, one woman left saying she had a better offer. While Tyler laments the impact of turnover on business and morale, in the longer view, he feels it to be beneficial. "Attrition is 15 percent; before that it was 10. That's 100 people a year. That's good in terms of the impact on society. It's a function of the industry's and the kid's immaturity. I've heard of 90 percent attrition in call centers. I've heard of 60–70 percent pay raises at captives [i.e., corporate subsidiaries]."

O'Shea, the CEO, says that what made Dynovate a viable business proposition was first and foremost labor arbitrage. When wages rise to

20 percent per annum, the company's raison d'être comes into question. Nevertheless, Tyler says the rising wages are "good," with an unexpected certainty. Josh, an American in his late twenties who had worked at an IT company in Bangalore, begs to differ. "What do you become more assertive about? Money? If so, then the country isn't gaining anything in terms of leadership. It doesn't do anyone any good." Josh also complains about the lack of loyalty and employees' tendency to put their own interests first. They are very competitive, he says, and there are times where they do not help colleagues on a project because it might undermine their own efforts to get ahead. "They don't recognize how helping a coworker can also help them in the longer run," he says. "In India there's no secret about wages. Everyone knows how much everyone is making. This breeds jealousy. People don't think like a team. . . . And some of the ancillary side effects are more materialism. People become more money-oriented."

Indian circumspection gives way to American directness, which is evidenced in the ratcheting up of expectations and demands, in the willingness to look the gift horse in the mouth. Tyler says that there are now "*a lot* of grievances around compensation and promotions." A promotion should have meaning, Tyler believes, but some employees think, "Why can't you make an exception for me?" Previously workers thought it was great to have the vice president come in and see how things work; now they walk into the office impudently and raise Cain. "But sir, what about my false hopes!" cried one worker. Tyler says that she said it six times, and while he found her plaint rather absurd—she had received a 40 percent pay raise recently—a suggestion of falsity, about her hopes, about the job, about the entire enterprise, seemed to linger in the back of his mind.[40]

Migrating to India alongside jobs are liberal hire and fire policies. One employee who has been with the company's legal services department for nine months as a senior production associate says there is "lots of competition" within BPO companies and that "one bad phase can pull you down." Asked about the relationship between Dynovate and its Western customers, he says that the "client catches the boss' neck; the buck stops at the client's neck. One bad client feedback and you're under scrutiny. There are no protections." Nonetheless were it not for the BPO jobs, "we would yet be looking. The U.S. has helped in building up a Third World country. The very fact that we're surviving in the market is a sign that we have potential."

I ask Tyler about the nature of work being outsourced, and whether the relatively low level of skill it required was a source of dissatisfaction. He notes how fascinating seemingly mundane work was for some. As Tyler's "right-hand woman" says about the early years of the industry, "All of us were very young. The BPO market hadn't really come into being. I had never heard of something like this. Making PowerPoint presentations was pretty exciting for me. I started understanding what the bankers wanted." This was essentially a happy narrative of Indian workers getting high-paying, if mundane, jobs they needed and learning some valuable business lessons on the side. Tyler, for his part, was filled with the gratifying feeling that he was serving a useful social purpose.

But as the excitement born of working for a multinational wanes and the drudgery dawns on people, laboring on PowerPoint slides for 18 months loses its appeal. Since I am not a reporter, Tyler says, he can be frank with me. In media interviews, he plays up the prospects of knowledge services, "high-end work" that "requires an MBA," such as doing research for a company and developing a business plan. But he would not tell reporters "anything about the vulnerability of vendors" in a competitive global market. Nor would he mention that so-called knowledge services constitute "only a fraction" of the company's revenues. Seventy percent of its revenues, he says, are from low-end EDGAR services. This is telling, as Tyler's company is routinely ranked as one of the best for knowledge and legal process outsourcing in various industry surveys. It is the same with their major competitors. "There is a limit to the complexity of what's going to be done here," Tyler says.

As one worker remarks, "We have SOPs [standard operating procedures]. We try to streamline the operation so that things don't go wrong. Somebody else is handling quality parameters. We don't put in a lot of our knowledge input. We can't make decisions." Another worker with two years of experience says that in SEC filings, "kids don't know what they're doing. For KPO, all they're doing is getting data and generating something in Excel. For legal processing, what are they doing? Preparing petitions, filings. Will they ever be involved in the contents of the case? They don't expect them to crack their brains and actually analyze things."

Conclusion: Full Circle

The currents of optimism and skepticism wash back and forth. For Tyler, the problems did not crowd out but, just as effectively, began to obscure the benefits. The question of *purpose* in work rose afresh, as if it had only gone into a brief remission. Once the transcendental support, the faith in the juggernaut, was removed, the edifice of daily work foundered. What was left was a meaningless shambles, a desire to quit India as soon as possible. At times a kind of melancholy overwhelms Tyler. The company's HR department, he says, is "falling apart." He says that "we have lapses and don't really treat people well," as if confessing a minor sin. He asks repeatedly, with doubt perceptible in his voice, whether I think that outsourcing is good for India.

Hume, with the Stoics, once observed that sympathy "with persons remote from us [is] much fainter than that with persons near and contiguous." Similarly, Viner writes that "spatial distance operates to intensify psychological distance."[41] When Tyler moved back to New York as the vice president of marketing, thus removing himself from the daily rigors and rewards of management, he gradually lost the sense of purpose that had previously sustained him on the job. Far from the madding crowd, an overwhelming sense of lassitude would divert him from work, would send him sauntering from his home office to the adjacent room to work on puzzles. His salary was adequate but the job lost its meaning as a vocation. He was haunted by what Sennett calls the "specter of uselessness."[42]

We are at a café in New York's Soho district and Leonard Cohen croons "Suzanne" softly on the stereo and we are drinking coffee, which would cost anywhere from four cents to $1.50 some 7,800 miles away in Bombay. Tyler has left Dynovate. "I became de-energized," he says forlornly. In offshoring, Tyler was able to reconcile the prods of an activist faith and the material need to make a living. However, as the days passed, the troubles and banalities intrinsic to the work had diminished its appeal and left him bothered and vaguely depressed. The capitalist juggernaut powered on but its spell—the sense of calling and the meaning it provided to worldly activities— had been broken. "I started dreading the days that I would have to force them to do something that they find boring. Being integrated into a multinational is exciting for them for a year. Then the cold, hard realty sets in," he says with hard-lived wisdom. That is why the business world is depressing and that is why Tyler left. He applied for a job counseling street children and started reading Piaget.

Tyler, like many who came to the subcontinent with high-minded dreams, is not alone in his inability to "pierce the veil" of India. As the writer Rabindranath Tagore put it in 1911:

> We hear about Europeans with feelings of devotion toward her, having been attracting by our scriptures or by the character or the words of some of our holy men . . . but they returned empty-handed, their sense of devotion waning over time and discarded in the end. They could not pierce the veil of poverty and incompleteness in the country as a whole to see what they had read about in the scriptures or what they had seen in the characters of holy men.[43]

So what is it about India that frustrates, that leads people to turn away empty-handed? On Chakrabarty's reading of Tagore, the error is a failure of imagination, an inability to see beyond the resplendent poverty and suffering of India, beyond its sad materiality: "His point was precisely that a view that was merely realist might not present an India that was lovable. To be able to love India was to go beyond realism, to pierce the veil of the real, as Tagore put it."[44] But most that come to India are already very well acquainted with its problems. I would suggest that what is wrong is the "mission" itself—whether it be a *desire to civilize*, which moved missionaries and some in the colonial apparatus, or a *yearning for salvation*, which drove the hippies and countless others to ashrams and Goan beaches. (As for the first, recall Tyler's quiet doubts about whether outsourcing is good for India after all. As for the latter, consider his bemusement at the shabby materialism of his workers.) One mission constructs Indians as objects of pity, and the other as spirituality incarnate. In either case, India is seen not as real but as ideal: a land of ideal beggars ready to be uplifted or ideal spiritual guides ready to instruct. Both, in their own ways, represent forms of escapism. It is true that one cannot live by bread alone, but neither can one live solely on dreams.

Some time later Tyler tells me that the counselor position never came through. The cycle of hope and toil that had ensnared his former workers was, for him, an ironic circle. As he wrote in an email from his apartment in New York: "I work at a big law firm doing the kind of work I used to outsource."

CHAPTER EIGHT

Cyber-Coolies and Techno-Populists

I usually have tea and fruit for breakfast. This morning, my tea, Wuyi Mao Feng, is from China, my overripe kiwis are from New Zealand, and my navel oranges were picked in some unspecified foreign locale. After a shower, I put on a cotton undershirt made in the Dominican Republic and underpants imported from Thailand. (The blue-gray songbird outside my window recently winged its way up from South America.) My transnationalism is mostly accidental and is born, in part, of slovenly convenience. ("You *should* have bought locally grown produce and union-made clothing," my rickety conscience tells me.) But my point is this: The dizzying cross-border trade in goods and services is now a settled part of our everyday reality. So much so that we scarcely notice it.

The purpose of this chapter is to explore the place-bound, but universalizing, ideals that help animate these accelerating flows. (As Tsing writes, "Global connections give *grip* to universal aspirations.")[1] This imaginative dimension of space has been variously characterized as "symbolic," "relational," and "representational."[2] This does not mean that it is "false" or any less real than empirical reality. However much they diverge from the facts on the ground, these visions motivate particular processes and have very real material impacts.[3] *Res extensa* and *res cogitans*, the objective and subjective dimensions of space, are "dialectically inseparable."[4]

Yet in keeping with our central motif, it is also necessary to look at how ideologies are transformed through people's daily activities. The notion of imitative counterpoint has been useful in understanding what happens when reality is forced into a mold in which it only partly fits.[5] I use the term *economy of utopia* to illustrate how universalistic ideals are pressed into the service of particular political strategies and agendas.[6] While social actors are doubtless inspired by grand visions (or even their absent presence), the economy of utopia denotes the cost-benefit calculation that is of necessity imposed by practical realities.

In this chapter I explore two broad perspectives on offshoring, that of capital and labor, and show how they are adjusted to accommodate distinct political and economic realities. First is a discussion of what I call business cosmopolitanism, the view that we are all denizens of an expanding global marketplace rather than of parochial nation-states. The realities of uneven development, poor infrastructure, and a labor shortage in India, however, lead executives and their political allies to espouse a vision of technological populism that is more politically viable. Second, I consider the ideal of worker internationalism. Faced with the threat of capital flight and individualistic worker identities, labor moves from a confrontational stance to a more accommodating posture in India—somewhere between standing ramrod straight in defiance and genuflecting to capital.

Business Cosmopolitanism

> The proprietor of stock is properly a citizen of the world, and is not
> necessarily attached to any particular country.
>
> —*Adam Smith, The Wealth of Nations*[7]

The exaggerated character of the globalization discourse has already been discussed. Suffice it to say, we are still a long way from a borderless world. Yet this fiction can be very persuasive, as evidenced by Thomas Friedman's best-selling paean to globalization, *The World Is Flat*. It limns a world in which national boundaries are irrelevant, where "knowledge centers" are linked together "into a single global network," and where corporations, not social movements, engage in social activism ("compassionate flatism"). The flat world, he predicts, will "superempower a whole new group of innovators," ushering in "an amazing era of prosperity and innovation." There is even a nod to multiculturalism. As opposed to the stodgy days of Western hegemony, the global economy will increasingly be driven "by a much more diverse— non-Western, nonwhite—group of individuals." Freed from the shackles of colonialism and also the yoke of nationalism and socialism, Fanon's "wretched of the earth" can now simply "plug and play" in the global economy. "You are going to see every color of the human rainbow take part," he writes, as if the developing world has finally awoken from a prolonged siesta.[8]

Friedman's periodization of globalization is instructive. He writes that while

> the dynamic force in Globalization 1.0 was countries globalizing, and while the dynamic in Globalization 2.0 was companies globalizing, the dynamic force in Globalization 3.0—the thing that gives it its unique character—is the newfound power of individuals to collaborate and compete globally.[9]

The subject and focal point is neither the nation nor the corporation; it is the individual and, more specifically, the sovereign consumer-entrepreneur. This idea of a deterritorialized gemeinschaft also undergirds consultants Vashishta and Vashishta's notion of the "Offshore Nation":

> The Offshore Nation is not one country or even one region. It is a world of buyers and sellers, all linked by a desire for higher productivity, lower costs, and matching supply with demand. It is the United States, which in 2003 spent over $10 billion on outsourced software and IT services alone. It is India, which is now exporting more than $15 billion a year in IT and business process services.[10]

They provide an equally breathless account of the offshoring of services:

> Services globalization is the next step in the evolution of trade and capitalism. It is progress. It is efficiency. It is the race for competitive advantage. It is not just offshore outsourcing but the wholesale elimination of borders as a means of restructuring the free flow of services.[11]

And so on. Quite appropriately, the Vashishta brothers dedicate their book to their "Globally Conscious Families."

In the blessed-out atmosphere of an outsourcing industry conference the ruminations are cosmic. The world, says a panelist, "feels more wide open." "Like the Wild Wild West?" asks the discussant. "This really is. This is a global services conference. . . . These are dramatic changes." Participants can hardly keep up with the excited momentum of their emotions. Superlatives cascade from trembling lips. There is talk of "nirvana." Attendees are advised on how to "futurize" their organizations. Insecure professionals are told how to succeed in a globally sourced world: "Take one step out of your comfort zone . . . Diversify . . . Take some risks . . . The leaders will have multiple skills, multifunctions. Be able to operate, empathize, stretch." One participant says that outsourcing has proceeded so far that a company like Cisco Systems is little more than a brand and website, as the vertically integrated corporation has become disaggregated. "Does this mean, are we talking about . . . the death of the corporation as we know it?" asks an Indian attendee who cannot contain his enthusiasm. It is as though the world has been turned upside down, as though the meek have inherited the earth, as though "all fixed, fast frozen relations" have been "swept away" by democratized technology.

With inverted Marxism, the business class universalizes itself. Compared to such visions of a placeless space and a timeless time of human progress, domestic considerations can seem downright provincial, even irresponsible. Globalization has changed how the world works; it is a Copernican revolution for our times. As Vikram, an Indian-American BPO executive, put it to me at a café in Bombay:

> In my experience, America generally is the most inward looking country. We get politicians like Kerry and his sidekick Lou Dobbs. They're losing an opportunity to build jobs. Opportunity is in the global economy, not in the heartland of America. The only way to grow the economy is to accept that the U.S. isn't the center of the world. The Internet eliminated physical borders. You have to take advantage of the global economy. You cannot look to old ways of doing things. It's political suicide but the right answer.

Similarly, according to the COO of a BPO company, American insularity may ultimately undermine American exceptionalism. Outsourcing is a harbinger of what is to come:

> The challenge for the U.S. is not outsourcing but when it truly globalizes. People [there] don't realize that the world is much bigger than the five-mile radius in which they stay. It'll be a real upheaval for U.S. society. . . . Right now the U.S. is so far ahead economically, but in 20 years?

Nonetheless, for Vikram, as well as Friedman, the unequivocal mark of progress is the ubiquity of Western multinationals. Where Friedman marveled that he could play golf in Bangalore against a spectral backdrop of corporate logos, Vikram talks about "pizzas, cellphones, cars, computers—goods and services. Microsoft, Dell, and Sun have opened up. It's just going to get better and better." A row recently erupted when the founder of Infosys, Narayana Murthy, refused to play the Indian national anthem with lyrics during a visit by Indian president Abdul Kalam, saying that it would "embarrass foreigners" working for the firm.[12] While he later apologized, the incident sheds light on the cosmopolitan aspirations of the business elite. Globalization produces an "outward-looking sense of place."[13]

In India, the new sensibility—the waxing of the global and the waning of the national—would not go unremarked upon. Shorn of the particularities of place, upwardly mobile Indians now see their country of birth as "merely one stopping place in a global employment market."[14] "Contributing to the inflow of foreign exchange," Chopra writes, "is seen as sufficient for realizing the dreams of national development and prosperity."[15] Tellingly, Nandan Nilekani, cofounder of Infosys, was awarded the Padma Bhushan, which is regarded as India's third highest civilian decoration, as recognition for distinguished service *to the nation*. According to Deshpande, "The darling of the national imagination is no longer the patriotic producer but the cosmopolitan consumer who has made the world his oyster."[16] For Khilnani, the globalized strand of the middle class is no longer "constrained by the territorial frame of the nation."[17] As Deshpande writes, "For the most influential and powerful elite fraction of this class (which would have supplied the second generation of Nehruvians), *the nation is no longer the canvas for their dreams and aspirations.*"[18] The poor are erased from the canvas altogether.[19]

Techno-populism and the Economy of Utopia

As a practical political program, then, business cosmopolitanism would not do. The BJP, for example, was soundly defeated at the polls in 2004 for its "India Shining" triumphalism, which was little more than the business class's romance of itself. It celebrates the rebirth of India, the releasing of repressed civilizational energies. But to cast contemporary India as a country belatedly freed of the shackles of autarky by a set of forward-thinking politicians and brave entrepreneurs is a bold try. It is true that many bureaucratic hindrances have been removed and that parts of India have benefited greatly from expanded international trade. What is eclipsed in such a rendering is the state's important role in developing the country's pipeline of tech-savvy, English-speaking labor; the very pipeline, that is, which allows India to reap the benefits of globalization.

By way of a backhanded compliment, an Indian executive acknowledges the state's contribution to education:

> I think the fact that India is doing relatively well despite the fact that we had all the wrong policies for a long time is just that, at least in the Nehruvian socialism, there was some peace and stability. And it allowed people to focus on education. And I think the only thing that Nehru gave us good was education. That allowed people to be in a good position when the knowledge boom came; people actually had some skill set. And now that we know what is working, we are trying to grapple away and get our policies in place. It's taking a lot time to get it there.

Thus they are quick to call upon the state to deliver a host of public goods from which the industry, incidentally, will also benefit. The two major concerns are infrastructure and the dearth of "employable" talent. In terms of the former, India spent $2 billion on its road network in 2004 as compared to the $30 billion spent by China.[20] As for talent, venture capitalist Vivek Paul said at an industry conference:

> To answer your question about labor availability, the entire IT and BPO business out of India constitutes less than 1 percent of the population in India. So as a result you have to ask yourself, if there's going to be a shortage of labor, that actually is a shortage of education capacity versus a shortage of labor.[21]

Thus the techno-populist slogan of the industry group, NASSCOM: *Roti, kapra, makan aur bijli and bandwidth* (food, clothing, housing, *and* electricity and bandwidth). *Roti, kapra, makan* was a popular political slogan in the 1970s—*bijli and bandwidth* is the industry's novel twist on that familiar theme. If business cosmopolitanism is the projection of the wish to be done with national strictures and limited expectations, techno-populism is its practical manifestation.

Executives view economic liberalization as consistent with development priorities. After an interview, the COO of one of India's leading outsourcing companies handed me a wire-bound copy of Will Durant's famous 1930 anticolonial tract, *The Case for India*. (Durant charges the British with no less than the "rape of a continent.") "Read this," he said, "it will teach you to take pride in India." He keeps a large stack of copies in his office. Globalization, he says, is in the national interest. It is a second independence. Chopra writes that "in the Nehruvian vision of independent India, scientific and technological progress was defined as essential to realizing India's unique modernity and destiny. A scientifically developed and socially progressive India was visualized as an embodiment of a timeless Indian ethos."[22] The industry's needs are grafted onto this historical narrative of national development.

Still, in a country that hosts about a third of the world's poor, the proper note of humility must be struck. One way of doing so is to argue that globalization-related wealth will trickle down to the poor. Vikram, an executive, describes himself as a "big free trader" and thinks that "all this talk" about the growing digital divide is "bullshit." Yet he has a real interest in the socioeconomic impact of outsourcing, arguing that the boom is percolating down to the lower classes. This can be seen, he says, in the increased purchasing power of workers as the money they spend most certainly finds it way back to the "villages." He also tells poor-boy-makes-good, Horatio Alger–like stories.

His former cleaning lady's son, for example, spoke English very well and dreamed of going to college. He had only a pair of slacks and a dirty shirt and worked at two tea stalls in the airport, earning around 3,000 rupees ($75) a month. Vikram's company hired him as an office administrator and he "basically made sure that there was paper in the printer, toilet paper in the bathroom, etc." They initially paid him 4,500 rupees ($110) but soon bumped his pay up to 7,000 ($172) as a result of his performance. And there was also the Dominoes Pizza delivery man who walked into Vikram's office and asked for a job. Admiring his initiative, they hired him and he quickly moved up the office chain. He eventually left the job because "it wasn't that challenging. His aspirations were in IT." This, Vikram says, is a case of someone who would have had a professional job but did not have the opportunity. Once given the chance, he excelled.

Another way to observe the trickle-down effect, says a BPO executive, is to consider "the overall employment generation including support staff." He reels off a list of people who support his office that "didn't have a job before or at least at the level they have now."[23] For all of these workers, this work is "much more valuable" than what they were doing before. According to the former executive Tyler Pfeiffer, his company employs 34 support personnel who earn between 30,000 rupees ($720) and 48,000 rupees ($1,155) a year. These individuals, he says as evidence of their modest backgrounds, mostly "don't speak English." (Extrapolating from these figures, the number of support staff employed by the industry could be around 29,500.)

Others argue that globalization is eroding status distinctions like caste. Whereas a typical Indian employer, Vikram says, would ask "a number of questions" about a prospective employee's family and caste background, outsourcing companies are equal opportunity employers and as such are unconcerned about social criteria in hiring. As the *Wall Street Journal* reports, "India's rapid economic expansion—and its booming high-tech sector—are beginning to chip away at the historical system that reserved well-paying jobs for upper castes and menial jobs for Dalits [untouchables]."[24] The article quotes the chairman of Microsoft India as saying, "We don't give a damn about any of these differences in caste or religion." Talent, he says, is all that matters. At a small IT service company I visited, 6 out of the 52 workers said they were from backward or scheduled castes. Says the company's CEO:

> I think the kind of people we hire, you would never hire otherwise. We are not hiring from the best schools, we are not hiring the best people. This because there's so much scarcity, we don't have too much flexibility. If we get somebody we have to hire them, it doesn't matter who he is. We have had developers that are barely able to speak a word of English and they're very good developers.[25]

Yet this is the exception to the rule; even the *Journal* reports that such instances are "rare."[26] A small survey of 150 workers I conducted found that 79 percent were Hindu, 84 percent of whom were of upper-caste or well-off middle-caste background. Another survey of IT workers found similarly that 86 percent came from upper castes or economically better-off communities.[27] This is because, while class and caste are not isomorphic, most Dalits are very poor, are discriminated against, and come from disadvantaged educational backgrounds. While the federal government reserves 23 percent of positions for Dalits and oppressed castes as part of an affirmative action program, only two private sector companies—Bharti Enterprises and Infosys—have said that they will also set aside jobs.[28] And even at multinational companies they often face biased recruiters. According to another study, informal barriers to employment like class and caste and most specifically parent's education mean that only "between 4 and 7 percent of rural Indians will qualify to gain entry."[29] Says an HR manager at a call center, "We hire from the middle, the higher middle class. Convent, private schools, good schools mostly. *The exceptions are very few.*"

An even larger problem with the trickle-down argument is that the industry remains at a remove from the domestic economy. According to consultants Gartner:

> India is one of the few countries in the world where the impact of the services export oriented business far outweighs that of the domestic

side. . . . The overall impact of ICT development in the country is skewed heavily around the unique dynamics of this services export trend, often to the detriment of the domestic opportunity.[30]

The COO of a BPO company discusses the limitations of outsourcing-generated employment: "It's too much hype. Travel and tourism have a bigger multiplier effect on the economy than the IT, ITES, and BPO sectors combined. In terms of jobs, it's a trickle. Where are the jobs going to come from? It's not a panacea for all ills." And Vikram's views on the digital divide aside, the country has extremely low rates of Internet and personal computer penetration.

Another factor to consider is the industry's dependence on the Western market. "Excessive dependence on outsourcing," writes D'Costa, "limits the synergy between vibrant domestic and foreign markets" and discourages "firms from taking on more complex projects at home."[31] Moreover, according to Taylor and Bain,

> The Indian outsourced sector emerged as a dependent niche market for developed nations' requirements. This reliance on labour arbitrage in the provision of low-value, standardized services was producing commoditization of the Indian industry . . . threatening profit margins and undermining efforts to diversify from mass production work.[32]

However globalized their supply chains, the ownership and corporate governance of multinational corporations "remain national rather than global. Shares are held by individuals and entities from the home country rather than from foreign countries. Most seats on the board of directors are held by home country nationals, enabling the retention of control within that country."[33] (Indeed, one study finds that fewer than half the firms in the Standard and Poor 500-stock index have a foreign national on their boards.)[34] This obtains for the ownership of intellectual property as well. In addition, most sophisticated work and R&D remains in the home country.

In other words, large multinationals have learned how to leverage the "flat" world to their advantage. Cross-border opportunities give corporations more power vis-à-vis the individual worker and the lower-level supplier. In terms of the latter, it carves out spaces for suppliers in developing countries, but they must understand their subordinate role in the global value chain. Large firms can use their considerable clout to demand that suppliers constantly cut costs and improve quality and productivity. (An ABN-AMRO contract with Infosys and Tata Consultancy Services, for example, includes a clause that mandates productivity gains.) *CIO* magazine suggests that companies use at least two subcontractors "and make them compete for your dollars."[35] And more and more suppliers are learning this lesson and acting in the same way. They are also beginning to outsource work to other developing countries like China, Sri Lanka, and the Philippines.[36]

Finally, the projection of past growth and employment rates into the future is likely to overstate the industry's real prospects, fueled as it is by inputs rather than innovation or efficiency. The pressing need for increased manpower suggests that the growth of the business services sector, impressive though it is, will only continue at the present rate as long as inputs also increase. But the doubling of the workforce cannot be repeated indefinitely.[37] Once the middle- and lower-middle-class "tranche" is exhausted, growth will likely slow. That is unless the industry advances technologically and becomes more productive and efficient.[38] The hope would seem to lie in the research and development centers created by a handful of multinationals, but not in input-driven, back-office services. As Baumol has argued, services are generally an area of limited productivity growth.[39] A strategy of brute informationalization cannot likely sustain growth at high rates over the long term. Nor can workers be squeezed much further.

Thus questions arise about gifting large incentives to a dependent industry that employs a relatively modest number of people. (At the generous estimate of 250 million, the "middle class" makes up 22 percent of the population.) Given that there is also no guarantee that the jobs will stay in India, Ross argues such concessions amount to the purchase of short-term employment.[40] According to Evalueserve, by 2010, India may become "too costly to provide low-end services at competitive costs."[41] As Vivek Paul put it, "We'll have to swallow the same medicine of globalization."[42] More generally, compared to its heavy spending on higher education, India invests a minuscule amount on primary education.[43] And while the Indian political establishment—spanning Hindu nationalists to secular moderates to reconstructed Communists—is largely supportive of economic liberalization and market reform, it is still unclear whether the large majority of the population has benefited. A report by the Indian Planning Commission's Special Group on Job Creation finds that "the number of jobs in the post-liberalization decade of the 1990s was less than a third of the corresponding number in the decade preceding liberalization."[44] The report predicts that, absent "corrective measures," the number of unemployed people will double to 45 million in the next five years.

Worker Internationalism

Labor's take on globalization is as sobering as capital's is euphoric. Although unions of all stripes are clamoring for "fair trade" and a more socially inclusive model of globalization, there is considerable disagreement about how best to realize these goals. Where technological advancements make it possible to move work seamlessly from Los Angeles to Bombay, does not the job security of the Angeleno vary in inverse relation to that of the Bombay-ite? What can fair trade possibly mean in a context where workers in developing countries have an interest in the insecurity of their counterparts in the developed world? The political opportunity structure for labor movements—at the national and transnational levels—has thus been altered significantly by globalization.

Organized labor has responded in essentially two ways to this situation. The first is largely domestic. Unions like the Communication Workers of America view offshoring as a threat to the job security of workers and the health of the U.S. economy. They brand companies that move work abroad "unpatriotic" and employ slogans such as "Keep Jobs in America." The AFL-CIO issued the following statement, which underlines the complexity of the issue: "We support raising living standards around the world, but we steadfastly reject and resist any notion that improving living standards elsewhere requires sacrificing good jobs and living standards for American workers and their families."[45] Likewise, the major Indian unions maintain a domestic focus. They say that they want outsourcing to continue as it provides jobs and foreign exchange and "are prepared to compromise on working conditions to make the country strong." Moreover, some unions along with the government have opposed the insertion of labor standards into trade agreements, coming out against, for example, the inclusion of a social clause at the World Trade Organization, arguing that it is motivated by "protectionist" intentions.

The second approach is internationalist. Unions of this persuasion argue that it makes little sense for unions to pursue an exclusively national agenda as the livelihoods of workers in developed and developing countries are linked through trade. There is a less a focus on stopping offshoring than on dealing with its consequences. While in India, I spent a considerable amount of time with a new union dedicated to organizing call center workers. Supranational in its conception, it is funded by a European nongovernmental organization. The purpose of the collaboration is to develop "rules and guidance for stakeholders for making offshoring sustainable in social and economic terms." The emerging consensus is to try to ensure that core labor rights are respected globally and to work toward some degree of uniformity in labor standards.

But while the *idea* of labor internationalism is very appealing, there are enormous obstacles to its realization. I have already mentioned the conceptual problems regarding conflicting interests in a global economy. In addition, unionization rates have been dropping steadily in the affected countries; labor laws everywhere are being "reformed"; and, while India is presently the global hub of offshore back-office services, China is not far behind, raising the specter of artificially depressed wages, poor working conditions, and the denial of labor rights.

False Consciousness and the Economy of Dystopia

Entering the offices of a union affiliated with the Communist Party of India, you have distinct the feeling that time stopped slightly before perestroika. Tables and desks and windows are all rimmed in bright red paint. Framed pictures of the Great Wall of China, Lenin, and a ponderous Ho Chi Minh with pen in hand, hang over doorways. My appointment is with the union secretary, a short bespectacled man in a windbreaker. A calendar pinned to the partition by his desk declares a more contemporary motto, "To fight global capital, global unity of workers."

None of the Indian trade unions say they are against international outsourcing. They do, however, have major misgivings about the political-economic framework in which it occurs. "There has been a serious development in the country for 10 to 15 years," the secretary says gravely. "All labor laws have been put on hold to face international competition. Hire and fire with social security and unemployment [insurance] is one thing. Without it, it's different. There's nothing to fall back on." Similarly, an official of a rival union points to things like privatization and voluntary retirement schemes. "We are opposing this tooth and nail, brother. Like hire and fire in your country," he says, pointing an accusatory finger. The government is of little help; its mind-set, the secretary says with understatement, is "not to indulge trade unions." And it is within this "framework that they've started BPO/ITES."

This strategy, he says, is being influenced by the reality of widespread unemployment: "The government feels like this is the best way create employment, for the jobs come to us." But while the "profitability of MNCs is increased, the country is not getting a share. For every dollar earned in America, only 30 cents comes to India. They are free from all income taxes. This is the law of the jungle now: 'Let the market prevail.' This is going to be counterproductive, Shehzad *bhai*." By "putting all eggs in one basket, in exports," moreover, the country is "vulnerable to ups and downs in American and European markets. China is doing far better; their domestic market is growing. Here the domestic market is growing only for a section of people." The government, he says, wants to promote India as a superpower in IT, which is "propaganda" for the privileged classes. While acknowledging that "BPO and IT are contributing a lot to GDP," he says they want a fairer distribution of the spoils.

Foreign capital is thus predatory; corporations "are making money at the cost of the people, the country." But perhaps the proper metaphor is not of a vulture circling overhead, but of a mother nurturing her child into lifelong dependence and incomplete individuality. Under Western tutelage, India moves forward but is held back. Globalization may signify a new "tryst with destiny," but it can only be redeemed on Western terms.

Work sites are branded electronic sweatshops and workers, cybercoolies.[46] But the stridency of the critique is qualified by a number of factors, such as the individualism of the workforce and its privileged employment base, the supply-demand imbalance that results in rising wages and decent work conditions, and the possibility of capital flight. Unions regard workers' individualism and indifference to unions as a species of false consciousness—the inability to understand the true conditions of one's productive existence. "For him the entire world is in the screen. It's like a prison he works in," says a call center worker and union member. High pay and free or subsidized transportation and food merely gloss over this fact: "They have that, but if you go into the employee, you'll find the problems." Writes a trade union official:

> A worker who performs duties in a call center would not like the use of the term "worker" to denote him/her, since the business puts the "respectable" tag of "executive." The use of the term "worker" does not go well with the neatly clad young men/women in their twenties working in cosy shops littered with computers and modern equipment that gives an ambience entirely different from the floors of a factory. They would rather like to be called IT professionals or knowledge professionals. . . . Yet, all this does not obliterate the fact that they are skilled labour working for a firm, hired by the management to expend labour for some hours under a set of rules framed by the management.[47]

Higher-than-average salaries, says another official, "lead to a false status": "There is no trade union movement in the IT industry. They're exploited. They get money but they're overworked. They are very upset but are afraid to speak out. There is no bar to forming a union. But they don't come near us because they're high paid." Workers do have a myriad of complaints, but the salaries they draw and their impressive titles convince them that they are upwardly mobile professionals and not downtrodden workers in need of collective organization. Such titles are also a corporate strategy to push workers outside the purview of labor laws: "Workmen" are covered; those performing managerial functions or entrepreneurial roles are not. In adopting the professional title, workers "forfeit rights for an intangible sense of status and social standing. . . . I don't mean to sound cruel, but if that's what they want, then I don't care. Go exploit yourself. I can't help you if you don't want to help yourself."

False consciousness is further exacerbated by the nature of the work. Whereas with the physical stress of manual labor "you feel it now," you experience "mental stress after some time," says an organizer. "This is the new economy," says another. "Physical exertion is self-evident. The long-term repercussions of mental stress are not." Of his son who works 12 hours a day in the IT industry, a union secretary says,

> The flexibility's there, but it's brainwork. I tell my son that the brain takes 80 percent of our blood circulation. If you go on taxing your brain like this, it will result in the long-term damage to the mind. At any other job, you stay up to 35 years. Not here. Safety is becoming a big problem; especially for girls. [The murder of a call center worker by her driver] was one incident; it showed how vulnerable they are.

Another official says that because outsourcing is new, "the health hazard impact has not been felt." Only later will workers begin to complain about "neck pain and chest pain. All these complaints will come. Youngsters are running a race; only after the race will they get tired. Today they are insensitive."

But even unions are afraid of capital flight, an example of what Jameson has called "the anxiety of Utopia," the fear of what would happen if their designs (to organize a majority of workers and bargain up wages and conditions) were fully realized.[48] They have thus scaled back their ambitions: modest organizing goals mixed with occasional agitation. It is a market-friendly strategy of "sustainable globalization." As an official of a Communist union puts it, "Our slogan is defend the industry, defend the interest of the worker. Both we follow, other trade unions don't. Industry has to grow and flourish, but a share of the profit has to come." The major unions are concerned about labor issues in the industry but generally feel that outsourcing employees are better off than other workers. Organizing them is not a top priority though they announce their intention to do so repeatedly in the press. As the same official explains, "Workers in IT and BPO aren't coming nearer to us. *We are there to lead them.* They are fearing that they will lose their jobs. We are now trying to go nearer to them. The possibilities are there."

It is from this Leninist approach that the new union dedicated to organizing ICT workers seeks to distance itself. As a participant at their executive council meeting in 2006 argued, "We must project the organization as something completely new." The reason for this recasting is that the political environment is currently hostile to unions, which "are seen as anticompany and antiestablishment." If they project themselves as free and democratic, they think, industry will prefer them to unions on the Communist left. The goal is to reach a point where employers are confident in the union as an honest broker, a point forcefully made at the meeting by a scholar and union advocate. He recalls meeting with the president of a large Indian IT firm and discussing the idea of unionization with him. The president viewed trade unions as ruinous rabble-rousers: "He said, 'For god's sake don't do this, not in my company, you'll spoil everything.' *That is the name we have and we need to remove it.*" The scholar-advocate advises the union not to dwell on the negatives. "Then you're challenging the employer. Then you're putting the employer on the defensive. You should appeal to them."

Traditional unions are portrayed as self-interested and combative. Someone says they sometimes function like "gangster organizations." Their attitude is that "my nose is more important than your job." The new union, by contrast, does not "want to sacrifice jobs to grow [its] strength." They should "take a different tack." They "don't have to show brawn or strength, we're dealing with knowledge workers. Not that we're losing our trade union values." For a slogan, someone suggests "Mobilize the intellectual capital in India."[49] Another proffers:

"Adding human value to the techno-culture." But there is one dissent. "It's hardcore union activity, brothers and sisters," says a veteran unionist. "We need a direct message. We're gathering people who have nothing to lose but their chains. 'You can't do it alone. You have to do it together.' That's it. We have to give a straightforward meaning." The consensus that emerges is to emphasize the immutably social character of labor. Unionists juxtapose workplace alienation with the possibility of a sense of "belonging, happiness, and security and power." As an organizer says:

> You're all doing routine, repetitive things where there isn't much satisfaction. You're tied down to technology. You are being individualized, compartmentalized. Money will not give you satisfaction. It will only reduce your dissatisfaction. We have to counter this. . . . You merely exchange words, you don't exchange feelings. That is something we have to exploit. Trade unions mean working collectively to achieve satisfaction. . . . How do you understand others? For you, this is through the screen. You are dealing with U.S. customers, how they treat you. What type of relationship are we trying to promote? Social needs where you want others to recognize you. In the BPO sector, workers have this need . . . to be recognized by your other employees.

In addition to satisfying the need for respect and recognition, organizers also seek to attend to workers' health issues. Employees complain of burning eyes from staring at monitors. In Bangalore, one worker says, most companies are sharing headsets: "We are landing into ear infections." Organizing campaigns could include eye and ear checkups, suggests a union member, so workers see that the union is also looking out for their welfare. And in the heady atmosphere, another suggests that eventually they could offer some form of "health insurance based on ear and eyes." Additionally, someone suggests the union try to educate workers' families, as "night work creates social problems in the house. Workers are becoming self-centered, aloof. They need some sort of counseling. . . . A trade union of a new type needs to handle this."

The comparatively good conditions of work also pose problems for organizers. As a government minister told me, they have "air-conditioned offices, free lunch, disco parties, and bonuses." Why would they need a trade union? According to a union member and organizer, "When you ask workers about unions, they ask why. It's Indian psychology: how's it going to benefit me?" The union's answer is that it is "shortsighted to see today's condition as something that is permanent. What's green today may be brown tomorrow. There is no guarantee that what has happened in the U.S., U.K., and Canada won't happen here." That is, they need to prepare members for the possibility of job flight, as one "cannot expect these jobs to be here forever." Additionally, an organizer says that "we need to prepare ourselves for a situation where the gap between supply and demand is not so large."

The response to both these dilemmas is to promote upskilling and technical training. Only a highly skilled workforce can ensure its own long-term employability—a sentiment that duplicates, albeit in a different moral register, loose free trade talk about employees' responsibility for losing their jobs. (As a consultant says of globalization's losers, "Shame on them for not developing their skills in seven years.") They consider offering skills training and even language classes in German and Spanish to appeal to an expanded service market. The union should work "hand in hand" with workers and industry on creating job security and a safety net, which would include things like retirement benefits. As workers are young, the union could offer to help them manage their funds, an innocent if ominous suggestion. "Contribute something toward your future." "Maintain the value of your investment." It is scarcely the diction of proletarian revolt.

Organizers "strive to create a distinct and cogent link between employees and employers at all levels." The emphasis is on cooperation rather than confrontation with management. They consider the possibility of a training-cum-placement service, where companies will actually go through the union to hire. They also discuss approaching companies about how to reduce turnover. The idea is to tread lightly. "We should work like a honeybee. The bee is the union, the flower is industry, the honey is profit," says an organizer. There is also a calculated appeal to nationalism: "The concepts of 'value addition' and 'intellectual capital' will ensure that the industry remains in India. All decision-making is over there. The heads of BPOs don't realize this. We have to bring this point to them in a more professional way."

To date, the union's progress has been slow. Despite the discursive fine-tuning, call center workers continue to see themselves as call center executives. In their main office, organizers have begun an experiment in creating a new BPO workforce that is more amenable to organizing. Each week a crowd of mostly female Dalits (untouchables) show up for computer literacy classes. They acknowledge that it is unlikely that these aspirants will ever land jobs in the BPO industry—mostly because they do not know English—but still feel that it may help them advance economically in some way. They have also had what they call a constructive meeting with the president of NASSCOM.

But despite the attempt to appeal to the good sense of companies, the union recognizes that its most persuasive framing device lies in exposing the seamy side of things; that is, in an *economy of dystopia*. At times the union office seems a clearinghouse for all that is unsavory about the industry. An official tells me about a call center worker who was beaten bloody by his manager when he tried to quit. They are organizing an event to commemorate the anniversary of the death of an HP worker who was murdered by her driver. (They held a candlelight vigil outside HP offices after the actual incident.) A news article is posted on their website about a 29-year-old call center worker who was struck and killed by a call center vehicle outside the gates of Bangalore University. "Ironically," the article wryly notes, the cab that hit him was from the same company that he worked for.

In the end, there is something ironic about the union itself. Because of the threat of capital flight, it must promote the very industry it stridently criticizes. It no longer uses terms like cyber-coolie, as it knows workers find them demeaning, but the union seems to feel that most call centers *are* "electronic sweatshops." Yet organizers know that exploitative conditions and the cheapness of labor are the country's chief comparative advantage. Rectify the conditions and bargain up the wages and companies may abscond. The union is not bent upon killing the golden goose, as critics allege, but wants to spread the lucre around. It is a delicate balance. But, again, I am writing *as if* the union exercised any real clout, as if it could bargain up wages and conditions so high that India would lose its cost advantage. A union seeking "partnership" with industry is especially unlikely to have any such effect. Its chief advantage, however, is that it is powered not by a message of resentment but one of inclusivity. And so, if it gains traction among workers, the industry cannot afford to ignore it.

CONCLUSION

There is a line in Kafka's diaries that reads, "'You are reserved for a great Monday.' Fine, but Sunday will never end."[1] I can think of no better way to summarize the general tenor of this book, no better way to synthesize the bubbling optimism and stoical cynicism we encountered early on in the figures of Prashant and Anil. Monday dangles tantalizingly on a near branch like an impossibly sweet fruit, but it is forever out of reach however much we grasp and drool. So it is with globalization's promises and India's "New Economic Policy." Is there a way out of this cycle? I do not know. But there may be ways of working through the impasse.

At the small call center I described at the beginning of chapter 4, I met Vishal, a tall, bleary-eyed 49-year-old who had been with the company for almost a year. Part of an experimental "senior shift" (49 is positively antique in this industry), Vishal was not very good at his work, and his monthly income of 6,000 rupees ($150) for 30 hours of work each week was in the control of his ailing, widowed mother, who subsisted mainly on a government pension. His glasses were coated with a thick film of dust that hid his enlarged, farsighted eyes. Vishal's manner was somewhat shabby and he inspired sympathy, if not pity. Yet he carried himself with a strange dignity. He spoke softly in regular conversation but on the phone his voice soared to an almost breathless yell. He would boom his opening lines—"Is this Mr. Leahy?!"— in such a loud and transparently Anglicized voice that the room seemed to shake. (One week of communication training had done little to smooth out the rough edges.) He was confused and delighted by the people he called. His greatest discovery about Americans was that wives fear their husbands: "They'll say, 'No, I don't think he'll want to talk to you.' It's like they're afraid," he said with a sweet chuckle. At the end of his shift he stood at attention and, addressing me, said, "Excuse me, sir, but I must be leaving," and with a soldier's salute, he marched into the night.

What are we to make of this office oddball? He would sit, scream his lines . . . and fail. Repeatedly. Endlessly. Loudly. Well, actually, he made a few sales; enough perhaps to justify his meager paycheck. He seemed a special kind of fool. But one line unlocked his mystery for me and uncovered his inner Bartleby. The Bartleby of Melville's famous short story, you may recall, was employed by a Wall Street lawyer as a copyist. He worked diligently, at least compared to the other two erratic employees, but one day things changed. When asked by his boss to examine a short document, Bartleby replied in "a singularly mild, firm voice," "I would prefer not to." The number of things that he preferred not to do escalated to the point that he did nearly nothing.[2]

When I asked Vishal how he felt about having to take a false name ("Peter"), he said simply, "I do not care as long they don't call me by it." He is none too bothered so long as he retains control over his self-definition.[3] This much is fine. But his position makes nonsense of the company's identity-shifting requirement. What good is a false name if customers cannot use it? At some point, someone would no doubt call him Peter. What then? Would he get enraged and slam down the receiver? Or perhaps curse him or her under his breath? When it did happen, he did nothing. He preferred not to care. Between West and East, original and copy, he refused to choose and this gave him an absurd kind of freedom.[4]

It may seem a stretch but I think Vishal's shrugging dismissal of dualistic dilemmas is helpful not only in addressing the problems of personal identity but also in thinking about larger issues like development, in the mode of Roberto Unger's "antinecessitarian" philosophy. (According to D. H. Lawrence, "Below what we think we are / we are something else / we are almost anything.") Seeking a left alternative to Marxism and social democracy, Unger encourages a "restless experimentation with institutions, ideas, and techniques for the sake of enhancing our practical capabilities."[5] Such a playful and joyful affirmation of what Bergson called the "perpetual creation of possibilities" can help us avoid the many false choices we are confronted with, such as that between free market radicalism and protectionist populism.[6] The prevailing policies, however, fall short of the goals of individual and collective empowerment, aspirations that are enshrined in the Indian Constitution.

Economic and Cultural Divides

> We now have the kind of government that is oriented towards the export ghetto of the economy on the false assumption that this can become the locomotive that will somehow drive the rest of society. For the rest of society it offers just a sort of charitable benevolence, the crumbs off the table.
>
> —*Roberto Unger*[7]

India has been cast as an unlikely, even "roaring" capitalist success story. Breaking the shell of its quasi-socialist past, it has been selectively integrated into the global economy, as its impressive economic growth over recent years attests. But the questions arise: is the industry sustainable and what are its implications for national development? Even industry backers recognize that flexible labor laws and special economic zones are short-term tactics and do not constitute a coherent development strategy. (Tax holidays, like all vacations from responsibility, cannot last forever.) Moreover, 88 percent of Indians work in the informal economy and are mostly excluded from export-oriented activity.[8] (Around 65 percent of Indians do not have bank accounts.) The offshore sector is an exception to national laws and regulations. Thus a trade union official said testily about the limits of concessions they are willing to make to foreign capital, "You can come here and invest but you have to follow the law of the country."

Moreover, the gains from trade must be put in the context of rising inequalities. The unevenness of globalization is nowhere more evident than in its differential impact on urban and rural areas. An issue of *India Today* in February 2006 reports on an outsourcing sector in which wages are rising astronomically and IT professionals are being gifted Mercedes as bonuses and incentives. But the same issue also details an epidemic of suicides among indebted Indian cotton farmers, the combined result of a local system of debt peonage, corporatized agriculture, and unequal trade relations. In 2008 alone, there were 16,196 reported farmer suicides, bringing the total since 1997 to an astonishing 199,132, according to the National Crime Records Bureau. (In a cruelly ironic twist, many of the farmers ended their lives by drinking the very pesticide that was intended to boost crop productivity.)[9] It is almost as if the reportage is of two different countries: one in which the skyscrapers of the "sunrise sector" point toward the heavens and another in which gazes are directed humbly downward to the barren soil.

When conducting interviews, I remember being baffled by a comment made by a HR manager. "This is the first time in India that there are more jobs than workers," he said. India currently has an unemployment rate of 10.7 percent. According to a World Bank estimate in 2005, 42 percent of Indians live below the international poverty line of $1.25 a day. The National Commission for Enterprises in the Unorganised Sector (NCEUS) estimates that 77 percent of Indians—about 836 million people—live on less than half a dollar a day.[10] Four hundred and twenty million Indians, 92 percent of India's total workforce, find precarious work as agricultural laborers, small farmers, and street vendors, or toil in brick kilns and quarries. So what, pray tell, is the HR manager talking about?

The manager may be forgiven his *bêtise*, for the economic divide is also a cultural one, and the rifts reinforce each other. Walter Bagehot once said that "poverty is an anomaly to rich people; it is very difficult to make out why people who want dinner do not ring the bell," and it is the same sort of cluelessness that informs the manager's remark.[11] He is talking about the world from a perspective where there may indeed be more jobs than workers, a place increasingly enclaved and walled-off from the rest of India. The same could be said of the COO who, in chapter 3, cheekily confessed his desire for a dictatorship that would be able to sidestep democratic niceties in shoring up India's technological infrastructure.

They ignore what the NCEUS describes as "the India of the Common People, [which] constitut[es] more than three-fourths of the population and consist[s] of all those whom the growth has, by and large, bypassed."[12] The "two worlds" thesis may be overly simplistic—India is of course composed of many different worlds—but the gaping inequalities give the notion some real-life credibility. As it stands, globalization in India rests on a thin social base. For it to be sustainable in the long term, its benefits must reach much deeper. As Amsden writes, historically, "capital formation and poverty alleviation went hand in hand; one created capable people and one created jobs to employ them."[13] Economic reforms that benefit specific class segments to the exclusion of others reinforce already existing divides.

So while India has certainly made the most of the expanded opportunities in global trade, Amartya Sen argues that it is important

> to avoid the much-aired simplification that argues that all India needs to do to achieve fast economic growth and speedy reduction of poverty is greater reliance on the global market and international trade. This reflects, in fact, a serious misreading of the variety of factors that have contributed to the kind of economic success achieved in China, South Korea, Thailand, and other countries in East and South East Asia. These countries did emphasize international trade. . . . But they also made it possible to have broad-based participation in economic expansion, through such policies as extensive schooling and high literacy, good health care, widespread land reforms, and considerable fostering of gender equity (not least through female education and employment).[14]

One has no special quarrel with state actions intended to improve the lot of the middle class—educated unemployment and underemployment are real problems—but there are trade-offs. As P. Sainath writes, "In 60 years, we haven't managed—except in three States—to push through any serious land reforms or tenancy reforms. But we can clear a Special Economic Zone in six months."[15] As a result of public disinvestment, the agricultural growth rate has declined steeply in the post-1991 era, and people are increasingly turning to overcrowded cities for employment.[16] And despite all the fretting about "good business climates," the opening of the country to trade does not require as its condition or corollary the gutting of labor laws, the withering of public investment in agriculture, deregulation, or class-biased economic growth, among other things.

The great irony about the economic reforms is that India's educational and technological and skills infrastructure was built in large part on a nationalist-minded attitude toward development.[17] Now the entrepreneurial class says it wants the state to stay out of its business. Bhabha's observation that it is "forgetting—a minus in the origin— that constitutes the beginning of the nation's narrative" helps us interpret discussion about India's "second independence."[18] For the country to genuinely begin anew, the state interventionism that characterized the independence to prereform era has to be repudiated, denied, and ultimately excised from the record. The state as such is an ontological scandal; its aggressive intervention (as opposed to the passive facilitation of capital) is an affront to the preferred ideological narrative.

Yet, at the same time, the business class wants reformed labor laws, guaranteed power, land subsidies, tax holidays, and greater investment in education to forestall an impending skills shortage. While the state obliges, it simultaneously deserts public arenas. As UN-Habitat points out in its report *The Challenge of Slums*, "The main cause of increases in poverty and inequality during the 1980s and 1990s was the retreat of the state."[19] Despite a growth rate of around 8 percent, India spends only 1.2 percent of its GDP on health expenditures, according to UN figures.[20] Since the mid-1990s, hunger and household-level food insecurity have increased. India has the largest number of undernourished people in the world and one of the highest levels of child malnutrition.[21] And while 563.7 million Indians have cellphones, only 366 million have access to modern sanitation.[22]

Thus some sectors of the economy are neglected while others are pampered like newborn children. The question then becomes: in what direction should state efforts be directed? Towards the maximization of global trade or the maximization of economic opportunities for a broad range of the populace? Towards expanded opportunities for the poor and the majority of the population who reside in the countryside, or towards expanded employment for the educated middle class? More broadly, will economic strategy stress adherence to a "Washington Consensus" that counsels countries to stabilize, privatize, and liberalize?[23] (Even China, which routinely defies the consensus, is finding it difficult to step out from the Western shadow. As Hung argues, "The PRC's export-oriented growth and vast dollar reserves have trapped it in a subordinate role—to which much of its elite remains committed.")[24] Or are unique and diverse paths of development possible?[25]

Outsourcing has always been driven by an imperative to cut labor costs; offshoring takes this rule to a catchpenny extreme. What recent business developments suggest is that more and more types of work will be globally dispersed. And workers in developed countries will increasingly be put into competition with their counterparts in poor nations on the basis of cost. For developed economies, the immediate concern is how to handle job losses. A longer-term and more pressing matter is the impact of trade on wages and labor conditions.

But perhaps even more lasting may be the effect of the outsourcing debate on the attitudes of business, policymakers, and the citizenry. Market liberals triumphantly declare that they have won the outsourcing debate. As one Indian executive turned American venture capitalist put it, "The backlash is over. It's finished." Backed by economists, business groups, politicians, and editorial boards, this expansion into the white-collar realm is depicted as inevitable. It signals the naturalization of offshoring; that is, the casting of concrete decisions by corporations to send work overseas as inevitable. It is a confirmation of a way of thinking that delegitimizes the state—it is to stand out of the way and do nothing (except, perhaps, reverse its previous misdeeds), as if this is the way things always have been and will be.

CEOs that offshore work are no longer so many Benedict Arnolds but rather patriotic citizens doing what is best for America (in the eyes of shareholders and politicians, at least) and whose efforts might even have the philanthropic benefit of job creation in the developing world. At the very least, views that just a few decades ago would have elicited great concern will cease to surprise. I recall a well-heeled corporate consultant telling a group of outsourcers that the mainstream climate in 2005 was such that outsourcing resulted in negative publicity and was "presidential political fodder." Between the years 2006 and 2010, she said, there will be some "activist opposition," but it will be dwarfed by a "general acceptance of globalization." Similarly, when I asked the founder of a legal services company if clients are wary of negative publicity, he said that "in the boardroom, behind closed doors, every CEO or executive is asking why they're not on Lou Dobbs' list. We've used that list to market ourselves; it's a fantastic resource. Leading companies are on the list."

In this light, the key task ahead is to denaturalize globalization and to construct alternative paths of development that allow for experimentation and creativity. Moreover, the prevailing desire for economic growth must be situated within a broader framework in which social goals can be pursued simultaneously. (Even the World Bank recognizes this: "To be sustainable, economic growth must be constantly nourished by the fruits of human development. Conversely, slow human development can put an end to fast economic growth.")[26] The children's story about the hare and tortoise is here instructive: short-term returns, however impressive, are no substitute for a considered, long-term development strategy. In other words, economic growth should be recognized not as an end in itself but as a means toward the realization of diverse human potentialities.

Research Methods

Too often, globalization is conceived of as a singular and inexorable process. We are constantly beset by provocative but simplistic questions about its effects: Is it flattening the world or producing new inequalities? Homogenizing it or intensifying difference? For such questions there are no easy answers. It is exceedingly difficult to study globalization *in general* because it is not a unitary phenomenon. It is possible, however, to study its particular figurations. The case study method is useful in that it allows you to explore large-scale processes in concrete detail. So while it is true that global forces are helping to redefine social relations, I tried to remain attentive to the ways in which they are collectively and politically constructed on the ground.[1] That is to say, globalization is not merely "localized." Rather, the global and the local are mutually constituted.[2]

The bulk of this book is based on fieldwork conducted between March 2005 and September 2006. In total, 129 semi- and unstructured interviews were conducted with workers, managers, employers, and trade unionists in India and the United States. (Some follow-up interviews were conducted in New York in 2009.) As offshoring is beginning to affect different segments of white-collar work, my goal was to cover different steps on what is called the service value ladder. No single company in India handled the full range of services, and so I thought it best to cast my net widely. In India, most of the fieldwork took place at four outsourcing companies, which were selected from a list provided by the National Association of Software and Service Companies. While I do not claim that the firms are representative of the entire industry, I do try to capture the range of diversity across the sector.

Three of the selected companies provide Business Process Outsourcing (BPO) and IT-enabled services (ITES), which includes customer support and back-office, financial, and legal services, while the fourth is the IT subsidiary of an investment bank. While they are often treated separately in the literature, the comparison is useful analytically in that we are able to see, for example, how time is "compressed" in one and "stretched" in the other. It also allows subtler distinctions to be made regarding the class and social background of workers— something the vague term *middle class* obscures. The firms, moreover, are located in four of India's outsourcing hubs—Delhi, Bangalore, Bombay, and Chennai—and this diversity provides a broader view of globalization's effects on the built and social landscape than would a study restricted to a single location.

As for the subjects, the majority of workers were in their midtwenties, and the gender ratio was close to 60:40 favoring men, with the caveat that men were overrepresented in management. Most employees, with the exception of those at the IT subsidiary, work the permanent night shift so that they are able to communicate directly with Western customers and clients. I used snowball sampling, relying on worker and employer networks, to arrange additional interviews in order to test the general applicability of my findings. These included interviews with top-level executives and managers at other outsourcing firms as well as with industry representatives.

I also conducted interviews with trade unions. In the case of the established unions, these were mostly with union officials as there were very few rank-and-file unionists to speak of in the outsourcing industry. Consequently, much of the discussion centered on how the organized Left should deal with the burgeoning sector. Fortunately, I came across a new union dedicated to organizing BPO and IT workers. I attended two of the union's executive meetings, which provided insight into its overall strategy. I also visited a regional office a few times, which allowed me to look at efforts to implement that strategy. Additionally, I spoke informally with support personnel (e.g., drivers of vehicles used by outsourcing companies, canteen staff, and maintenance workers) at a few outsourcing companies to help gauge the broader effects of the industry.

While the emphasis was not on the broad political-economy of globalization, I do believe that commodity chain analysis is useful in concretely tracing transnational flows. Illustrating how production and service "networks are situationally specific, socially constructed, and locally integrated," moreover, is especially important in demystifying globalization.[3] Consequently, I interviewed personnel at the home and client offices of companies that I visited in India. First, visiting the U.S. offices allowed me to better understand how offshoring works. It provided insight into the types of work being moved and how global processes are managed locally. It also shed light on the ways in which particular managerial techniques and values are exported to developing countries. I also attended four outsourcing industry conferences in New York City, which allowed me to observe candid discussions about the benefits and pitfalls of offshoring. They also helped situate my interviews within a broader context.

While the interviews often focused on workers' and employers' subjectivity, identities are of course relational.[4] Or as Montaigne put it, "Others form man."[5] To properly understand the process of identity formation, one must attend to a variety of factors that influence self-perceptions. In the workplace, I interviewed HR managers, supervisors, and executives. As societal and familial perceptions exercise considerable influence, I spent time with workers in a variety of settings, from homes to malls, cafés, and nightclubs. This was also necessitated by the restrictive nature of some of the interviews, as subjects were sometimes handpicked by managers. While even these subjects could be remarkably frank about their hopes and disappointments, the workplace setting has certain inherent limitations. At one company I was not allowed to observe the labor process for long periods as it would breach client privacy agreements, or so I was told. And in some cases, I was not permitted to record conversations on company premises. Given the difficulty of gaining access, these are constraints I had to accept.

If, as Geertz writes, the field "is a powerful disciplinary force: assertive, demanding, and even coercive," how then to surmount the epistemic instability?[6] I did my best. In the event that I could not spend time with workers in the office or canteen, we met outside. And when I could not record I took copious notes. Even this imperfect method was not foolproof. Early on (mercifully), I lost one of my notebooks on a night train to Agra and spent the next sleepless night transcribing from memory. Substitutes, I know, but is this not oddly consistent with my overall theme? I mimicked a tape recorder and, in the last case, my memory mimicked a lost notebook, which mimicked interviews.

Another thematic coincidence: the convention of changing names to preserve anonymity. Like a roman à clef, this book is composed of characters that have different names than their real-world originals. And names are not all that change as any act of representation involves some departure from verisimilitude. To make sense of a fluid reality we abstract some things and delete others and string the choice elements together to create narratives and arguments. To craft this book, I coded transcripts and field notes thematically. This made it easier to analyze the genial jabberings and gesticulations, the "discourse," of my subjects.[7] Abstract notions like identity, professionalism, and class consciousness came into clearer view when I took them as lived experiences (rather than coded categories imposed from on high). Individual subjects were chosen for inclusion in the interest of providing a balanced and nuanced account of the industry and its effects. I also tried to heed Briggs's emphasis on reflexivity, though, initially, this made me a tad stiff and self-conscious.[8] My experience supports Flyvbjerg's observation that researchers engaged in in-depth case studies "typically report that their preconceived views, assumptions, concepts, and hypotheses were wrong and that the case material forces them to revise their hypotheses on essential points."[9] While my analytical approach was inductive in that I tried to keep an open mind to the ways in which people's lives are altered by economic change, my ideas, too, took on strange new shapes in the field.

While there are inherent limits to the "generalizability" of case studies, I did find the field—with its opportunities for intense observation—to be a fruitful ground for generating ideas and even theorizing, and so have many others.[10] Indeed, my foray into survey research—I conducted a survey of 150 Indian workers at work sites—provided useful data on the demographics of the workforce, among other things, but failed to produce many compelling insights. That is to say, it did not shed adequate light on people's "situational self-interpretation," something that was central to my research goals.[11] Consequently, I rely heavily on interviews and observations. My findings also have multiple sources of support in the secondary literature. Particularly, I draw on the scholarly literature on workplace culture, identity, labor discipline, modernity, and globalization. I also became very well acquainted—too well for my liking—with the various media, marketing, and sales materials on the subject. This proved vital in keeping abreast of industry-wide trends in things like salaries and the labor market situation. Finally, the analysis, particularly in the opening chapters, is also informed by a review of over 300 U.S. and Indian English-language newspaper articles on outsourcing from 2000 to the present.

Notes

Introduction

1. Paul Krugman, *The Accidental Theorist* (New York: Norton, 1999).

2. Brendan Burchell, David Ladipo, and Frank Wilkinson, eds., *Job Insecurity and Work Intensification* (London: Routledge, 2002); Edmund Heery and John Salmon, eds., *The Insecure Workforce* (London: Routledge, 2002); Arne L. Kalleberg, "Precarious Work, Insecure Workers: Employment Relations in Transition," *American Sociological Review* 74(1):1–22 (2009); Vicki Smith, *Crossing the Great Divide: Worker Risk and Opportunity in the New Economy* (Ithaca, N.Y.: Cornell University Press, 2002).

3. Ulrich Beck, *The Brave New World of Work* (Malden, Mass.: Blackwell, 2000).

4. David Brady, Jason Beckfield, and Wei Zhao, "The Consequences of Economic Globalization for Affluent Democracies," *Annual Review of Sociology* 33:313–34 (2007).

5. The term *globalization* covers both "offshoring," the movement of work abroad through subsidiaries, and "international outsourcing," which denotes the subcontracting of foreign firms.

6. Manjeet Kripalani, "Satyam Revelation Rocks Indian Markets," *BusinessWeek*, January 8, 2009:14.

7. Florian-Arun Taube, "Transnational Networks and the Evolution of the Indian Software Industry: The Role of Culture and Ethnicity," in Dirk Fornahl, Christen Zellner, and David B. Audretsch, eds., *The Role of Labour Mobility and Informal Networks for Knowledge Transfer* (New York: Springer, 2005), 115.

8. There are also cases of credit card fraud and data and identity pilfering at outsourcing companies. Satyam itself had been barred from World Bank contracts in late 2008 on the suspicion that it had installed spyware on some of the agency's computers. It was also accused of providing "improper benefits" to bank staff, among other things. None of these were scandals in their own right, but cumulatively they cast a pall on the earlier enthusiasm for the new postindustrial India. On rationalization, see Yong Suk Jang, "Transparent Accounting as World Societal Rule," in Gili S. Drori, John W. Meyer, and Hokyu Hwang, eds., *Globalization and Organization* (Oxford: Oxford University Press, 2006), 167–95; John Meyer, John Boli, George Thomas, and Francisco Ramirez, "World Society and the Nation State," *American Journal of Sociology* 103(1):144–81 (1997).

9. In 1999, a credulous Lawrence Summers, then deputy Treasury secre-

tary and now director of Obama's National Economic Council, said of transparency in corporate accounting: "If you ask why the American financial system succeeds, at least my reading of the history would be that there is no innovation more important than that of generally accepted accounting principles: it means that every investor gets to see information presented on a comparable basis; that there is discipline on company managements in the way they report and monitor their activities" (quoted in Paul Krugman, "The Big Zero," *New York Times*, December 28, 2009:A27. See also Haridimous Tsoukas, *Complex Knowledge: Studies in Organizational Epistemology* (Oxford: Oxford University Press, 2005).

10. Max Weber, *The Protestant Ethic and the Spirit of Capitalism* (New York: Penguin, 2002 [1905]).

11. Nietzsche was a particularly astute observer of this: "The course of logical thoughts and inferences in our brains today corresponds to a process and battle of drives that taken separately are all over illogical and unjust" (*The Gay Science* [Cambridge: Cambridge University Press, 2001], 120). According to Hume, "Reason and sentiment concur in almost all moral determinations and conclusions" (*An Enquiry Concerning the Principles of Morals* [Oxford: Oxford University Press, 2006 (1751)], 5).

12. George Akerlof and Robert Schiller, *Animal Spirits: How Human Psychology Drives the Economy, and Why It Matters for Global Capitalism* (Princeton: Princeton University Press, 2009).

13. So politically sensitive is the matter in the United States and Europe that subcontractors often have to sign confidentiality agreements that bar them from revealing their clients' names publicly.

14. Francis Fukuyama loudly proclaims the first view: "There has emerged in the last few centuries something like a true global culture, centering around technologically driven economic growth and the capitalist social relations necessary to produce and sustain it" (*The End of History and the Last Man* [New York: Harper Perennial, 1993], 126).

15. In its fascination with "hybrid," "negotiated," "fluid" identities, this school too often sidelines issues of power. See Achille Mbembe, *On the Postcolony* (Berkeley: University of California Press, 2001), 5.

16. Hence George Ritzer's use of the portmanteau term *grobalization* as counterpoint to *glocalization* (*The Globalization of Nothing* [Thousand Oaks, Calif.: Sage], 2004).

17. Fredric Jameson, "Progress versus Utopia: or Can We Imagine the Future?" in Brian Wallis, ed., *Art after Modernism: Rethinking Representation* (New York: New Museum of Contemporary Art, 1984), 287.

18. As Oswaldo de Rivero writes, "In the face of the great emerging power of the new transnational aristocracy and the policies of the . . . IMF and World Bank, the power of the so-called developing countries is marginal. Even the

most powerful of the group, such as Brazil and India, are unable to influence the rules of the international economic game" (*The Myth of Development* [London: Zed Books, 2001], 61).

19. "The Call of the Call Centres," *The Hindu,* December 27, 2004; "The Call Centre Drawl," *Indian Express,* June 4, 2003; "Nasscom Flays Reports on Labour Issues in BPOs," *Financial Express,* October 25, 2005; Sramana Mitra, "The Coming Death of Indian Outsourcing," *Forbes,* February 29, 2008.

20. Timothy Mitchell, "Dreamland," in Mike Davis and Daniel Bertrand Monk, eds., *Evil Paradises: Dreamworlds of Neoliberalism* (London: Verso, 2007), 1–33.

Chapter One: Leaps of Faith

1. While I do use these categories, mostly out of convenience, we should, of course, recognize that all societies are in states of becoming.

2. Edmund Andrews, "Democrats Criticize Bush over Job Exports," *New York Times,* February 11, 2004:A26; Jacob Weisman, "Bush, Adviser Assailed for Stance on 'Offshoring' Jobs," *Washington Post,* February 11, 2004: A6.

3. Hence the need, in consultant Michael Corbett's clumsy terms, to "manage outsourcing's people impacts" (*The Outsourcing Revolution: Why It Makes Sense and How to Do It Right* [Chicago: Dearborn Trade Publishing, 2004], 64).

4. More recently, presidential contender Senator John McCain claimed that outsourcing strengthens the U.S. economy, while his opponent, then-senator Barack Obama, vowed to "stop providing tax breaks for companies that are shipping jobs overseas."

5. Not only may the list have "indirectly boosted offshoring by providing free publicity for the BPO industry" but it reads like a who's who of corporate America (Andrew Ross, *Fast Boat to China: Corporate Flight and the Consequences of Free Trade* [New York: Pantheon, 2006]).

6. Pew Research Center, "Public Says American Work Life Is Worsening, But Most Workers Remain Satisfied with Their Jobs" (Washington, D.C.: Pew, 2006), 3.

7. Whatever the term's ideological connotations, it did describe a certain yet fuzzy reality. While service workers numbered around 64.9 million in 1979, they almost doubled to 113.9 million by 2006 (Uric Dufrene and James Altmann, "The Professional and Business Service Sector," *Indiana Business Review* 82[2]:1–6 [2007]).

8. Carrie Kirby and John Shinal, "Offshoring's Giant Target," *San Francisco Chronicle,* March 7, 2004:A1.

9. Ashok Bardhan and Cynthia Kroll, "The New Wave of Outsourcing," Fisher Center for Real Estate and Urban Economics, University of California, Berkeley (2003); Jon Haveman and Howard Shatz, *Services Offshoring: Background and Implications for California* (San Francisco: Public Policy Institute of California, 2004).

10. According to UNCTAD, 70–80 percent of companies in various studies mention lower costs as the reason for offshoring, with cost-savings ranging from 20 percent to 40 percent (*World Investment Report: The Shift towards Services* [New York: United Nations, 2004], xxv). Another survey of executives finds that "it was a given that savings on a given activity would have to be at least 40 percent to make the relocation worthwhile" (Rafiq Dossani and Martin Kenney, "Went for Cost, Stayed for Quality? Moving the Back Office to India," Asia Pacific Research Center, Stanford University [2003], 7).

11. Sandra Polaski, "Job Anxiety Is Real—and It's Global," Carnegie Endowment for International Peace Policy Brief 30 (May 2004), 1.

12. Carolyn Locheed, "Tech Bosses Defend Overseas Hiring," *San Francisco Chronicle*, January 8, 2004:A1.

13. The company's website declares that "Autodesk Solutions Fulfill Criteria for the American Recovery and Reinvestment Act" and that "Autodesk's solutions allow government agencies and their contractors to implement the funded projects in a cost effective, more transparent, and more efficient manner."

14. "Looking Offshore: Straight from the Mouth: Executives Speak Out," *San Francisco Chronicle*, March 7, 2004:I1.

15. "The average pay of the leading outsourcing CEOs is 3,300 times the pay of an average Indian call center employee and 1,300 times more than the pay of an average Indian computer programmer" (Sarah Anderson, John Cavanagh, Stacey Chan, Chris Hartman, and Scott Klinger, *Executive Excess: Campaign Contributions, Outsourcing, Unexpensed Stock Options, and Rising CEO Pay* (Washington, D.C.: Institute for Policy Studies), 1.

16. Ron Hira and Anil Hira, *Outsourcing America* (New York: American Management Association, 2005).

17. Douglas Brown and Scott Wilson, *The Black Book of Outsourcing: How to Manage the Changes, Challenges, and Opportunities* (New York: Wiley, 2005).

18. Daniel Drezner, "The Outsourcing Bogeyman," *Foreign Affairs*, May 2004:22–34.

19. Jagdish Bhagwati, "Why Your Job Isn't Moving to Bangalore," *New York Times*, February 15, 2004:A11.

20. Thomas Friedman, "A Race to the Top," *New York Times*, June 3, 2005:A23.

21. Friedman, *The World Is Flat* (New York: Farrar, Straus and Giroux, 2005), 236, 229.

22. "Where the Good Jobs are Going," *Time*, August 4, 2003:36–39; Lael Brainard and Robert Litan, "Offshoring Service Jobs: Bane or Boon—and What to Do?" Brookings Institution Policy Brief, No. 132 (April 2004).

23. Catherine Mann, "Globalization of IT Services and White-Collar Jobs: The Next Wave of Productivity Growth," Washington, D.C.: Institute for International Economics (2004); Joshua Bivens, "Truth and Consequences of Offshoring," Economic Policy Institute Briefing Paper 155 (2005).

24. Global Services Conference, New York City, January 31, 2007.

25. Corbett, *The Outsourcing Revolution*, 54.

26. Dufrene and Altmann, "Professional and Business."

27. Atul Vashishta and Avinash Vashishta, *The Offshore Nation: Strategies for Success in Global Outsourcing and Offshoring* (New York: McGraw-Hill, 2006), 16.

28. "Offshoring Issue Guide," Economic Policy Institute; retrieved from http://www.epinet.org/content.cfm/issueguide_offshoring.

29. Steve Lohr, "Nobel Laureate, Critic of Outsourcing Theory, Dissects 'Polemical Untruth,'" *International Herald Tribune*, September 8, 2004:F14.

30. Ralph Gomory and William Baumol, *Global Trade and Conflicting National Interests* (Cambridge: MIT Press, 2000), 8.

31. John Cassidy, "Winners and Losers: The Truth about Free Trade," *New Yorker*, August 2, 2004:26–33.

32. Polaski, "Job Anxiety Is Real," 1.

33. Lohr, "Nobel Laureate," 14.

34. Anderson, Cavanagh, et al., 1; Carrick Mollenkamp, "Bank of America to Cut 4,500 More Jobs," *Wall Street Journal*, October 8, 2004:C5; David Lazarus, "Train Your Replacement, or No Severance Pay for You," *San Francisco Chronicle*, June 9, 2006:D1.

35. Saritha Rai, "India Concern to Design I.B.M. Chips," *New York Times*, November 18, 2005:C4; "IBM and the Rebirth of Outsourcing," *Time*, March 26, 2009; retrieved from http://www.time.com/time/business/article/0,8599,1887779,00.html.

36. Aneesh Aneesh, *Virtual Migration: The Programming of Globalization* (Durham, N.C.: Duke University Press, 2006); Carol Upadhya and A. R. Vasavi, "Work, Culture, and Sociality in the Indian IT Industry," National Institute of Advanced Studies, Bangalore (2006).

37. UNCTAD, *World Investment Report*, xxv.

38. Global Services Conference, New York City, January 31, 2007.

39. Churchill Club, "Outsourcing: Sorting Out the Hype, Reality, Risks and Benefits," Palo Alto, California, June 28, 2005.

40. Global Services Conference, 2007.

41. Robert Reich, "The New Rich-Rich Gap," *Common Dreams*, December 12, 2005.

42. Alan Blinder, "Offshoring: The Next Industrial Revolution?" *Foreign Affairs* 85(2):113–28 (2006).

43. Quoted in Amit Prasad, "Capitalizing Disease: Biopolitics of Drug Trials in India," *Theory, Culture and Society* 26(5):1–29 (2009).

44. Surrogacy is a largely unregulated, multi-billion-dollar business in India. See Amanda Gentleman, "India Nurtures Business of Surrogate Motherhood," *New York Times*, March 10, 2008:A9.

45. UNCTAD, *World Investment Report*, xxiv.

46. Or as an executive puts it: "Venture capitalists today require that product design be distributed across continents." See also Paul Blustein, "Implored to 'Offshore' More: U.S. Firms Are Too Reluctant to Outsource Jobs, Report Says," *Washington Post*, July 2, 2005:E1.

47. Geetanjali Pathole, "Catering to the Americans," *Times of India*, September 28, 2000.

48. "Stressed Youth Turn to Acupressure," *Times of India*, October 26, 2004; Siddhartha Kashyap, "Stressed Techies Losing Sex Drive," *Times of India*, November 27, 2004.

49. "BPO Jobs: No More Than a Stopgap Option for Youth," *Hindu*, December 17, 2004.

50. Rohit Chopra writes more generally: "In the contemporary conversation on Indian economy, politics and society, it is usually the pro-globalization and pro-liberalization narrative that is affirmed as more credible than the opposing viewpoint" ("Neoliberalism as Doxa: Bourdieu's Theory of the State and Contemporary Indian Discourse on Globalization and Liberalization," *Cultural Studies* 17[3–4]:419–44 [2003], 420).

51. Karl Marx, *Capital*, vol. 1 (New York: Penguin, 1976 [1867]).

52. United Nations Development Programme, *Making New Technologies Work for Human Development* (New York: Oxford University Press, 2001); International Labour Organization, *World Employment Report 2001: Life at Work in the Information Economy* (Geneva: International Labour Office, 2001).

53. "Economist Outsourcing Survey: A World of Work," *The Economist*, November 11, 2004:3–4.

54. Bardhan and Kroll, "New Wave of Outsourcing"; NASSCOM and McKinsey and Company, *The NASSCOM-McKinsey Report: 2002* (New Delhi: NASSCOM and McKinsey and Company, 2003).

55. Consultants McKinsey and Company note ruefully, however, that in India as with other low-wage countries, "only a fraction (10 to 25) of these people are suited for work in multinational companies." Nonetheless, India

"produces a higher proportion of suitable graduates than China" (Diana Farrell, Noshir Kaka, and Sasha Sturz, "Ensuring India's Offshoring Future," *The McKinsey Quarterly*, September 2005:76.

56. UNCTAD, *World Investment Report*, xxiv–xxv, xxvii.

Chapter Two: Variations on a Theme

1. Speaking to the *Financial Express*, Seagram's marketing head explains the rationale behind the first competition in 2004: "BPO executives are pretty young and they view corporate participation in such rock music and dance carnivals as a part of good HR practices. For marketers like us, the fast growing BPO segment means a lot of disposable income in the hands of young executives, who are open to new changes and influences. The employee base of these dozen firms participating in Gurgaon itself is over 50,000" ("BPOites Dance to Seagram's Tunes," *Financial Express*, August 7, 2004.) See also A.P.S. Malhotra, "A Spirited Evening," *The Hindu*, December 22, 2005.

2. See Friedman, *The World Is Flat*; Robert Reich, *The Work of Nations* (New York: Vintage Books, 1992).

3. Kenichi Ohmae, *The Borderless World: Power and Strategy in the Interlinked Economy* (New York: HarperCollins, 1990), 116. Ohmae reportedly exercised considerable influence on the Clinton administration's trade policies via Labor secretary Robert Reich.

4. Karl Marx and Friedrich Engels, *The Communist Manifesto* (New York: Verso, 1998 [1848]), 38.

5. This is not to downplay the massive flows of labor migration, which are well documented. See David Bacon, *Illegal People: How Globalization Creates Migration and Criminalizes Immigrants* (Boston: Beacon Press, 2008) and Arlie Hochschild and Barbara Ehrenreich, eds., *Global Woman: Nannies, Maids, and Sex Workers in the New Economy* (New York: Metropolitan Books, 2003) among many others. The focus here is on corporate mobility and its effects.

6. Henry Yeung, "Capital, State, and Space: Contesting the Borderless World," *Transnational Institute of British Geography* 23:291–309, 299 (1998). Or as Peter Dicken puts it, "Every component in the production chain, every economic activity is, quite literally, 'grounded' in specific locations. Such grounding is both physical, in the form of sunk costs, and less tangible in the form of localized social relationships" (*Global Shift: Transforming the World Economy* [New York: Guilford Press, 1998], 11).

7. As Manuel Castells writes, "We are not living in a global village, but in customized cottages globally produced and locally distributed" (*The Rise of the Network Society* [Oxford: Blackwell, 1996], 341).

8. Ibid., 409.

9. Yi Fu Tuan, *Space and Place: The Perspective of Experience* (Minneapolis: University of Minnesota Press, 2001), 6.

10. Tuan, *Space and Place*, 36–37.

11. Henri Lefebvre, *The Production of Space* (Oxford: Blackwell, 1991).

12. Huw Beynon and Ray Hudson, "Place and Space in Contemporary Europe: Some Lessons and Reflections," *Antipode* 25(3):177–90, 192 (1993).

13. Jamie Peck, *Work-Place: The Social Regulation of Labor Markets* (New York: Guilford Press, 1996), 238.

14. David Harvey, *The Condition of Postmodernity: An Enquiry into the Origins of Cultural Change* (Cambridge, Mass.: Blackwell, 1989), 254.

15. Lefebvre, *Production of Space*, 334. Harvey writes, if place is the "site of Being," then "becoming entails a spatial politics that renders place subservient to transformations of space" (*Condition of Postmodernity*, 257).

16. Karl Polanyi characterized the oscillation between market self-regulation and social intervention as the "double movement" of capitalism (*The Great Transformation* [New York: Rinehart, 1944]).

17. David Harvey, "The Geopolitics of Capitalism," in D. Gregory and J. Urry, eds., *Social Relations and Spatial Structures* (London: Macmillan, 1985), 145.

18. Global Services Conference, 2007.

19. Harvey, *Condition of Postmodernity*, 141.

20. Alain Lipietz, *Mirages and Miracles: The Crises of Global Fordism* (New York: Verso, 1987), 71.

21. Jan Nederveen Pieterse, "Globalisation as Hybridisation," *International Sociology* 9(2):161–84 (1994).

22. On this free traders and socialists agree: capital and the market are amoral and without conscience, all nerves and instinct; genuine corporate social responsibility would suggest that this hardwiring has frayed.

23. Gilles Deleuze and Felix Guattari, *A Thousand Plateaus: Capitalism and Schizophrenia* (Minneapolis: University of Minnesota Press, 1987).

24. Xiang Biao, *Global "Body Shopping": An Indian Labor System in the Information Technology Industry* (Princeton: Princeton University Press, 2006).

25. Neil Brenner and Nik Theodore, "Cities and the Geographies of 'Actually Existing Neoliberalism,'" *Antipode* 34(3):349–79, 366 (2002).

26. See Rupal Oza, "Special Economic Zones: Space, Law and Dispossession," in Waquar Ahmed, Amitabh Kundu, and Richard Peet, eds., *India's New Economic Policy: A Critical Analysis* (New York: Routledge, 2010).

27. David Harvey, "The Right to the City," *New Left Review* 53:23–40, 34 (2008). On China, see Jun Jing, "Villages Dammed, Villages Repossessed: A

Memorial Movement in Northwest China," *American Ethnologist* 26(2):324–43 (1999).

28. As a former IMF chief economist puts it, "Emerging-market governments and their private-sector allies commonly form a tight-knit . . . oligarchy, running the country rather like a profit-seeking company in which they are the controlling shareholders" (Simon Johnson, "The Quiet Coup," *The Atlantic*, May 2009:1–11).

29. See Oza, "Special Economic Zones."

30. Aiwha Ong, "The Gender and Labor Politics of Postmodernity," in Lisa Lowe and David Lloyd, eds., *The Politics of Culture in the Shadow of Capital* (Durham, N.C.: Duke University Press, 1997), 64.

31. Ibid.

32. International Labour Organization, *Employment and Social Policy in Respect to Export Processing Zones* (Geneva: ILO, 2003), 2.

33. Lefebvre, *Production of Space*, 395.

34. Ryan Bishop, John Phillips, and Wei Wei Yeo, *Post-colonial Urbanism: Southeast Asian Cities and Global Processes* (London: Routledge, 2003).

35. Bradford DeLong, "India since Independence: An Analytic Growth Narrative," in Dani Rodrik, ed., *Modern Economic Growth: Analytical Country Studies* (Princeton: Princeton University Press, 2003); Dani Rodrik and Arvind Subramanian, "From 'Hindu Growth' to Productivity Surge: The Mystery of the Indian Growth Transition," KSG Working Paper No. RWP04-13 (2004).

36. Prabhat Patnaik, "On the Political Economy of Liberalisation," *Social Scientist* 13(7–8):3–17 (1985).

37. Atul Kohli, "Politics of Economic Liberalization in India," *World Development* 17(3):305–28 (1989).

38. Jorgen Dige Pedersen, "Explaining Economic Liberalization in India: State and Society Perspectives," *World Development* 28(2):265–82 (2000); K. J. Joseph, *Industry under Economic Liberalization: The Case of Indian Electronics* (New Delhi: Sage, 1997).

39. Montek Ahluwalia, "Economic Reforms in India since 1991: Has Gradualism Worked?" *Journal of Economic Perspectives* 16(3):67–88 (2002).

40. See Waquar Ahmed, "From Mixed Economy to Neo-liberalism: Class and Caste in India's Economic Transition," *Human Geography* 2(3):37–51 (2009).

41. Ahluwalia, "Economic Reforms in India," 74.

42. Barry Lynn, *End of the Line: The Rise and Coming Fall of the Global Corporation* (New York: Doubleday, 2005).

43. See Biao, *Global "Body Shopping."* Over half the companies started in the last decade or so in Silicon Valley were founded by immigrants (Vivek

Wadhwa, "Don't Blame H-1B Workers for Woes," *BusinessWeek*, February 10, 2009:28).

44. Paul Krugman, "Feeling No Pain," *New York Times*, March 6, 2006:A21.

45. News reports and Vashishta and Vashishta, *The Offshore Nation*.

46. Bardhan and Kroll, "New Wave of Outsourcing"; National Association of Software and Services Companies, "Indian IT Industry Fact Sheet" (2008); UNCTAD, *World Investment Report*.

47. C. J. Fuller and Haripriya Narasimhan, "Engineering Colleges, 'Exposure' and Information Technology Professionals in Tamil Nadu," *Economic and Political Weekly* 41:258–62 (2006); Anirudh Krishna and Vijay Brihmadesam, "What Does It Take to Become a Software Professional?" *Economic and Political Weekly* 41:3307–14 (2006); U. Oommen and A. Meenakshisundararajan, "Social Structuring of Human Capital of the New Global Workforce," paper presented to International Conference on New Global Workforces and Virtual Workplaces, National Institute of Advanced Studies, Bangalore, August 12–13, 2005; Upadhya and Vasavi, "Work, Culture, and Sociality."

48. NASSCOM, *Strengthening the Human Resource Foundation of the Indian IT Enabled Services/IT Industry* (New Delhi: NASSCOM and Government of India, 2004).

49. For a critical assessment, see Kiran Mirchandani, "Gender Eclipsed? Racial Hierarchies in Transnational Call Centres," *Social Justice* 32(4):105–19 (2006).

50. Babu Ramesh, "'Cyber Coolies' in BPO: Insecurities and Vulnerabilities of Nonstandard Work," *Economic and Political Weekly* 39:492–97 (2004). BPO/ITES also recruits heavily from the liberal arts background, while IT relies on the sciences. Software exports generate more revenue but employ less people than BPO/ITES.

51. "The Insidious Charms of Foreign Investment," *Economist*, March 3, 2005.

52. Aneesh, *Virtual Migration*, 160–61.

53. "Millennium Business Processing Outsourcing Policy," Department of IT and Biotechnology, Government of Karnataka (2002); retrieved from http://www.karnatakaindustry.gov.in/documents/The%20%20Millenium%20BPO%20Policy.pdf.

54. "West Bengal IT Policy," Department of Information Technology, Government of West Bengal (2003). As a result of these actions, Calcutta holds the distinction of being the "least riskiest [*sic*]" outsourcing destination in India, according to an industry survey ("Black Book of Outsourcing, 2009: The Year of Outsourcing Dangerously," Clearwater, Fla.: Brown-Wilson Group [2009]).

55. "Press Release: Haryana Government Makes Changes in Labor Policy to Benefit IT-ITES Sectors," *BPO Newsline* 52 (2006).

56. Focus on the Global South, "When the Wind Blows: An Overview of Business Process Outsourcing in India" (2006); Upadhya and Vasavi, "Work, Culture and Sociality."

57. Walter Benjamin, "Doctrine of the Similar," *New German Critique* 17:65–69, 65 (1979 [1933]).

58. Fredric Jameson, *Postmodernism; or, the Cultural Logic of Late Capitalism* (Durham, N.C.: Duke University Press, 1991), 314.

59. Susan Willis, *A Primer for Daily Life* (New York: Routledge, 1991), 52.

60. Jameson, *Postmodernism*, 314.

61. Fred Alford, "Nature and Narcissism: The Frankfurt School," *New German Critique* 36:174–92, 186 (1985).

62. Jurgen Habermas, *The Theory of Communicative Action: Reason and the Rationalization of Society* (Boston: Beacon Press, 1984), 382, 453.

63. Ibid., 390.

64. Benjamin, "Doctrine of the Similar," 65.

65. Theodor Adorno and Max Horkheimer, *The Dialectic of Enlightenment* (New York: Verso, 1986), 187.

66. Ibid., 180–81.

67. Michael Taussig, *Mimesis and Alterity: A Particular History of the Senses* (New York: Routledge, 1993, 52).

68. Homi Bhabha, *The Location of Culture* (New York: Routledge, 1995), 6.

69. Susan Sontag, *Styles of the Radical Will* (New York: Farrar, Straus and Giroux, 1969), 261.

70. Deleuze and Guattari, *A Thousand Plateaus*, 11.

71. Ernst Bloch, "Nonsynchronism and the Obligation to Its Dialectics," *New German Critique* 11:22–38, 22 (1977 [1935]).

72. Theodor W. Adorno, *Prisms* (Cambridge: MIT Press, 1983), 139.

73. Edward W. Said, *On Late Style* (New York: Vintage, 2006), 127.

74. Bloch, "Nonsynchronism," 29.

75. As Pankaj Mishra writes, "Our modern fantasies of a simple and whole past are fragile. Perhaps that's why we hold on to them so tenaciously" (*Temptations of the West: How to Be Modern in India, Pakistan, Tibet, and Beyond* [New York: Farrar, Straus and Giroux], 306).

76. Arif Dirlik, "Spectres of the Third World: Global Modernity and the End of the Three Worlds," *Third World Quarterly* 25(1):131–48, 142 (2004).

77. Nigel Thrift, "Afterword," *Environment and Planning D: Society and Space* 18:213–55, 222 (2000).

78. Bloch, "Nonsynchronism," 27.

79. Michel de Certeau, *The Practice of Everyday Life* (Berkeley: University of California Press, 1984), 25.

80. Harvey, *Condition of Postmodernity*, 214.

81. As Henri Lefebvre puts it, "The birth of 'modernity' . . . coincided with the beginnings of doubt and questioning; the world we call modern was born with the shattering of the modern world, carrying within its heart the principle of its destruction and self-destruction" (*Introduction to Modernity: Twelve Preludes* [New York: Verso, 1995], 105).

82. At some point, today's celebrated flexible professional will share a similar fate.

83. See Nicholas Dirks, *Castes of Mind: Colonialism and the Making of Modern India* (Princeton: Princeton University Press, 2001); Eric Hobsbawm and Terence Ranger, eds., *The Invention of Tradition* (Cambridge: Cambridge University Press, 1983); Timothy Mitchell, *Colonising Egypt* (Berkeley: University of California Press, 1998); Edward Said, *Orientalism* (New York: Vintage, 1979).

84. Dirlik, "Spectres," 139.

85. Pieterse, "Globalisation as Hybridisation," 161.

86. Anna Tsing, *Friction: An Ethnography of Global Connection* (Princeton: Princeton University Press, 2005).

87. Taussig, *Mimesis and Alterity*, xiv.

88. While all Hindu gods and goddesses embody contradictory qualities, Parvati is generally considered a benevolent mother goddess that domesticated the unruly Shiva, and Lakshmi is thought of as the goddess of wealth or good fortune. See Stanley Wolpert, *A New History of India* (Oxford: Oxford University Press, 1977).

89. Gita Mehta, *Snakes and Ladders: Glimpses of Modern India* (New York: Doubleday, 1997), 85.

90. Adorno and Horkheimer, *The Dialectic of Enlightenment*, 181.

91. Alford, "Nature and Narcissism," 186.

92. Benjamin, "Doctrine of the Similar," 65.

93. Susan Buck-Morss, *The Dialectics of Seeing: Walter Benjamin and the Arcades Project* (Cambridge: MIT Press, 1991), 267.

94. Lefebvre, *Production of Space*, 48.

95. Ash Amin, "Spatialities of Globalisation," *Environment and Planning A* 34:385–99, 388 (2002).

96. Henri Lefebvre, *Everyday Life in the Modern World* (London: Althone Press, 2000 [1971]), 64–65.

97. Ian Burkitt, "The Time and Space of Everyday Life," *Cultural Studies* 18(2–3): 211–17, 224 (2004).

98. The appeal of tea is double, both as a work stimulant and, historically,

as a luxury, as in "the tea," a middle-class social occasion in England and elsewhere. See Sidney Mintz, *Sweetness and Power: The Place of Sugar in Modern History* (New York: Penguin, 1985), 141, 186.

99. In Polanyi's words, social conditions during the Industrial Revolution were "a veritable abyss of human degradation" (*Great Transformation*, 39).

100. Doreen Massey, "Traveling Thoughts," in Paul Gilroy, Lawrence Grossberg, and A. McRobbie, eds., *Without Guarantees: In Honor of Stuart Hall* (London: Verso, 2000), 225.

Chapter Three: Macaulay's (Cyber) Children

1. Raymond Williams, *Marxism and Literature* (Oxford: Oxford University Press, 1978).

2. See Sharon Zukin, "Mimesis in the Origins of Bourgeois Culture," *Theory and Society* 4(3):333–58 (1977).

3. Emma Rothschild, "Globalization and the Return of History," *Foreign Policy* (Summer):106–16, 106 (1999).

4. Manuel Castells, *The Power of Identity: The Information Age: Economy, Society and Culture*, vol. 2 (Oxford: Blackwell Publishers, 1997), 1; Anthony Giddens, *Central Problems in Social Theory: Action, Structure, and Contradiction in Social Analysis* (Berkeley: University of California Press, 1991); Mauro Guillén, "Is Globalization Civilizing, Destructive or Feeble? A Critique of Five Key Debates in the Social-Science Literature," *Annual Review of Sociology* 27:235–60 (2001).

5. George Ritzer provides a nuanced and sophisticated example of this perspective in *McDonaldization of Society*, 6th ed. (Thousand Oaks, Calif.: Pine Forge Press, 2010). According to Forbes correspondent Robyn Merdith, outsourcing "is costing Americans jobs but allowing the United States to export its way of life" (*The Elephant and the Dragon: The Rise of India and China* [New York: Norton, 2007], 123).

6. W. W. Rostow, *The Stages of Economic Growth: A Non-Communist Manifesto* (Cambridge: Cambridge University Press, 1960).

7. Daniel Bell, *The Coming of Post-Industrial Society* (New York: Basic Books, 1999), li.

8. Arjun Appadurai, "Deep Democracy: Urban Governmentality and the Horizon of Politics," *Public Culture* 14(1):21–47, 29 (1996).

9. Arturo Escobar, "Culture Sits in Places: Reflections on Globalism and Subaltern Strategies of Localization," *Political Geography* 20(2):139–74 (2001); Jonathan Friedman, *Cultural Identity and Global Process* (Thousand Oaks, Calif.: Sage, 1994); Saskia Sassen, "Spatialities and Tempor-

alities of the Global: Elements for a Theorization," *Public Culture* 12(1):215–32 (2000).

10. Marwan Kraidy, *Hybridity: Or the Cultural Logic of Globalization* (Philadelphia: Temple University Press, 2005).

11. The terms are Thorstein Veblen's (*The Theory of the Leisure Class* [New York: Dover, 1994 (1899)]).

12. Leela Fernandez, *India's New Middle Class* (Minneapolis: University of Minnesota Press, 2006).

13. Mark Liechty, *Suitably Modern: Making Middle-Class Culture in a New Consumer Society* (Princeton: Princeton University Press, 2002), 7.

14. Jean Comaroff and John Comaroff, "Millennial Capitalism: First Thoughts on a Second Coming," *Public Culture* 12(2):291–343, 299 (2002).

15. McKinsey Global Institute, "The Bird of Gold: The Rise of India's Consumer Market," McKinsey & Co. (September 2007), 6.

16. Bell, *Coming of Post-Industrial Society*.

17. Andre Beteille, "Caste in Contemporary India," in C. J. Fuller, ed., *Caste Today* (Delhi: Oxford University Press, 1997), 150–79.

18. Fernando Coronil, "Towards a Critique of Globalcentrism: Speculations on Capitalism's Nature," *Public Culture* 12(2):351–74 (2000).

19. Kiran Mirchandani, "Practices of Global Capital: Gaps, Cracks and Ironies in Transnational Call Centers," *Global Networks* 4(4):355–73, 361 (2004).

20. Fredric Jameson, "On Cultural Studies," *Social Text* 34:17–52, 34 (1993).

21. Claire Cowie, "The Accents of Outsourcing: The Meaning of Neutral in the Indian Call Centre Industry," *World Englishes* 26(3):316–30 (2006).

22. See Arlie Hochschild, *The Managed Heart: The Commercialization of Human Feeling* (Berkeley: University of California Press, 2003) and Robin Leidner, "Emotional Labor in Service Work," *Annals of the American Academy of Political and Social Science* 561(1):81–95 (1999).

23. According to *The Hindu* newspaper, one company makes unique allowance for such frustrations: "Her friendly BPO has a yelling room even. A soundproof room that lets you yell and bawl!" (Harish Bijoor, "Stress, Suicide, and Sales," *Hindu Business Line*, December 22, 2005).

24. Aneesh, *Virtual Migration*, 93–94.

25. See, for example, Laurie Cohen and Amal El-Sawad, "Lived Experiences of Offshoring: An Examination of UK and Indian Financial Service Employees' Accounts of Themselves and One Another," *Human Relations* 60(8):1235–62 (2007); Mirchandani, "Practices of Global Capital"; Winifred Poster, "Who's On the Line? Indian Call Center Agents Pose as Americans for U.S.-Outsourced Firms," *Industrial Relations* 46(2):271–304 (2007); Phil

Taylor and Peter Bain, "'India Calling to the Far Away Towns': The Call Centre Labour Process and Globalization," *Work, Employment and Society* 19(2):261–82 (2005).

26. "Call Centers 'Bad for India,'" *BBC News*, December 11, 2003; retrieved from http://news.bbc.co.uk/2/hi/south_asia/3292619.stm.

27. Mark Landler, "Hi, I'm in Bangalore (but I Can't Say So)," *New York Times*, March 21, 2001:A1.

28. According to one survey, Bangalore ranks as the riskiest outsourcing destination in terms of "uncontrolled environmental waste and pollution" ("Black Book of Outsourcing").

29. Pavan Varma, *The Great Indian Middle Class* (New Delhi: Penguin, 1999), xii.

30. Leela Fernandes, "Nationalizing the Global: Media Images, Cultural Politics, and the Middle Class of India," *Media, Culture and Society* 22:611–28 (2000).

31. Nicos Poulantzas, *The Crisis of the Dictatorships* (London: New Left Books, 1976).

32. As Eric Wolf writes of the Indian textile industry under colonialism: "Within each mill the administrative and technical staff were at first British, but soon Indians were recruited. The key figure in the organization of the mill was the 'jobber,' a kind of foreman charged with recruiting and supervising unskilled laborers. He wielded a great deal of power" (*Europe and the People without History* [Berkeley: University of California Press, 1997], 289).

33. Christopher Lasch, *The Revolt of the Elites* (New York: Norton, 1996); William Mazzarella, "Indian Middle Class," in Rachel Dwyer, ed., *South Asia Keywords*; retrieved from http://www.soas.ac.uk/csasfiles/keywords/Mazzarella-middleclass.pdf.

34. Such views are not uncommon among the privileged classes. What is of special interest is not the flirtation with authoritarianism, though that too is alarming, but the manner in which development is conceived. In this narrow view, it is acceptable to sacrifice soft "rights" and "privileges" like democracy for the "hard" goal of economic development. But, as Amartya Sen points out, freedom is itself constitutive of development, not simply a beneficial by-product (*Development as Freedom* [New York: Anchor Books, 2000]). For example, the freedom of literacy and education, not to mention freedom from hunger, ill health, and homelessness, form the basis of a skilled workforce that can drive long-term economic development.

35. Saswati Chakravarty, "Sex in the City: BPOs Rock," *Economic Times*, September 7, 1994.

36. As one executive says, "Even the *Economic Times*, a business paper," is obsessed with "these culture issues."

37. Such thinking inspired the creation of the website bposhaadi.com (*shaadi* is Hindi for marriage), the "first matrimonial service for BPO employees."

38. Dean Nelson, "India's Call-Centre Staff Tune in to Decadence," *Sunday Times*, March 19, 2006.

39. Richard Sennett, *The Corrosion of Character: The Personal Consequences of Work in the New Capitalism* (New York: Norton, 1998), 139.

40. Nelson, "India's Call Centre Staff ."

41. S. Mitra Kalita, "Hope and Toil at India's Call Centers: Up-All-Night Culture Develops Around Outsourced U.S. Jobs," *Washington Post*, December 27, 2005:A1.

42. Focus on the Global South, "When the Wind Blows."

43. Pierre Bourdieu, "The Space of Points of View," in Pierre Bourdieu, ed., *The Weight of the World* (Stanford: Stanford University Press, 1999), 3–5, 4.

44. She also received a certificate from management that bore the inscription: "Amazing Job and good achievement . . . MY BEST WISHES TO THE WHOLE TEAM !!!!!!!!!!!!!!!!!!!!!1 Cheers & Beers☺ Joe."

45. Winifred Poster, "Emotion Detectors, Answering Machines, and e-Unions: Multi-Surveillances in the Global Interactive Service Industry," *American Behavioral Scientist* (forthcoming).

46. Bhabha, *The Location of Culture*; Franz Fanon, *White Skin, Black Masks* (New York: Grove Press, 1952); V. S. Naipaul, *The Mimic Men* (New York: Picador, 1967).

47. Plato, *The Dialogues of Plato* (New York: Macmillan, 1892), xlii.

48. Arjun Appadurai, *Modernity at Large: Cultural Dimensions of Globalization* Minneapolis: University of Minnesota Press, 1996).

49. Fernand Braudel, *Capitalism and Material Life, 1400–1800* (New York: Harper Row, 1975).

50. See William Mazzarella, *Shoveling Smoke: Advertising and Globalization in Contemporary India* (Durham, N.C.: Duke University Press, 2003).

Chapter Four: The Uses and Abuses of Time

1. Eric Simonson, "Part I: What's Driving the Growth of BPO? The Impact of Labor Arbitrage," *BPO Outsourcing Journal* (2002); retrieved from http://www.bpo-outsourcing-journal.com/nov2002-everest.html.

2. "A World of Work," *The Economist*, November 11, 2004:3–4; Stephanie Overby, "2006 Global Outsourcing Guide," *CIO Magazine* 19(19): 64–69.

3. Harvey, *Condition of Postmodernity*, 240.

4. Barbara Adam, "Reflexive Modernization Temporalized," *Theory, Culture & Society* 20(2):59–78 (2003); Castells, *Rise of Network Society*; Robert Hassan, "Network Time and the New Knowledge Epoch," *Time and Society* 12(2/3):225–41 (2003).

5. Castells, *Rise of Network Society*, 101.

6. Richard Heeks, S. Krishna, Brian Nicholson, and Sundeep Sahay, "Synching or Sinking," *IEEE Software* 18(2):54–60 (2001).

7. Sassen, "Spatialities and Temporalities."

8. Friedman, *The World Is Flat.*

9. Bennett Harrison, *Lean and Mean: Why Large Corporations Will Continue to Dominate the Global Economy* (New York: Guilford Press, 1997), 47; Lynn, *End of the Line.*

10. Pietro Basso, *Modern Times, Ancient Hours: Working Lives in the Twenty-first Century* (London: Verso, 2003); Juliet Schor, *The Overworked American: The Unexpected Decline of Leisure* (New York: Basic Books, 1991).

11. Peter Bain, Aileen Watson, Gareth Mulvey, Phil Taylor and Gregor Gall, "Taylorism, Targets and the Pursuit of Quantity and Quality by Call Centre Management," *New Technology, Work and Employment* 17(3):170–85 (2002); Aihwa Ong, *Neoliberalism as Exception: Mutations in Citizenship and Sovereignty* (Durham, N.C.: Duke University Press, 2006); Phil Taylor and Peter Bain, "'An Assembly Line in the Head': Work and Employee Relations in the Call Centre," *Industrial Relations Journal* 30(2):101–17 (1999).

12. Adam, "Reflexive Modernization Temporalized."

13. Aaditya Mattoo and Sacha Wunsch, "Pre-empting Protectionism in Services: The WTO and Outsourcing," World Bank Policy Research Working Paper 3237 (2004).

14. Martin Baily and Diana Farrell, "Exploding the Myths of Offshoring," *The McKinsey Quarterly* (2004).

15. Basso, *Modern Times, Ancient Hours.*

16. At a call center I visited, 32 percent of compensation was performance-based. A broader survey found that 17.5 percent of compensation is performance-based in international call centers and 15.5 percent in domestic centers (Rosemary Batt, Virginia Doellgast, Hyunji Kwon, Mudit Nopany, Priti Nopany, and Anil da Costa, "The Indian Call Centre Industry: National Benchmarking Report Strategy," Center for Advanced Human Resource Studies, Working Paper 5-7, Cornell University ILR School [2005]).

17. Ibid., 17.

18. Dinesh Sharma, "Shining India's Swanky New Sweatshops," *Hindustan Times*, October 24, 2005.

19. Tamara Hareven, *Family Time and Industrial Time* (Cambridge: Cambridge University Press, 1982).

20. Erran Carmel, "Building Your Information Systems from the Other

Side of the World: How Infosys Manages Time Zone Differences," *MIS Quarterly Executive* 5(1):43–53, 46 (2006).

21. Ibid., 50–51.

22. Dataquest, "BPO Employee Survey 2004: Industry Stress Factors"; retrieved from http://www.dqindia.com/content/dqtop202k4/empSurvey2004/2004/104110816.asp.

23. Leslie Perlow, "Time to Coordinate: Towards an Understanding of Work Time Standards and Norms in a Multicountry Study of Software Engineers," *Work and Occupations* 28(1):91–111 (2001).

24. International Labour Organisation, *Encyclopedia of Occupational Health and Safety*; retrieved from http://www.ilo.org/encyclopedia.

25. Ibid.; Muhammad Jamal, "Burnout, Stress and Health of Employees on Non-standard Work Schedules: A Study of Canadian Workers," *Stress and Health* 20(3):113–19 (2004).

26. Scott Davis, Dana Mirick, and Richard Stevens, "Night Shift Work, Light at Night, and Risk of Breast Cancer," *Journal of the National Cancer Institute* 93(20):1557–62 (2001).

27. "Night Shifts Spark Cancer Payout," *BBC News*, March 15, 2009.

28. L. Alfredsson, T. Åkerstedt, M. Mattson, and B. Wilborg, "Self-Reported Health and Well-Being amongst Night Security Guards: A Comparison with the Working Population," *Ergonomics* 34:525–30 (2001); P. Knauth and M. Härmä, "The Relation of Shift Work Tolerance to the Circadian Adjustment," *Chronobiology International* 9(1):46–54 (1992); Anders Knutsson, "Health Disorders of Shift Workers," *Occupational Medicine* 53:103–8 (2003).

29. Another survey of female BPO workers finds that "32 percent of the employees suffered from sleep disorders, 25 percent had developed digestive problems, and about 20 percent suffered from eyesight problems" ("Sleep and Travel Hamper Women BPO Staff," BPO Watch India, September 17, 2008).

30. J. Barton, L. Smith, P. Totterdell, E. Spelten, and S. Folkard, "Does Individual Choice Determine Shift System Acceptability?" *Ergonomics* 36(1–3):93–99 (1993).

31. International Labour Organisation, *Encyclopedia*.

32. S. Al-Naimi, S. M. Hampton, P. Richard, C. Tzung, and L. M. Morgan, "Postprandial Metabolic Profiles Following Meals and Snacks Eaten during Simulated Night and Day Shift Work," *Chronobiology International* 21(6):937–47 (2004).

33. N. R. Kleinfeld, "Modern Ways Open India's Doors to Diabetes," *New York Times*, September 13, 2006:A1.

34. A study in the *Indian Journal of Sleep Medicine* found that 40 percent of call center workers surveyed smoked, against 7 percent of a control group. What is more, 36 percent had more than two alcoholic drinks a week, com-

pared to 2 percent of the control group. Close to a third of respondents said they used sleeping pills or other drugs to help them fall asleep (Laurie Goering, "Outsourced to India: Stress," *Chicago Tribune*, April 20, 2008:D1).

35. Hans Van Dongen, Greg Maislin, Janet M. Mullington, and David F. Dinges, "The Cumulative Cost of Additional Wakefulness," *Sleep* 26(2):117–27, 117 (2003).

36. P. Meerlo, M. Koehl, K. van der Borght, and F. W. Turek, "Sleep Restriction Alters the Hypothalamic-Pituitary-Adrenal Response to Stress," *Journal of Neuroendocrinology* 14:397–402 (2002).

37. Van Dongen et al., "Cumulative Cost," 117.

38. Amartya has a room in the company's cold-water flat. His belongings are stuffed into two duffle bags and the room traversed by a clothesline. He sleeps on a small metal cot placed in the center. During the day, when he is often sleeping, the sunlight is dimmed and diffused by a diaphanous curtain. Pictures of his family and magazine cutouts are taped to the walls.

39. L. F. Portela, L. Rotenberg, and W. Waissman, "Self-Reported Health and Sleep Complaints among Nursing Personnel Working Under 12h Night and Day Shifts," *Chronobiology International* 21(6):859–70 (2004); International Labour Organisation, *Encyclopedia*.

40. Mirchandani, "Practices of Global Capital," 365.

41. Henry David Thoreau, *Walden* (Oxford: Oxford University Press, 1999), 114.

42. BBC News, "Boss Faces Call-Centre Death Case," *BBC News*, February 22, 2008; retrieved from http://news.bbc.co.uk/2/hi/business/7258837.stm.

43. Ravi Sharma, "Murder Most Foul," *Frontline*, January 13, 2006.

44. T. A. Johnson, "BPO Rape, Murder Clouds Bangalore," *Indian Express*, December 17, 2005.

45. Phil Taylor, Dora Scholarios, Ernesto Noronha, and Dr. Premilla d'Cruz, "Union Formation in Indian Call Centres/BPO," Strathclyde Business School, Glasgow, and Indian Institute of Management, Ahmedabad (2008), 6.

46. Teresa Rodriguez, *The Daughters of Juárez* (New York: Simon & Schuster, 2007), 2.

47. Ibid., 71.

48. Ibid., 21.

49. "Cover Up, Cabbies Tell BPO Women," *CNN-IBN*, February 23, 2006.

50. "We Don't Dread the Night," *Daily News and Analysis*, August 15, 2008.

51. Melissa Wright, *Disposable Women and Other Myths of Global Capitalism* (London: Routledge, 2006).

52. Shantha Rajaratnam and Josephine Arendt, "Health in a 24-Hour So-

ciety," *Lancet* 358:999–1005, 999 (2001); Torbjorn Akerstedt, Bjorn Peters, Anna Anund, and Goran Kecklund, "Impaired Alertness and Performance Driving Home from the Night Shift: A Driving Simulator Study," *Journal of Sleep Research* 14(1):17–20 (2005).

53. E. P. Thompson, "Time, Work-Discipline, and Industrial Capitalism," *Past and Present* 38:56–97 (1967).

54. Henri Lefebvre, *Rhythmanalysis: Space, Time, and Everyday Life* (London: Continuum, 2004).

55. More generally, see Arlie Hochschild's *The Time Bind: When Work Becomes Home and Home Becomes Work* (New York: Holt, 2001).

56. Frida Fischer, Lúcia Rotenberg, and Claudia Roberta de Castro Moreno, "Equity and Working Time: A Challenge to Achieve," *Chronobiology International* 21(6):813–29 (2004).

57. Albert O. Hirschman, *Exit, Voice, and Loyalty: Responses to Decline in Firms, Organizations, and States* (Cambridge: Harvard University Press, 1970).

58. Erik Olin Wright, "Working-Class Power, Capitalist-Class Interests and Class Compromise," *American Journal of Sociology* 105(4):957–1002, 962 (2000).

59. Beverly Silver, *Forces of Labor: Workers' Movements and Globalization since 1870* (Cambridge: Cambridge University Press, 2003), 13.

60. The figures companies give are somewhat inflated. While experienced personnel are indeed receiving large salary increases and bonuses, entry-level and junior workers are somewhat expendable and have not seen major increases.

61. Castells, *Rise of Network Society*, 6.

62. T. S. Eliot, *Four Quartets* (New York: Norton, 1968), 13.

63. Silicon India, "One Lakh Layoffs in IT Service Sector by September," *Silicon India*, April 28, 2009; Mini Tejaswi, "Techies Say 'No' to Pink Slips," *Times of India*, May 1, 2009:B15.

64. John Maynard Keynes, *Essays in Persuasion* (London: Macmillan, 1931), 131–32.

65. Thompson, "Time, Work-Discipline," 73.

66. Basso, *Modern Times, Ancient Hours*, 163.

67. Thompson, "Time, Work-Discipline," 93.

Chapter Five: The Rules of the Game

1. "Smartsourcing: The New Way to Drive Innovation," *Industry Week*, June 14, 2005; retrieved from http://www.industryweek.com/ReadArticle.aspx?ArticleID=12129; Vivek Paul, "It Was the Right Time to Go," Rediff.

com, July 8, 2005; retrieved from http://www.rediff.com/money/2005/jul/08inter.htm.

2. The result of Welch's downsizing and outsourcing was that more than 100,000 workers were pushed off the GE payroll (James Lardner, "The Specter Haunting Your Office," *New York Review of Books*, June, 14, 2007).

3. Paul, "Right Time to Go"; Shelley Singh and Snigdha Sengupta, "The Inside Story: Why Vivek Paul Quit Wipro," *Rediff.com*, July 8, 2005; retrieved from http://in.rediff.com/money/2005/jul/08bspec.htm; Jyoti Thottom, "Vivek Paul," *Time*, December 17, 2004:109.

4. Ravi Aron, "Confessions of an Aspiring Venture Capitalist," Wharton School of Business (November 21, 2005); retrieved from http://knowledge.wharton.upenn.edu/article.cfm?articleid=1276.

5. Ibid.

6. Paul Attewell, "Big Brother and the Sweatshop: Computer Surveillance in the Automated Office," *Sociological Theory* 4:77–89 (1987); Harry Braverman, *Labor and Monopoly Capital* (New York: Monthly Review Press, 1975); Larry Hirschhorn, *Beyond Mechanization: Work and Technology in a Postindustrial Age* (Cambridge: MIT Press, 1984); David Noble, *America by Design: Science, Technology, and the Rise of Corporate Capitalism* (New York: Knopf, 1977); Harley Shaiken, *Work Transformed: Automation and Labor in the Computer Age* (New York: Holt, Rinehart and Winston, 1985).

7. By Indian standards, these workers are privileged (only 10 percent of Indians get any kind of postsecondary education). But educational standards at even reputable institutions are lagging. Of India's 300-plus universities, only two are ranked in the top 300 in the world, and as a result, in the global labor market, workers enter with what corporations consider to be a relatively low level of skills (James Surowiecki, "India's Skills Famine," *New Yorker*, April 16, 2007:28).

8. Monica Prasad, "International Capital on 'Silicon Plateau': Work and Control in India's Computer Industry," *Social Forces* 77(2):429–52 (1998), 429.

9. Aneesh, *Virtual Migration*.

10. Taylor and Bain, "India Calling," 277.

11. Ibid.

12. "BPO Employee Survey 2005: Call Centre Maladies," *Dataquest*, November 8, 2005; retrieved from http://www.dqindia.com/content/dqtop202k4/empSurvey2004/2004/104110814.asp.

13. Braverman, *Labor and Monopoly Capital*; Leidner, "Emotional Labor."

14. Aneesh, *Virtual Migration*.

15. C. Wright Mills, *White Collar* (Oxford: Oxford University Press, 1951), 233.

16. Jeremy Leonard, "Offshoring of Information Technology Jobs: Myths and Realities," American Sentinel University (2006), 3.

17. Shyamanuja Das, "BPO Pricing: Are Companies Risk Averse?" *Global Services*, September 25, 2006.

18. A BPO trainer says they sometimes hire high school graduates between 19 and 20 years of age, without any college education. Before the BPO market, "It was hard to find jobs. The starting age for earning was 23 to 24, now its 18 to 19. People are less mature; you need to give guidance. Education is taking a backdrop. I have a feeling that BPO might undermine the importance of education." He believes the industry "will grow at the base."

19. Or as the CEO of Motorola puts it, "You have to draw a line. . . . Core intellectual property is above it, and commodity technology is below" (Peter Engardio and Bruce Einhorn, "Outsourcing Innovation," *BusinessWeek*, March 21, 2005:84–94).

20. Heather Timmons, "India Feels Less Vulnerable as Outsourcing Presses On," *New York Times*, June 2, 2009:B1.

21. Mirchandani, "Gender Eclipsed?"

22. Marianne McGee, "Recession Takes a Bite Out of Pay-for-Performance Outsourcing," *Information Week*, March 21, 2009.

23. While there is some intraoffice mobility within call centers, the jobs do not provide much leverage in landing higher positions. One study finds that only 1 percent of workers are able to do so. "Call center jobs," the authors conclude, "typically do not serve as entry-level positions for careers outside of the centers in the larger corporation" (Batt et al., "Indian Call Center Industry").

24. In more abstract terms, it began as a subsidiary of a subsidiary, which serves as an outsourcing provider for other companies. In this, Amandeep Sandhu is correct in describing international outsourcing as "Russian doll capitalism" ("Russian Doll Capitalism: An Essay on Work in the IT-City of Bangalore," *Biblio*, May–June 2006, 41–42).

25. Louis Uchitelle, *The Disposable American: Layoffs and Their Consequences* (New York: Vintage, 2006), 143.

26. Or else face the consequences: sluggish research and development, negligible productivity gains, and stagnant or declining long-term shareholder value.

27. And these future nonhires, of course, will find no way into the job loss estimates.

28. Richard Sennett, *The Culture of the New Capitalism* (New Haven: Yale University Press, 2006), 90.

29. According to one consultant, the emphasis shifts in such situations from managing *process* delivery to managing deliverables, as it is difficult to micromanage a process 9,000 miles away.

30. As an American IT worker observes: "The real decision making posi-

tions are still held by the American IT worker, where jobs like coding are done by the Indians" (Stephanie Overby, "Inside Outsourcing in India," *CIO Magazine*, June 1, 2003:60).

31. Al Gini, *My Job, My Self: Work and the Creation of the Modern Individual* (New York: Routledge, 2001), 18; Samuel Johnson, *Dictionary of the English Language: A Modern Selection* (New York: Pantheon Books, 1963), 22; Sennett, *Corrosion of Character*, 9.

32. Bill Worthen, "Extreme Outsourcing," *CIO*, May 1, 2007:32–40.

33. Nicos Poulantzas, "On Social Classes," *New Left Review* 1(78), March–April (1973).

34. Claus Offe, *Industry and Inequality: The Achievement Principle in Work and Social Status* (New York: St. Martin's, 1977); Shoshana Zuboff, *In the Age of the Smart Machine: The Future of Work and Power* (New York: Basic Books, 1988), 236.

35. Chopra, "Neoliberalism as Doxa," 437.

36. Mills, *White Collar*, 233.

37. Uchitelle, *Disposable American*, 3.

38. Carl Dalhman and Anuja Utz, *India and the Knowledge Economy* (Washington, D.C.: World Bank, 2005).

39. Incidentally, a web search for *Chindia* turns up a few scattered business reports as well as an Indian medical tourism site, India Health Guru, that advertises the cost and quality of outsourced chin surgeries. See also Peter Engardio, *Chindia: How China and India Are Revolutionizing Global Business* (New York: McGraw-Hill, 2006).

40. Aaditya Matoo and Sacha Wunsch, "Pre-empting Protectionism in Services: The WTO and Outsourcing," Policy Research Working Paper 3237, World Bank, Washington, D.C. (2004), 6–7.

41. Sangeetha Chengappa, "Can Academia Bail Out Industry from Manpower Shortage?" *Deccan Herald*, January 16, 2006.

42. Surowiecki, "India's Skills Famine."

43. This is not to say that English is not important. It is an "essential prerequisite for obtaining a quality higher education in India" (Chopra, "Neoliberalism as Doxa," 439). It is also a major differentiator in the Indian labor market: "Salary differences between equally qualified (non-professional/technical) candidates can be as high as 400 to 500%. In fact, the more fancied jobs in airlines, hotels, media, banks and financial services [go] only to those who know English. . . .The best jobs with the upmarket shopping malls, multinational fast-food chains and tony restaurants go to those who can speak English along with the mandatory fluency in local languages" (Sucheta Dalal, "BPOs and the Economics of English," *Indian Express*, November 6, 2005).

44. NeoIT, "Offshore and Nearshore ITO and BPO Salary Report," Offshore Insights Market Report Series 4(4):1–23 (2006).

45. A recent case found one company guilty of poaching. According to an

associate at the law firm Baker and McKenzie, in *Wipro Ltd. v. Beckman Coulter International*, the Delhi High Court "held that the defendant had breached the non-solicitation provision by publishing a recruitment advertisement specifically targeted at the plaintiff's employees."

46. Asked his thoughts on unionization, the executive of a KPO remarked surprisingly, "Truthfully, I'd love a union contract. . . . Unions have order. It might actually place restrictions on employees like a notice period."

47. Dataquest, "BPO Employee Survey 2004: Industry Stress Factors." Another reason for high turnover is the graveyard shift. An executive explains: "You may be able to train, indoctrinate 10 people when they come over, but what happens when they leave because they don't want to work the night shift? Attrition is a fact of life in our industry. It's a nascent industry."

48. For engineering, the quality of education is often lower in India than the West. As a result, one study found that "if you define 'engineer' by U.S. standards, India produces just a hundred and seventy thousand engineers a year, not four hundred thousand. Infosys says that, of 1.3 million applicants for jobs last year, it found only two per cent acceptable" (Surowiecki, "India's Skills Famine"). Moreover, the large figures of Indian and Chinese engineering graduates include not only four-year degrees, but also three-year training programs and diploma holders (Vivek Wadwa, Gary Gereffi, Ben Rissing, and Ryan Ong, "Where the Engineers Are," *Issues in Science and Technology*, April 9, 2007:73–84).

49. Farrell, Kaka, and Sturz, "Ensuring India's Offshoring Future," 78–79.

50. To the mass of inexperienced entry-level workers, those who do not see their salaries double each year, this commitment is also lacking in terms of investment in personal and skill training.

51. NeoIT, "Offshore and Nearshore." Nonetheless, employers still carp about increasing labor costs. An executive of a KPO company at an industry conference says that a few years ago "people making $250,000 to $300,000 in the U.S. were replaced by workers in Bangalore making $25,000. "Now," he says ruefully, "the latter is going up." Others at the conference voiced concerns about having to pay more for work once it is labeled KPO.

52. Mohit Chhabra, "The DQ-IDC India Salary Survey," *Dataquest*, October 6, 2004. There is also an increasing use of variable pay in the industry ("TCS Withholds Variable Pay of BPO Employees," BPO Watch India, April 21, 2009). As one venture capitalist with work experience at Infosys says, "There is an increasing variable percent of people's salaries. Sixty percent will be fixed and 40 percent is variable and depends on things like the company's overall performance. On paper wages go up 17 percent but not in reality. They give you much less. The pay was so low at Infosys . . . that's why people were upset about wages."

53. Shyamanuja Das, "Five Outsourcing Myths that 2006 Busted," *Global Services*, January 1, 2007.

54. Ramesh, "Cyber Coolies."

55. As Marx wrote of the "equilibrium" condition of labor supply and demand: "Finally, the law which always holds the relative surplus population or industrial reserve army in equilibrium with the extent and energy of accumulation rivets the worker to capital more firmly than the wedges of Hephaestus held Prometheus to the rock" (*Capital*, 799).

56. In an effort to exert greater control over workers, NASSCOM, the industry association, has started a National Skills Registry—the first-ever centralized database of employees of IT services and BPO companies (https://nationalskillsregistry.com/).

Chapter Six: The Infantilizing Gaze, or Schmidt Revisited

1. Quoted in Kundera, *The Art of the Novel* (New York: HarperCollins, 2000), 113.

2. Frederick Winslow Taylor, *The Principles of Scientific Management* (New York: Harper and Brothers, 1911), 59.

3. Ibid.

4. Daryl D'Art and Thomas Turner, "Independent Collective Representation: Providing Effectiveness, Fairness, and Democracy in the Employment Relationship," *Employee Responsibilities and Rights Journal* 15(4):169–80, 172 (2003).

5. Susan Schneider, "Human and Inhuman Resource Management: Sense and Nonsense," *Organization* 6(2):277–84, 281 (1999).

6. Jane Collins, *Threads: Gender, Labor, and Power in the Global Apparel Industry* (Chicago: University of Chicago Press, 2003), 16. See also, Carol Upadhya and A. R. Vasavi, eds., *In an Outpost of the Global Economy Work and Workers in India's Information Technology Industry* (New Delhi: Routledge, 2007).

7. Ross, *Fast Boat to China*, 157.

8. Dataquest, "BPO Employee Survey 2004."

9. C. Wright Mills, *The Sociological Imagination* (Oxford: Oxford University Press, 1959), 40–41.

10. Luc Boltanski and Eve Chiapello, *The New Spirit of Capitalism* (New York: Verso, 2005).

11. Reinhard Bendix, *Work and Authority in Industry* (New York: Harper and Row, 1963); Michael Burawoy, *Manufacturing Consent: Changes in the Labor Process under Capitalism* (Chicago: University of Chicago Press, 1979);

P. K. Edwards, *Conflict at Work: A Materialist Analysis of Workplace Relations* (London: Blackwell, 1986).

12. Peter Berger, Brigitte Berger, and Hansfried Kellner, *The Homeless Mind: Modernization and Consciousness* (New York: Vintage, 1973), 32.

13. Mills, *White Collar*, 233.

14. Cornelius Castoriadis, *The Imaginary Institution of Society* (Cambridge: MIT Press, 1987), 16.

15. See Attewell, "Big Brother"; Irena Grugulis, Tony Dundon, and Adrian Wilkinson, "Cultural Control and the 'Cultural Manager': Employment Practices in a Consultancy," *Work Employment and Society* 14:97–116 (2001); Steven McKay, *Satanic Mills or Silicon Islands? The Politics of High-Tech Production in the Philippines* (Ithaca, N.Y.: Cornell University Press, 2006); Patrice Rosenthal, "Management Control as an Employee Resource: The Case of Front-Line Service Workers," *Journal of Management Studies* 41(4):601–22 (2004); Patrice Rosenthal, Stephen Hill, and Riccardo Peccei, "Checking Out Service: Evaluating Excellence, HRM and TQM in Retailing," *Work, Employment and Society* 11(3):481–503 (1997); James Rui and Peter Brantley, "Computerized Surveillance in the Workplace: Forms and Distributions," *Sociological Forum* 7(3):405–23 (2002).

16. Ali Mir and Raza Mir, "Producing the Governable Employee: The Strategic Deployment of Workplace Empowerment," *Cultural Dynamics* 17(1):51–72 (2005).

17. Zuboff, *Smart Machine*, 322–23; Carla Freeman, *High Tech and High Heels in the Global Economy* (Durham, N.C.: Duke University Press, 2000), 199.

18. Freeman, *High Tech*, 199.

19. Ernesto Noronha and Premilla D'Cruz, "Being Professional: Organizational Control in Indian Call Centers," *Social Science Computer Review* 24(3):342–61 (2006).

20. As Michel Foucault argues, the individual is not merely affected by disciplinary power but is, in part, its creation, "one of its prime effects" (*Power/Knowledge* [New York: Pantheon Books, 1980], 98).

21. Hence Steven McKay's call for a "place-sensitive notion of production politics" ("Zones of Regulation: Restructuring Labor Control in Privatized Export Zones," *Politics & Society* 32(2):171–202, 173 [2004]).

22. Alan Roland, *In Search of Self in India and Japan* (Princeton: Princeton University Press, 1988).

23. Meaghan Morris, "Metamorphoses at Sydney Tower," *New Formations* 11:5–18, 10 (1990); Mbembe, *On the Postcolony*; Akhil Gupta, *Postcolonial Developments: Agriculture in the Making of Modern India* (Princeton: Princeton University Press, 1998).

24. Dipesh Chakrabarty, "Provincializing Europe: Postcoloniality and the Critique of History," *Cultural Studies* 6(3):337–57, 339–40 (1992).

25. The reference is to Louis Dumont, *Homo Hierarchicus: The Caste System and Its Implications* (Chicago: Chicago University Press, 1981).

26. Both, of course, are ideal types, stylized representations of how people think and act.

27. Boltanski and Chiapello, *New Spirit of Capitalism*; Christian Marazzi, *Capital and Language: From the New Economy to the War Economy* (Cambridge, Mass.: Semiotext(e), 2008); Ong, *Neoliberalism as Exception*; Richard Sennett, *Culture of New Capitalism*.

28. E. M. Forster, *A Passage to India* (New York: Modern Library, 1940), 86.

29. On a four-week project, for example, all is said to be well during the first few weeks, but "when the project is due tomorrow, they say it's not going to be done for another two weeks. Or they won't respond to email until it's done or will just say everything's fine."

30. The phrase is Freud's (*Civilization and Its Discontents* [New York: Norton, 1989 (1930)], 72).

31. Sundeep Sahay and Geoff Walsham write that in Indian bureaucracy the "rigid adherence to procedure combines with a ready susceptibility to personal pressure and intervention" ("Social Structure and Managerial Agency in India," *Organization Studies* 18[3]:415–44, 420 [1997]).

32. Adorno and Horkheimer, *The Dialectic of Enlightenment*, 181–82.

33. This illustrates how "culture and its representations remain in important ways rooted in the assumptions of the colonial modern in spite of the complex processes . . . of political independence and decolonization" (Saloni Mathur, *India by Design: Colonial History and Cultural Display* [Berkeley: University of California Press, 2007], 166).

34. For example, an IT worker says that the employees at his old job were "oldies"; that is, they were in their thirties and forties. The "atmosphere here is lively. We have office parties, an annual day were teams are nominated for best hub. We celebrate birthdays and we have a social group in the hub itself."

35. Russell Muirhead, *Just Work* (Cambridge: Harvard University Press, 2004), 72–73.

36. Ibid, 72. This condition might be characterized as partial servitude; partial, because of the element of volition: a freedom-in-obedience to superiors and social customs.

37. Roland, *In Search of Self*, 32.

38. Bruce Nicholson and Sundeep Sahay, "Some Political and Cultural Issues in the Globalization of Software Development," *Information and Organization* 11(1):25–44.

39. What bothers Das is that feudal relations are bad for business. He does not question the treatment of the domestic qua domestic, but only says that professionals deserve something better.

40. Guruchan Das, *India Unbound* (New York: Anchor, 2002), 274. Das accuses Indian companies of "a lack of attention to human capital." They do not invest enough in workers' training, "and just throw" the employee into her job, in contrast with "the detailed training plans" at multinationals. Josh, an American who worked at an IT company for two years in Bangalore, said that despite his repeated requests, he was never assigned a mentor, which he said bodes ill for the development of human capital and leadership skills in the industry.

41. Sahay and Walsham, "Social Structure," 421.

42. As the Bhagavad Gita counsels: "And do thy duty, even if it be humble, rather than another's, even if it be great. To die in one's duty is life; to live in another's is death" (New York: Penguin Classics, 2003, 20).

43. Ernesto Noronha and Premilla D'Cruz, *Employee Identity in Indian Call Centres: The Notion of Professionalism* (New Delhi: Sage, 2009).

44. Batt et al., "Indian Call Center Industry," 16.

45. As Freeman writes, "The open office is, at one and the same time, factorylike in its labor process and officelike in its muffled quiet ambience" (*High Tech*, 200).

46. Kalita, "Hope and Toil," A1.

47. Noronha and Cruz, "Being Professional."

48. Berger, Berger, and Kellner, *The Homeless Mind*, 31.

49. Kundera, *Art of the Novel*, 112.

50. As Sahay and Walsham write, "The Hindu virtues of contentment, absence of desire and stability oppose the dynamic striving for success and unlimited consumption that capitalist systems emphasize" ("Social Structure," 420).

51. See Peter Van der Veer, "Virtual India: Indian IT Labor and the Nation-State," in Thomas Hansen and Finn Stepputat, eds., *Sovereign Bodies: Citizens, Migrants, and States in the Postcolonial World* (Princeton: Princeton University Press, 2005), 276–90.

52. To be sure, the jobs also relate to self-approval. As one worker puts it, "The job has affected my social and family life positively. It has helped me enhance my job and personal skills, which enhances my confidence and abilities overall."

53. T.V. Mahalingam, "Where Dreams End," *Outlook India*, June 27, 2009:12.

54. Ong, *Neoliberalism as Exception.*

55. Brenner and Theodore, "Cities and Geographies," 364.

56. Lionel Trilling, *The Moral Obligation to Be Intelligent: Selected Essays* (New York: Farrar, Straus and Giroux, 2001 [1950], 118).

57. This even applies to the cab drivers who ferry workers to and from work: "I don't have to be servile, saying, 'Yes, sir' and 'Yes, madam' all day

and carry my boss's briefcase everywhere," one driver says. "In this job, I just focus on the time and the road" (Rama Lakshmi, "Ferrying the Night Owls Who Fix the World's Glitches," *Washington Post*, August 30, 2007:A12).

58. Robert Jackall, *Moral Mazes: The World of Corporate Managers* (Oxford: Oxford University Press, 1989), 193.

59. Ibid., 5.

60. Ibid., 3.

Chapter Seven: The Juggernaut of Global Capitalism

1. John Stuart Mill, *On Liberty* (Oxford: Oxford University Press, 1998), 63.

2. See Greg Grandin, *Fordlandia: The Rise and Fall of Henry Ford's Forgotten Jungle City* (New York: Macmillan, 2009).

3. William Dalrymple, *White Mughals: Love and Betrayal in Eighteenth-Century India* (New York: Penguin, 2004); Jeremy Prestholdt, *Domesticating the World: African Consumerism and the Genealogies of Globalization* (Berkeley: University of California Press, 2008).

4. Frederick Cooper, *Colonialism in Question: Theory, Knowledge, History* (Berkeley: University of California Press, 2005), 149.

5. One worker notes, however, that this is not always a "cultural issue": "It takes employees a long time to get places because of traffic, distance, and infrastructure. Many things intervene to delay, like power outages."

6. Other managers I have spoken to say similarly that they only allow select workers to speak or communicate with clients directly, and not just for reasons of poor grammar.

7. Arthur Schopenhauer, *The Pessimist's Handbook* (Lincoln: University of Nebraska Press, 1964 [1851]), 226.

8. Sudhir Kakar, *The Inner World: A Psycho-analytic Study of Childhood and Society in India* (Delhi: Oxford University Press, 1978); Dinesh Sharma, "Psychoanalysis and Sociocultural Change in India: A Conversation with Sudhir Kakar," *International Journal of Group Tensions* 29(3–4):253–83 (2000).

9. Kakar, *The Inner World*, 107.

10. Sen, *Development as Freedom*.

11. Mbembe, *On the Postcolony*, 2.

12. Alexis de Tocqueville, *Democracy in America* (New York: Harper, 2006), 526.

13. Ibid., 528.

14. Adam Smith, *The Theory of Moral Sentiments* (Oxford: Oxford University Press, 2004), 11.

15. Mike Davis, *Planet of Slums* (New York: Verso, 2006).

16. Theodor W. Adorno, *Minima Moralia: Reflections from a Damaged Life* (New York: Verso, 2006 [1951]).

17. As Rousseau wrote more generally about the limits of sympathy and concern: "It appears that the feeling of humanity evaporates and grows feeble in embracing all mankind. . . . It is necessary in some degree to confine and limit our interest and compassion in order to make it active" (*Discourse on Political Economy* [London: Dent, 1946 (1755)], 246).

18. See Nezar Alsayyad and Ananya Roy, "Medieval Modernity: On Citizenship and Urbanism in a Global Era," *Space and Polity* 10(1):1–20 (2006); Setha Low, *Behind the Gates: Life, Security and the Pursuit of Happiness in Fortress America* (New York: Routledge, 2003).

19. Benjamin Friedman, *The Moral Consequences of Economic Growth* (New York: Vintage, 2006).

20. Ferdinand Tönnies, *Community and Society: Gemeinschaft und Gesellschaft* (East Lansing: Michigan State University Press, 1957 [1887]).

21. Emile Durkheim, *The Division of Labor in Society* (New York: Free Press, 1997 [1893]).

22. Varuna Verma, "Fear in the City: 'I Don't Feel Safe in Bangalore Anymore,'" *The Telegraph* (2005); retrieved from http://www.telegraphindia.com/1051225/asp/opinion/story_5636735.asp.

23. Quoted in Varma, *Great Indian Middle Class*, 184.

24. "Software in India: Bangalore Bytes," *The Economist*, March 23, 1996:67.

25. Sennett, *Corrosion of Character*, 9.

26. Bell, *The Cultural Contradictions of Capitalism* (New York: Basic Books, 1996), 89.

27. Boltanski and Chiapello, *New Spirit of Capitalism*, 10.

28. In a similar vein, *Forbes* correspondent Meredith writes that "capitalists from corporate America and elsewhere surely did not set out to help Asia's downtrodden, but they did. Call them accidental activists" (*The Elephant and the Dragon* [New York: Norton, 2007], 12).

29. Of the penchant for not saying no and taking on too much work: "Commerce is changing this. Vendors now make a point of only committing to what they can do."

30. See Harald Fischer-Tine and Michael Mann, *Colonialism as Civilizing Mission: Cultural Ideology in British India* (London: Anthem Press, 2004).

31. Joanne Waghorne, "Chariots of the God(s): Riding the Line between Hindu and Christian," *History of Religions* 39(2): 95–116 (1999).

32. *American Heritage* dictionary.

33. Anthony Giddens writes of the juggernaut of modernity as "a runaway

engine of enormous power which, collectively as human beings, we can drive to some extent but which also threatens to rush out of control and which could rend itself asunder" (*The Consequences of Modernity* [Cambridge: Polity Press, 1990], 139).

34. Andrew Leyshon writes that "most of the globalization discourses ... tend to be far more simplistic in their general tenor, if not evangelical in tone, and display a burning faith in the 'natural' benevolence and 'obvious' utility of markets" ("True Stories? Global Dreams, Global Nightmares, and Writing Globalization," in Roger Lee and Jane Willis, eds., *Geographies of Economies* [London: Arnold, 1997], 143).

35. Compare this to Marx's portrayal of the capitalist juggernaut: "All means for the development of production transform themselves into means of domination over, and exploitation of, the producers; they mutilate the labourer into a fragment of a man, degrade him to the level of an appendage of a machine, destroy every remnant of charm in his work and turn it into a hated toil; they estrange him from the intellectual potentialities of the labour-process in the same proportion as science is incorporated in it as an independent power; they distort the conditions under which he works, subject him during the labour-process to a despotism more hateful for its meanness; they transform his life-time into working-time, and drag his wife and child beneath the wheels of the Juggernaut of capital" (*Capital*, 799). Nevertheless, Marx did argue that British imperialism would bring progressive change to India.

36. Despite the sobering reality of over 10 percent unemployment and over 17 percent underemployment in late Novermber of 2009, Goldman Sachs has resumed awarding large bonuses, eliciting public anger. See John Arlidge, "I'm Doing 'God's Work.' Meet Mr. Goldman Sachs," *Times of London*, November 8. 2009; retrieved from http://www.timesonline.co.uk/tol/news/world/us_and_americas/article6907681.ece. On Datini see Iris Origo, *The Merchant of Prato, Francesco di Marco Datini, 1335–1410* (New York: Knopf, 1957).

37. See Albert O. Hirschman, *The Passions and the Interests: Political Arguments for Capitalism before Its Triumph* (Princeton: Princeton University Press, 1997).

38. Joseph Brodsky, *Less Than One: Selected Essays* (New York: Farrar, Straus and Giroux, 1986), 157.

39. Although they provide a home drop from 10:30 at night to 4:30 in the morning, many parents are concerned about their daughters riding the train at night.

40. She had been promised an annual salary of 1.8 lakhs ($4,090), but was given only 1.7 lakhs ($3,862).

41. Hume, *Principles of Morals*, 44; Jacob Viner, *The Role of Providence in the Social Order: An Essay in Intellectual History* (Princeton: Princeton

University Press, 1972), 80; See also, Fonna Forman-Barzilai, *Adam Smith and the Circles of Sympathy: Cosmopolitanism and Moral Theory* (Cambridge: Cambridge University Press, 2010).

42. Sennett, *Culture of New Capitalism*, 83.

43. Dipesh Chakrabarty, *Provincializing Europe* (Princeton: Princeton University Press, 2000), 150.

44. Ibid.

Chapter Eight. Cyber-Coolies and Techno-Populists

1. Anna Tsing, *Friction: An Ethnography of Global Connection* (Princeton: Princeton University Press, 2005), 1.

2. Lefebvre, *Production of Space*; Ernst Cassirer, *The Philosophy of Symbolic Forms* (New Haven: Yale University Press, 1965); David Harvey, "Neoliberalism as Creative Destruction," *Annals of the American Academy of Political Science* 610 (1):21–44 (2006).

3. Etienne Balibar, "The Nation Form: History and Ideology," in Etienne Balibar and Immanuel Wallerstein, *Race, Nation, and Class: Ambiguous Identities* (New York: Verso, 1991); Benedict Anderson, *Imagined Communities: Reflections on the Origin and Spread of Nationalism* (New York: Verso, 1983); Phillip Kelly, "The Geographies and Politics of Globalization," *Progress in Human Geography* 23(3):379–400 (1999).

4. Phillip Wegner, *Imaginary Communities: Utopia, the Nation, and the Spatial Histories of Modernity* (Berkeley: University of California Press, 2002), 14.

5. In other words, to resolve what Robert Wuthnow calls the "problem of articulation" between ideas and social context, one needs to look at how symbols and ideologies are interpreted in the face of concrete events (*Communities of Discourse: Ideology and Social Structure in the Reformation, the Enlightenment, and European Socialism* [Cambridge: Harvard University Press, 1989], 5).

6. I use the notion of an *economy of morality* in an earlier piece: Shehzad Nadeem, "The Living Wage Movement and the Economics of Morality," *Research in Social Movements, Conflicts, and Change* 28:137–67.

7. Adam Smith, *The Wealth of Nations* (New York: Modern Library, 2000 [1776]), 800.

8. Friedman, *The World Is Flat*, 10–11, 297.

9. Ibid., 11.

10. Vashishta and Vashishta, *The Offshore Nation*, 13.

11. Ibid., ix.

12. Habib Beary, "Infosys Boss Makes Anthem Apology," *BBC News*, April 10, 2007.

13. Pieterse, "Globalisation as Hybridisation," 177.

14. Sunil Khilnani, *The Idea of India* (New York: Farrar, Straus and Giroux, 1999), 149.

15. Chopra, "Neoliberalism as Doxa," 439.

16. Satish Deshpande, "After Culture: Renewed Agendas for the Political Economy of India," *Cultural Dynamics* 10(2):147–69, 148 (1998).

17. Khilnani, *The Idea of India*, 148.

18. Desphande, "After Culture," 160.

19. Leela Fernandes, "The Politics of Forgetting: Class Politics, State Power and the Restructuring of Urban Space in India," *Urban Studies* 41(12):2415–30 (2004).

20. Edward Luce, "India to Dip into Forex Reserves to Build Roads," *Financial Times*, October 6, 2004:14.

21. Churchill Club, "Outsourcing."

22. Chopra, "Neoliberalism as Doxa," 435.

23. Ramesh, the cleaner, makes 2,000 rupees per month (part-time); Mahendra makes 3,500 rupees per month; Vinod works at night, making photocopies and performing various chores and earns 2,800 rupees; the "coffee guy" makes five rupees on each cup of coffee and six rupees per cup of tea. Their driver's base wage is 5,000–6,000 rupees a month, but can reach 12,000, even as high as 20,000 depending on how late they keep him at the office.

24. Paul Beckett, "Caste Away: India's High-Tech Revolution Helps 'Untouchables' Rise," *Wall Street Journal*, June 23, 2007:A1.

25. Working conditions, incidentally, are better in large companies, which suggests that caste and class inequalities are also reproduced within the industry.

26. As a trade union official writes, "If we keep in mind the hierarchical caste-based division of Indian society, the workers in this sector predominantly belong to the upper castes with a marginal presence of people from the backward or scheduled castes or scheduled tribes" (Pradeep Kumar, "The Outsourcing of Services: The Case of India," All India Federation of Trade Unions, New Delhi [2004]).

27. Upadhya and Vasavi, "Work, Culture and Sociality."

28. Emily Wax, "India's Lower Castes Seek Social Progress in Global Job Market," *Washington Post*, August 20, 2007:A1.

29. Krishna and Brihmadesam, "What Does It Take," 3310.

30. Gartner, "India ICT is at a Crossroads" (2005); retrieved from http://www.gartner.com/press_releases/asset_134972_11.html.

31. Anthony D'Costa, "Software Outsourcing and Development Policy Implications: An Indian Perspective," *International Journal of Technology Management* 24(7–8):705–23, 705 (2002).

32. Taylor and Bain, "India Calling," 270.

33. Yeung, "Capital, State, and Space," 300.

34. "How Global Are You?" *BusinessWeek*, December 8, 2008:12.

35. Worthen, "Extreme Outsourcing." Such strategies are particularly problematic for smaller vendors, as the CEO of one company notes: "The cost has come down. Part of it is the fact that you have vendors. In fact, we get killed because you can always get freelancers and the freelance cost is minimum. So let's say you want to get something done. You want to get your whole thesis written, for example. You could outsource it, right? And you could get it done for minimum cost, which would make it worthwhile for you." Needless to say, I did not avail myself of this option.

36. Multinationals are increasingly insisting on geographic diversity so that in the event of a natural disaster or power outage work will not grind to a halt. As one executive put it, "They want disaster recovery and want providers to have two different functioning facilities, where data is redundant and things can be worked on."

37. The same could be said of liberalization—it has unlocked many forces, but India cannot liberalize over and over again.

38. As economist Robert Solow famously illustrated, 87.5 percent of labor productivity in the United States over the past 150 years has been the result of technological changes, while the rest can be attributed to growth in the number of workers and capital equipment (*Technical Change and the Aggregate Production Function* [Cambridge: MIT Press, 1957]).

39. William J. Baumol, "Macroeconomics of Unbalanced Growth: The Anatomy of Urban Crises," *American Economic Review* 57(3):415–26 (1967).

40. Ross, *Fast Boat to China*.

41. "The Next Big Opportunity: Moving up the Value Chain from BPO to KPO," Evalueserve, Gurgaon, India (2004), 11.

42. Amy Waldman, "India Takes Economic Spotlight, and Critics Are Unkind," *New York Times*, March 7, 2004:A3.

43. Pamela Shurmer-Smith, *India: Globalization and Change* (London: Arnold, 2000).

44. Quoted in Chopra, "Neoliberalism as Doxa," 420.

45. AFL-CIO, "Outsourcing America," AFL-CIO Executive Council (2004); retrieved from http://www.aflcio.org/aboutus/thisistheaflcio/ecouncil/ec03112004i.cfm.

46. While the working conditions compare favorably with other "traditional" Indian industries, a major obstruction to organizing efforts is the high level of monitoring. "From day one," says an official, "they say come in, work here, but don't talk about trade unions." In workspaces, there are closed-circuit cameras and nearly "everything is recorded and monitored in call centers."

47. Kumar, "The Outsourcing of Services."

48. Jameson, *Postmodernism*, 207.

49. Neoclassical economists like Gary Becker used the term *human capital* to describe the stock of education, knowledge, and training that a worker acquires over time and invests in work. By contrast, businesses and this union, at least, prefer *intellectual capital*, perhaps to hint at the cerebral and thus distinguished nature of white-collar work.

Conclusion

1. Franz Kafka, *The Diaries of Franz Kafka*, ed. Max Brod (New York: Schocken Books, 1949), 397.

2. The story's narrator refers to Bartleby's refusal as a form of "passive resistance." Herman Melville, *Great Short Works of Herman Melville* (New York: Perennial, 1969), 47, 50.

3. As anthropologist Eric Wolf writes, "Meanings are not imprinted into things by nature; they are developed and imposed by human beings. . . . The ability to bestow meanings—to 'name' things, acts, and ideas—is a source of power" (*Europe*, 388).

4. Mimicry, as I have used the term, is duplicative but not strictly so. There is room for subtlety and invention. The copied thing becomes something else. As Eric Wolf put it, "In the rough-and-tumble of social interaction, groups are known to exploit ambiguities of inherited forms, to impart new evaluations or valences to them, to borrow forms more expressive of their interests, or to create wholly new forms to answer changed circumstances" (ibid., 387).

5. Roberto M. Unger, *False Necessity: Anti-Necessitarian Social Theory in the Service of Radical Democracy* (London: Verso, 2004), 594.

6. Henri Bergson, *The Creative Mind* (New York: Citadel Press, 1946), 22.

7. Sukumar Muralidharan, "Some Heresies of Development: An Interview with Roberto Unger," *Frontline* 18(8):1–14 (2001).

8. Barbara Harriss-White, *India Working: Essays on Society and Economy* (Cambridge: Cambridge University Press, 2002).

9. P. Sainath, "Nearly Two Lakh Farm Suicides since 1997," *The Hindu*, January 22, 2010; Kounteya Sinha, "UN Report Slams India for Farmer Suicides," *Times of India*, September 24, 2006; *Frontline*, "Seeds of Suicide: India's Desperate Farmers," *PBS*, July 26, 2005.

10. National Commission for Enterprises in the Unorganised Sector, *Report on Conditions of Work and Promotion of Livelihoods in the Unorganised Sector* (New Delhi: Government of India, 2007).

11. Bagehot is quoted in Lewis Lapham, *The Agony of Mammon* (New York: Verso, 1998), 1.

12. National Commission for Enterprises in the Unorganised Sector, *Conditions of Work*, 8.

13. Alice Amsden, *Escape from Empire: The Developing World's Journey from Heaven to Hell* (Cambridge: MIT Press, 2007), 9.

14. Amartya Sen, *The Argumentative Indian: Writings on Indian History, Culture and Identity* (New York: Picador, 2007), 197.

15. P. Sainath, "The Decade of Our Discontent." *The Hindu*, September 8, 2007. Land reforms, writes Achin Vanaik, "greatly facilitate mass literacy, creating a more skilled labour force that contributes to rising industrial productivity, as well as preparing a wider domestic market for more sophisticated consumer goods" ("Myths of the Permit Raj," *New Left Review* 29:153–60 [2004], 159).

16. Ahmed, "Mixed Economy," 42.

17. As Alice Amsden writes of India, "Output rose over time, soaring in the early 1990s even before market reforms began. Software services boomed in the remote region of Bangalore, which benefited from former government investments in electronics, telecommunications, aerospace, and a prestigious Indian Institute of Science" (*Escape from Empire*, 8). For an historical view, see Vivek Chibber, *Locked in Place: State-Building and Late Industrialization in India* (Princeton: Princeton University Press, 2006).

18. Bhabha, *The Location of Culture*, 310.

19. UN-Habitat, *The Challenge of the Slums: Global Report on Human Settlements* (London: Earthscan, 2003), 2.

20. And as John Pilger notes, "Spending on private health, which only the well-off can afford, is one of the highest in the world" ("Not Shining, but Drowning," *New Statesman*, September 2004).

21. Sinha, "UN Report."

22. Roger Cohen, "Toilets and Cellphones," *International Herald Tribune*, May 24, 2010:6.

23. See Dani Rodrik, "Goodbye Washington Consensus, Hello Washington Confusion?" *Journal of Economic Literature* 44(4):973–87 (2006).

24. Ho-fung Hung, "America's Head Servant," *New Left Review* 60:5–25 (2009).

25. Unger, *False Necessity*; Mauro F. Guillén, *The Limits of Convergence: Globalization and Organizational Change in Argentina, South Korea, and Spain* (Princeton: Princeton University Press, 2003).

26. World Bank, "Beyond Economic Growth: Meeting the Challenges of Global Development," The World Bank (2000), 8.

Appendix: Research Methods

1. Michael Burawoy, Joseph Blum, Sheba George, Zsuzsa Gille, Teresa Gowan, Lynne Haney, Maren Klawiter, Steven Lopez, Sean O Riain, and Mil-

lie Thayer, *Global Ethnography: Forces, Connections, and Imaginations in a Postmodern World* (Berkeley: University of California Press, 2002); Thomas Eriksen, *Globalization: Studies in Anthropology* (London: Pluto Press, 2003); Melissa Fisher and Greg Downey, *Frontiers of Capital: Ethnographic Reflections on the New Economy* (Durham, N.C.: Duke University Press, 2006); Zsuzsa Gille and Sean O Riain, "Global Ethnography," *Annual Review of Sociology* 28:271–95 (2002); Biao, *Global "Body Shopping."*

2. James Clifford, *Routes: Travel and Translation in the Late Twentieth Century* (Cambridge: Harvard University Press, 1997); Cooper, *Colonialism in Question*; Alan Hudson, "Placing Trust, Trusting Place: On the Social Construction of Offshore Financial Centres," *Political Geography* 17(8):915–37 (1998).

3. Gary Gereffi and Miguel Korzeniewicz, *Commodity Chains and Global Capitalism* (Westport, Conn.: Praeger, 1994), 2.

4. Margaret Somers, "The Narrative Constitution of Identity: A Relational and Network Approach," *Theory and Society* 23:605–49 (1994).

5. *Complete Essays of Montaigne* (Stanford: Stanford University Press, 1965), 610.

6. Clifford Geertz, *After the Fact: Two Countries, Four Decades, One Anthropologist* (Cambridge: Harvard University Press, 1995), 119.

7. Norman Fairclough, *Critical Discourse Analysis: The Critical Study of Language* (London: Longman, 1995).

8. Charles Briggs, *Learning How to Ask* (Cambridge: Cambridge University Press, 1985).

9. Bent Flyvbjerg, *Making Social Science Matter* (Cambridge: Cambridge University Press, 2001), 82.

10. Anthony Giddens, *The Constitution of Society: Outline of the Theory of Structuralism* (Cambridge: Polity Press, 1984); Charles Ragin and Howard Becker, eds., *What Is a Case? Exploring the Foundations of Social Inquiry* (Cambridge: Cambridge University Press, 1992).

11. Flyvbjerg, *Making Social Science Matter*, 47.

Index

due to, 116; offshoring and, 30; outsourcing and standardization, 22; "ownership"
and personal investment in product, 104;
ownership of work undermined by, 134;
productivity increases linked to, 104; repetitive or routine tasks and, 21–23; research and development limited by, 103;
responsibility, individual and, 104, 107;
rote, monotonous tasks as result of, 3–4,
10, 12, 96, 106; Taylor and, 132–133
regulation, 3; deregulation as incentive for industry, 33, 215; of IT industry, 36; labor
law modifications to benefit call center industry, 91; taxes and tariffs, 32, 33, 38;
transportation safety guidelines, 92; of
working time, 84–85
reification, 40–41
religion, disruption of socio-religious participation, 90
research & development: in India, 103, 109;
offshoring of, 26
research methodology, 221–225
resistance, 9
responsibility. *See* ownership, responsibility
and accountability for work
restriction, 11
Ross, Andrew, 134, 202
Roy, Raman, 22
Royal Stag Corporate Music Carnival, 28, 48

safety issues, 91–95
Said, Edward W., 43
Sainath, P., 217
salaries. *See* wages
Samuelson, Paul, 20, 21
satisfaction, worker, 106
Satyam Computer Services, 5–7
Scheyer, Mark, 144–147
Schneider, Susan, 134
Schopenhauer, Arthur, 175
self-direction. *See* agency
Sen, Amartya, 217
service sector, outsourcing of, 16–18, 194–
195; global cost reduction as result of, 121;
and Indian economy, 200–201; research
and development linked to, 103; service
work as emotional labor, 58, 106
sexuality: BPO industry and reputation for
sexual promiscuity, 56; conservative values
challenged by changing attitudes about,

62–63, 65; reputed promiscuity of employees, 93–94; victim-blaming in rape and ha-
rassment cases, 93–94
shifts, length of workday, 83–85; elasticity
and unpredictability of, 96; labor law
amendments regarding, 91
Singh, Manmohan, 34
skills: and bargaining power, 98; "creative"
work, 104; rationalization of work/fragmen-
tation as barrier to skill development, 114–
115; required BPO jobs, 21–22; the "skill
ceiling," 104, 105; "skills extinction," 112;
standardization and, 104
social rhythms (sociotemporal patterns), 12;
long and irregular working hours and, 84;
night shift schedules and disruption of, 86,
89–91; time regulation in the workplace
and, 96
Sontag, Susan, 42
space: absolute *vs.* abstract, 48; capital, territorialization cycle of, 30–31; capital and
placeless space, 29–30; dislocation from
social spaces and social rhythms, 90–91;
offshore work spaces as constructs, 8–9;
and place, 29; place-space and the relationship to labor and capital, 29–30; spatial discontinuity, 43; technology parks and
campuses as separate from place, 60
spatialization, 3
Special Economic Zones (SEZs), 32–33, 38,
40, 92, 215, 217
standardization of work, 12; dissatisfaction
linked to, 109–110; globalization and, 30
status, social: caste as, 53–54, 61, 64–65,
151, 158–159, 178, 179, 199–200, 259;
consumer culture and constitution of, 53–
54, 61; cultural distancing and perceived,
11; "culture of deference" and, 102–104,
138–141, 150–152, 161, 173–174, 176–
177; employment and increase in, 90, 153,
158–159; within global organization, 105;
job-hopping as response to status insecurity, 124–125; mimicry and, 58; servility
and, 149–152
stigma, social: BPO work and, 67; income as
compensation for, 68, 69; night shift workers as stigmatized, 63–64, 68, 72
stress: BOSS (burn-out stress syndrome), 88;
emotional labor and, 58; long work hours
and, 83; repetitive tasks and, 87–88; sleep